ISLAM IN RELATION TO THE CHRIST IMPULSE

An Anthroposophic Inquiry

Islam in Relation to the Christ Impulse

A Search for Reconciliation between Christianity and Islam

Andrei Younis

SteinerBooks | 2015

2015
SteinerBooks
An imprint of Anthroposophic Press/SteinerBooks
610 Main St., Great Barrington, MA
www.steinerbooks.org

Copyright © 2015 by Andrei Younis. All rights reserved. No part of this publication may be reproduced, stored in a retrieval system, or transmitted, in any form or by any means, electronic, mechanical, photocopying, recording, or otherwise, without the prior written permission of the publisher.

Cover and book design: William Jens Jensen
Cover image: The Dome of the Rock
(*Qubbat As-Sakhrah,* Arabic; *Kipat Hasela,* Hebrew)
on the Temple Mount in the Old City of Jerusalem
viewed at night from the Austrian hospice
© by Stéphanie Gromann (used by permission)

Library of Congress Control Number: 2015942755

ISBN: 978-1-58420-184-7 (paperback)
ISBN: 978-1-58420-185-4 (eBook)

Contents

Preface   vii

1. **The Need to Understand Islam through Anthroposophic Wisdom**   1

   Noteworthy contrasts between Christianity and Islam   7

   Reasons concealed behind the emergence of Islam as a new Yahweh Moon religion   20

   Influences on the descendants of Ishmael during the Kali Yuga period   26

   The critical situation 333 years after the coming of Christ   31

   The advent of Christ in relation to the crisis of 333: Lucifer's involvement in blunting the Sorathic intervention   37

2. **Sorath's Intervention in AD 666 and the Role of Ishmael's Descendants**   42

   The aftermath of the invasion of the Gondishapur Academy   45

   Yahweh's transformation into Allah: The beginning of the denial of spirit   49

   Further considerations on the absence of the concept of spirit in Islam: Confusion of three significant Hebraic terms   65

   What are the fundamental messages of the Koran? How did Muhammad's verses influence pagan Arabs?   72

   Is the principle of freedom indicated anywhere in the Koran?   80

   Sharia law, the rule of retaliation, and the new principle of forgiveness in the Koran   86

   Are there any signs of the Christ impulse in the Koran?   93

3. **In What Ways Has Arabism Influenced Islam?**   98

   Absence of the concept of spiritual freedom as a result of Arabism   101

   Absence of a concept of reincarnation   109

   Absence of the concept of karma and confined to the fatalistic concept of qadar   115

	Confusing Islam today with incidents and verses related only to Muhammad's time	122
	What is Arabism? How are we to define it?	129
	What does Islam mean for Muslims, and how do they regard other religions?	132
4.	**Muhammad as the Last Prophet Sent by Allah: Lucifer's Involvement in Islam**	139
	Lucifer's role in Arabism's increase in power: The influence of luciferic morality on Islam	143
	Other reasons why the Koran has been misunderstood and misinterpreted	154
	Influence of apocryphal gospels on koranic verses and Islam: The influence of folk souls	160
	Is Islam related to Christ in any way?	165
	Consequences of the reappearance of Abraham's monotheistic faith	168
	Why is the Antichrist (Dajjal) mentioned in Islam?	172
	How do Muslims interpret the Second Coming of Christ?	175
5.	**How Is Jesus of Nazareth Conceived in Islam?**	179
	Reasons behind the denial of the Holy Trinity and God's Son	187
	What did Abraham's monotheistic faith mean to Muhammad and to Muslims?	193
	The Prophet Muhammad's two sons	195
	Further consequences of adhering to the old principle, "I and Father Abraham are one"	198
	Denial of the Crucifixion and its consequences	200
	Conclusion	209
	Can Christianity and Islam find a key to reconciliation?	216
	Bibliography	240

Preface

During the last three decades, I often visited Islamic lands and had the opportunity to live in one of them for several years. At the beginning, my stay in this Islamic country was due to my work, but later I decided to live here for a longer period, for it was quite intriguing to live in an Islamic land. Since I found myself in the midst of a different cultural and religious setting from that to which I was accustomed, my foremost aim was to achieve a better understanding of the members of this culture who evidently had a different soul and spiritual constitution than I did and lived in a somewhat "separate reality"—that is, they had a different worldview compared to the general worldview prevalent in Western cultures.

As my inquiry deepened, I realized that their different understanding of the world was generated by the "spirit of Islam" peculiar to adherents of the Islamic religion and that this spirit of Islam had a distinct influence on their souls. As time went by, my relationship with them developed and transcended the boundaries of the formal definition of my work. As I got to know them better, it became apparent that we were different in many ways, but we were always able to meet on common ground as members of humanity. As a result, I become good friends with them, and what made me feel at ease during my stay in this Islamic country was that they were not friendly just because they tolerated me as a Christian, but that they had accepted me as a fellow human being in a most natural way. For a while I was under the impression that Muslims in every Islamic culture were able to evaluate Christians in a similar way, but I found out this was not the case and that their approach differed to a great extent from one Islamic land to another and from person to person. Accordingly, some of my friends were not very involved in traditional Islam, whereas others were somewhat conservative.

Still, they were not fundamentalist, radical, or extremist Muslims, and of course were definitely not jihadist. This made me realize that I shouldn't generalize Muslims or place them in one category, for many shades of the Islamic spirit exist in different Islamic lands.

As time went by, my curiosity about Islam deepened, and I realized that my friends were also curious about Christianity. As a result, we often had deep conversations concerning our religious faiths. Since my friends had sensed that I did not have a judgmental approach and embraced them without any discrimination, they felt free to ask questions and delve into a wide range of subjects regarding Christianity. Gradually, I realized that, to be able to provide better explanations regarding Christianity, it was necessary to learn more about their religious teachings and find out if there were any Islamic terms and concepts that corresponded to the terms and concepts found in Christian teachings, and this is how my inquiry about Islam began.

Of course one could learn many things about traditional Islam by having conversations with its members and by observing how they perform their religious duties, but I knew that—because Islam was founded firmly on the teachings in the Koran (or *Qur'an*)—I had to study and analyze the Koran to be able to achieve a deeper understanding of the core of Islam. While I carried on with my research into Islam and the Koran, I also had the opportunity to meet and have discussions with scholars of Islamic teachings. These discussions proved to be very valuable, for besides learning many things about traditional Islamic teachings, I also learned that the concept of reincarnation does not exist in Islam (although I later found out that it does exist in the koranic verses in a somewhat different and indirect way that can be misleading). During our discussions, I found out, too, that Muslims apprehend the concept of *karma* in a fatalistic way. Furthermore, when I combined the information I received from these scholars with the results of my inquiries, I discovered that, although the concept of what is *divine* has a place in Islam—for example, Allah is the exalted divine being—the concept of *spirit* does not exist in Islamic teachings. Accordingly, derivations of this word—spirit, spiritual, and spiritualization—do not exist in the Koran as distinct terms.

In fact, my findings were very indicative of more than just a simple and negligible problem. The absence of such concepts, or their misconception, leads to certain consequences, since these fundamental terms and certain other spiritual concepts are needed to comprehend the concealed truths concerning human existence in this cosmos and the reasons behind the very existence of religions. During my inquiries—regarding external Islam—I realized that Islam is no Friday-go-to-mosque kind of religion (as believed by many Westerners). It is a system of law and an all-encompassing way of life, and it is in a sense a political faith with a yearning for expansion. As I visited different Islamic countries, I also realized that, although religious observance varies somewhat from community to community and from person to person, to most Muslims their faith is much more prominent in everyday life than Christianity is for people in most Western lands.

Although my friends really appreciated my endeavor to understand Islam and the Koran, from time to time they warned me that it would be a fruitless effort for a foreigner—that is, a Christian—to unravel its teachings, for the koranic verses are very complicated, even for a Muslim. In a sense, they were quite right; the content of the Koran is indeed not easy to fathom, but for several years I had also been studying Anthroposophy. I had come across many invaluable elucidations concerning the reasons behind the emergence of Islam and the "spiritual forces" that had been influential within it ever since. Thus, although my friends had indicated that I could get lost in the maze of the koranic verses—and were right from a certain point of view—they were not aware of the fact that anthroposophic wisdom is able to provide a special light that illumines intricate parts and concealed meanings found in the Koran.

Anthroposophic elucidations are not limited only to teachings pertaining to Christianity; they are actually profound revelations of cosmic wisdom that cover every aspect of human spiritual evolution and have the quality of being absolutely objective. After a while, I decided to share the results of my inquiries (guided by anthroposophic wisdom) with my friends and—because I did not know how they would react—I was somewhat cautious at the beginning. To my surprise, although they were astounded to hear about many unknown views regarding Christianity and Islam, I was not confronted with any negativism or objection. Apparently, they were very intrigued by what they heard. Of course, there was no way of knowing for sure to what extent they were influenced by what I conveyed and whether this would bring about any changes in their religious beliefs or opinions, but there was no doubt that their interest was genuine. Besides, it was not my intention to change their beliefs or opinions or to persuade them to believe in something else. What I shared with them were only objective answers to their questions.

Throughout those years, every now and then we heard news reports of various unpleasant events having to do with hostile attacks by radical, extremist, and jihadist Muslims, or about some unfounded anger or the arrogant demands of fundamentalist Muslims. Although I would rather not mention them in this book, it is necessary to give some examples of these disturbing events. Nonetheless, my reason for including them is not to judge the Islamic world or to underline how horrible Muslim terrorists are; rather, it is an endeavor to show that there was something wrong going on in the Islamic world—which is, in fact, an issue that concerns the whole world—and that we are all confronted with a serious problem that need solutions. It is very distressing and alarming when we see ten- or twelve-year-old Muslim children handed guns—especially machine guns—and taught how to shoot, or given the task of beheading an enemy of Islam—one either from a different religion or from another Islamic sect. As a result, all these unpleasant events that have happened over the years have combined to focus the Western world's attention on Islam.

Some might claim that a revival or resurgence of Islam started many years ago with the revolution in Iran, when the oil wealth of the Arabian Peninsula became very important, and that we should regard those recent events as the continuation of this resurgence. Accordingly, some may also believe that Islam is somehow being used as a vehicle for striking out at the West in an effort to reclaim a greatly damaged sense of self-esteem, for Muslims (in general) feel that for the past 160 years the Western world has overpowered them culturally and in many other ways. This claim cannot be totally dismissed, and there might be some truth in it. However, anyone who has been following world events closely in recent years and, as a result, is distressed and alarmed about the future of the world, will not be satisfied with the explanation of an Islamic "resurgence."

Because I had close relationships with many Muslims while those events were taking place, I was able to witness that they, too, were alarmed and upset, saying, "This is not the Islam we know; we do not approve of any of the despicable acts of those fundamentalist, radical, extremist, or jihadist Muslims. We do not identify with them or with their acts, and we do not see them as true representatives of Islam." Sometimes I had to console them: "Westerners have witnessed such dreadful events and were at the receiving end of the hatred and hostility radiating from some people who emphasized their Muslim identity. It is inevitable that negative propaganda against Islam—even Islamophobia—would develop in the West. Nevertheless, the people who committed these acts should not be regarded as the true representatives of Islam, and Muslims as a whole should not take Westerners' negative reactions personally; most Western peoples surely know that the majority of Muslims are against hatred, hostility, and aggression, and that they are not involved in such unacceptable and disturbing events."

Hostile and deplorable assaults executed by certain fanatical Muslim groups in Western cultures (and in the other parts of the world) cannot be explained away as a resurgence of Islam; so much hatred, hostility, and aggression cannot be the result of a revival of a religion—the kind of negativism that connotes "evil" cannot be the manifestation of a religion that speaks of peace, friendliness, and forgiving in its sacred book. Therefore, when we consider from different angles how all these antagonistic Islamic groups behave, one can sense the distinct presence of a different kind of force that motivates fundamentalist, radical, extremist, and jihadist Muslims. One wonders if their thoughts, feelings, and actions must be under the influence of a kind of non-divine spiritual power that impels them to act in ways that defy worldwide norms of humane behavior—conscience, compassion, ethics, and morality.

Whether we are Muslims, Christians, Buddhists, or members of some other religion, we are confronted by many serious problems, including worldwide pollution, serious climate changes, natural disasters, the threat of global economic crises, shortages of food and water, starvation, epidemics, political upheavals, and local wars in emerging countries. Insofar as humanity is concerned, this is already more than enough to cope with. Therefore, when additional hatred, hostility, and aggression is frequently imposed on members of different religions and cultures by certain Muslims, it is understandably alarming for people on the receiving end, and that, as a consequence, they become concerned for their future. It is also understandable, too, that negative feelings are generated in those communities as a reaction. Nonetheless, we must not forget that a great many Muslims are likewise disturbed and worried by the hostile behavior of certain Muslims. It is necessary to realize that once the door of a certain type of negativism is opened, pure evil can come in through that door from a spiritual dimension parallel to ours; as a result humankind can face more tribulations. However, since it has been clearly indicated in the Gospels and emphasized by anthroposophic wisdom that humanity shall be confronted by many tribulations in future times, it would not be realistic to expect that we will be able to live blissfully in a trouble-free world at this stage of our spiritual evolution. Under these conditions, to blame, judge, and condemn the "other" will never be helpful; on the contrary, it will hinder our chances of finding common ground that might enable us to live in a neighborly and peaceful way in this world we all share.

Following several years of analyzing different aspects of Islam and studying the Koran—and observing that my Muslim friends do not raise serious objections nor seem to have negative reactions to objective anthroposophic facts—I was encouraged to write a book in which I could suggest a common meeting point for us all and also attempt to indicate the reasons that hinder some Muslims from achieving a higher spiritual understanding that could help them embrace members of other religions. In this context, my endeavor was actually a search for reconciliation between Christianity and Islam, for as I witness the recent state of affairs in the world I can sense this reconciliation is absolutely necessary so that the future of humanity's spiritual evolution is not endangered, and that we—as members of humanity—could create the opportunity to be permeated by cosmic consciousness and be able to attain a highly spiritualized state of love.

I.

The Need to Understand Islam through Anthroposophic Wisdom

When we visit an Islamic land ruled by *sharia*, it quickly becomes clear that the recitation (*azan*)[1] heard from minarets is inseparable from Islamic culture. Due to its perpetual recitation five times a day since the dawn of Islam, the *azan* has become the "voice of Islam." The euphonious way of reciting can be enchanting for some Western visitors, but what does this call for prayer actually say? It says, "There is only one Allah [there is no deity other than him], and Muhammad [c. 570–632] is his prophet." As *Allah* is God's name in Islam, and Muhammad is the prophet of this religion, we may suppose that the message of the *azan* is appropriate. However, the impartiality of its meaning is disputable, for these words have a more serious connotation than we imagine, and we cannot evaluate them superficially. Actually, this maxim, which forms the foundation of Islamic faith, has concealed implications, and *certain cosmic forces*—whose influences are reflected on humankind in manifold ways—have found expression in it.

When we bear in mind that this maxim is not just a simple expression of the Muslim faith in Allah, it becomes clear that we need to gain a deeper understanding of this monotheistic religion that has more than a billion adherents all over the world. Thus, to acquire an insight into the intricacies and essence of Islam, we shall attempt to analyze its different aspects and consider certain questions of

---

1 *Azan*: The Islamic call to prayer recited five times at specific hours during the day and night.

importance from an anthroposophic point of view.² This objective analysis could be helpful in forming a deeper understanding of Islam's relation to the Christ impulse.³

Another significant issue related to Islam needs to be examined. According to Rudolf Steiner's anthroposophic disclosures, besides the *Christ impulse*—which is the most vital and important impulse that has unfolded in the evolution of humankind—there was also the *impulse of Islam* that appeared in the Arabian Peninsula approximately 600 years after the Advent of Christ—after the Christ impulse came to the world. Each impulse was absolutely necessary in its own way for the balance and continuation of human evolution in the direction intended by the beings of the divine–spiritual realm. The existence of Islam is not the outcome of any coincidence; in fact, there are very special cosmic reasons behind its birth. However, although both of them have been classified as impulses, it must be emphasized that fundamentally their quintessence, mission, and the nature of the spiritual force behind each of them was very different. With these facts as the background, when we ponder the encounters the Western world has had with Islam and Muslims in the last three decades, our overall impression of Islam is not that of a placid religion in search of spiritual truths, but that of a politicized "peculiar force" in which anger is inherent and that can often be fierce, intolerant, and aggressive. As a result of what we perceive, important questions arise: Why is there an immense difference between the worldview of Western Christian peoples and Muslims? Why it is difficult for Muslims, in general, to integrate to the Western way of life although many have been living in Christian cultures for decades?

Contemplation on these questions leads to a third significant question: Is Islam harmonious with the Christ impulse? When we bear in mind various examples of how Islamic teachings manifest in negative

---

2   Throughout our endeavor to gain a different understanding of Islam other than that which is founded on outer history, we shall be referring to anthroposophic elucidations of Rudolf Steiner and Valentin Tomberg.

3   Throughout the evolution of humanity certain impulses have come from the spiritual world—mainly from the divine–spiritual world—and the Christ impulse, inaugurated by the Christ, is the most important and vital impulse that has come to the world and is the fulcrum of human evolution.

ways in our daily lives, we sense that this is a central question that we must explore. Since existence of the Christ impulse was first revealed to modern humankind by Steiner's anthroposophic wisdom, it is necessary to delve into anthroposophic explanations to find out the concealed factors and underlying spiritual forces that affect the whole Islamic world and have been influential in shaping the mind soul and spiritual constitution of Muslims.

The Muslim way of life and worldview, although they vary from culture to culture, is very much affected by Islamic upbringing and its rules and teachings. Nearly every day we encounter news related to Islam and Muslims. Yet, how much do we really know about the meanings of koranic verses and the content of the *sharia* laws that govern Islamic life? For instance, when we ponder the fact that in some countries ruled by *sharia* the punishment for renouncing Islam is death, we may realize it is not so easy to understand "the spirit of Islam," which at the core of its understanding lacks the concept and the principle of freedom—thus, freedom of spiritual belief—and readily enacts such a harsh punishment. Admittedly, being subjected to the penalty of death because one has renounced one's creed is not easy to comprehend with the Western outlook, or to approve of it. Furthermore, Western and Islamic cultures have never shared a mutual understanding—apart from certain trade relationships. Difference of religious beliefs has often caused disagreement over a variety of subjects—for example, whether the content of the Gospels has been changed since the time it was written; or whether Jesus is God's Son; or if the Christian concept of the Holy Trinity is a blasphemy. Regarding several other subjects, there is a growing gulf between these two cultures, and one may posit that, as time goes by, this gulf is becoming harder to bridge.

On the one hand we may find it hard to relate to a religion that has an oppressive trait at its core. However, since humankind is the representative of freedom in the divine–spiritual hierarchy, it would not be wrong to state that everyone is free to believe in whatever creed or opinion[4] he or she chooses. Although an oppressive trait may be inherent in the Islamic teachings and belief system, every person's

---

4   For example, agnosticism or atheism.

choice is indisputable. Such an understanding reflects the importance of the "principle of freedom" and the fact that every person on Earth is entitled to it. Do Muslims also agree that members of other religions are entitled to this freedom, or do they have other convictions and unrevealed aims? Recent confrontations with the Islamic culture indicate that Muslims have different opinions, values, and aims that do not seem to be in harmony with the goals of human evolution. Actually, this is the very least that can be said about their radically different convictions. The question is, under these circumstances, will there be any chance of reconciliation between these cultures, which are diametrically opposed?

To understand the influences that have shaped Islam and have been motivating its members since it began is a matter of urgency for our times. It would not be wrong to say that Islam is like a closed chest. Just as one examines the fruit of a tree to get an idea about the nature of that particular tree, likewise peoples of Western Christian cultures have been observing Muslims so as to form objective ideas about Islam. However, because their recent encounters with Muslims have been upsetting—infused with negativism and even hostility—the impressions they received were far from objective and have led them to sentimentally form negative impressions regarding Islam and Muslims.[5] Consequentially, the term *Islamophobia*[6] sprung out of these encounters. Although Islamophobia was the unavoidable result of several unpleasant experiences Westerners had with Islam, fortunately all Christians have not yet made a final verdict. If extremist

---

5   In this book, the term *Muslims* will be used often. However, it is necessary to underline that this is not intended to generalize all Muslims and place each person under the same definition. As in all religions, various shades of gentleness, modesty, conservative beliefs, extreme opinions, and acts of fanaticism exist among adherents of Islam. It would not be correct to adopt a generalized idea about all Muslims, for generalizing may lead us to being judgmental, and judgments may hinder us while trying to gain a true and objective understanding about adherents of Islam.

6   *Islamophobia* is a hatred or fear of Islam or Muslims, especially as a political force. According to a Wikipedia entry, *Islamophobia* is prejudice against, hatred toward, or fear of Muslims or of ethnic groups perceived to be Muslim. Whereas the term *Islamophobia* is widely recognized and used, people who do not agree with fostering a negative attitude toward Islam have criticized both the term and the underlying concept.

Muslims insist on being hostile and violent while living in Western societies—or if Westerners continue witnessing Muslims using *sharia* law in a harsh and unjust manner in their own countries—it is very likely that Western people will have increasingly negative thoughts and feelings. Furthermore, the attitude of Islamophobia may spread, for once a negative opinion becomes widely accepted public opinion, it is not so easy to change or eradicate; this may negatively influence the existence of all Muslims who live in Western countries. Moreover, this fixed negative attitude will quite possibly affect the international relations between Western and Islamic countries. It has already been seen how Muslims' recent attempts to build new mosques in both European countries and the United States have deeply disturbed many people and have become a subject of debate. Just so, European countries have increasingly been banning certain garments worn by Muslim women that reflect their identification with radical Islam. In Europe, the *burqa*[7] is largely regarded as apparel that is oppressive and regressive to the advancement of women.

As we begin to consider different aspects of the unknown Islam, issues concerning Islamic culture and its relation to Christian culture cannot be easily dismissed or ignored, for every human being originated from the same divine–spiritual source, and we are all taking part in *a spiritual evolution that is moving toward a future spiritual goal*. This knowledge brings with it certain responsibilities concerning our neighbors. We see that—since the human is the microcosm—these responsibilities are asserting themselves at a microcosmic level and, in certain instances, even at a macrocosmic level. Therefore, trying to find humane resolutions to the problems that confront us rather than dismissing them would be in accordance with what the divine–spiritual world expects of humanity. When we consider the relationship between Christian and Islamic cultures, we find that we cannot afford to remain indifferent to these matters of grave importance. And the most important factor that could help us to understand "the other" is empathy. Inflexible, permanent judgments could hinder our endeavors to achieve the degree of empathy needed

---

7   *Burqa*: A garment (usually black) worn by Muslim women to cover themselves from head to toe (except the eyes).

to understand Muslims and Islam, and to establish reconciliation between the cultures.

Until recently, there was no particular reason why Islam should have become the center of attention in Western countries. In the West, Islam has been viewed as a monotheistic religion adopted by most Middle Eastern and North African countries, whose adherents believe in Allah, have a sacred book called the Koran, and go to a mosque for prayer. It has also been assumed that Muslims lead a reserved way of life. On the surface, it looked as if there was no major misunderstanding between Muslims and Christians; everybody seemed to go about their own way of life and adhere to their own religious belief. The two World Wars fought in Europe and the consequent division of Europe into two opposing political blocks shifted Europe's attention to their own internal matters, which also contributed to its slackening relationships with Islamic countries. However, in recent years Muslims who live in Europe and in the US began to assert themselves and their Islamic beliefs in various ways. As a consequence of shocking incidents perpetrated by certain people, this former opinion has totally changed. For example, there are serious allegations that Muslim terrorists committed the September 11th attack on the Twin Towers in New York City. As a result of this attack, both towers collapsed and nearly three thousand people died. This was an incident that is not likely to be easily forgotten.[8]

We might recall other dreadful attacks carried out by Muslim terrorists. In 2005, two of London's underground stations and a bus were bombed. In these devastating incidents fifty people died and 700 were wounded. Muslim terrorists' bombings were not aimed only at

---

[8] This event is given here as an example, since it has been officially alleged that Muslim terrorists were responsible for the attack. Others, however, have serious doubts about this conviction, because they find it hard to believe that such an intricately planned and determined execution of three simultaneous attacks (in fact, a fourth building also collapsed in the vicinity) could have been so easily accomplished by terrorists who had entered the US as tourists for the first time in their lives. With this perspective and reasoning, the notion is that "one can believe with no doubt when hearing that Muslim terrorists have exploded a bus or an underground station or similar attacks, but the 9/11 event sounds far too technical and complex to be inspired and conceived by terrorists who came from the deserts of Arabia."

the Western world, however. In 2008, in the month of Ramadan (a time of fasting for Muslims), there was a bombing in a luxury hotel in Islamabad, Pakistan, and sixty people died, including women and children. In Holland in 2005, a Dutch filmmaker was killed for making a documentary film about the oppression and suffering of Muslim women. We might also recall the time when a caricature of the Prophet Muhammad—depicting him as a bomb that was about to explode—aroused much anger in the Islamic world, to the extent that some Muslims began to threaten war between the cultures. The Danish artist who made that drawing had to go into hiding because Muslim fundamentalists threatened his life. The author Salman Rushdie had a similar experience in 1989 and went into hiding. In January 2010, a young Muslim suicide bomber from Nigeria tried to blow up a jumbo jet, but luckily his attempt was unsuccessful. To these, we could also add the bombing of a church in Egypt during a service in December 2010, resulting in the death and wounding of many Christians. In 2015, the French journal *Charlie Hebdo* came under attack by Muslim extremists for perceived blasphemy against Islam and the Prophet Muhammad. Other incidents of Islamic terror are on record, but these few examples sufficiently draw our attention to certain points. As a consequence of such attacks, the Western world no longer regards Islam as a peaceful or benevolent religion in the Middle East.[9]

Noteworthy contrasts between Christianity and Islam

When we analyze the nature and structure of Islam, it becomes clear that this religion is based mainly on submission and obedience to Allah. For example, their formal way of worshipping involves prostrating themselves five times a day—a clear gesture of submission and obedience. Comparing their understanding of worshipping Allah with how Christians revere their God, we find that Christianity does not demand this kind of worship, and that *freedom of belief* is inherent in the nature of "true Christianity." Therefore,

---

9   All of these examples are viewed from an objective and unbiased standpoint; in this book, the intent is not to accuse or judge Islam or any particular Muslim.

members of Western Christian cultures may find it hard to understand why this kind of worship—based on obedience to and fear of Allah—is practiced in Islam. Christians may also wonder if the deity that Muslims have named Allah is actually demanding this kind of worship and obedience. As a matter of fact—strangely enough—the answer to this question is both "yes" and "no." However, this answer will make more sense if we approach the subject from a historical angle. There was a time when this kind of obedience and worship had to be demanded of the Arabic people, for it was very much necessary at the outset of Islam. Then a time came when it was no longer necessary, owing to certain reasons that shall be explained in later sections.

We could look for indications of obedience and surrender in the Gospels. In contrast to the prevalent Islamic doctrine, the content of the Gospels reveals that the God of Christianity does not demand obedience, submission, and worship from humanity (especially since the Advent of Christ). According to John 15:15, Jesus Christ declares, "I no longer call you servants, because a servant does not know his master's business. Instead, I have called you *'friends,'* for everything that I learned from my Father I have made known to you." In Mark 10:45, he says, "For even the Son of Man did not come to be served, but to serve, and to give his life as a ransom for many."

Christ's words indicate a radical change in the status of human beings. In a sense, Christ's declaration is the turning point away from the downward direction of humanity's evolution since the "Fall" from Paradise. Before the Fall, although humankind was within the bosom of the divine-spiritual world, they could not yet be called "friends"; to call someone a friend, we must be able to perceive the presence of an "I" in that other person. However, humankind did not yet possess an "I," a true sense of self, while in heaven.[10] Jesus

---

10 It is interesting to see that this particular primal "paradise condition" of humanity—when humankind did not yet possess an individualized ego—has also been mentioned in the Koran in a different way. Surah 76:1 questions, "Has there not been over Man a long period of Time, when he was nothing—(not even) mentioned?" Another rendering of the same verse states, "There has certainly come upon man a period of time when he was not a thing spoken of." The meaning of this is that humans only began to

Christ was able to address human beings as "friends" in the fourth post-Atlantean epoch, when the human intellectual (mind) soul was developing. This was the time when the human was able to stand in front of Christ with a developed "I." When we ponder on how Christ (as a god) chose to express his relationship to humankind, we can see that the word he used is very meaningful; one does not expect worship from a friend, and a friendship cannot be founded on obedience or submission. The quality inherent as the basis of a deep friendship is *love*. Insofar as humankind's relationship with Christ is concerned, the more a person is imbued with Christ, the more this love will be transformed into a spiritualized higher form of love. Although human beings will acquire this higher and spiritualized form of love in the far-distant future, divine–spiritual love has always been part of Christ's intrinsic nature, and this personal quality manifests in the cosmos as a cosmic principle.[11] Christ's words "I called you friends" is a natural reflection of his divine love for humanity. When he proclaimed, "I did not come to be served but to serve," these words reflect the profound understanding prevalent among the beings of the divine–spiritual hierarchy, for beings of the hierarchy offer their service to beings who occupy a lower rank than their own. This is the opposite of how a relationship is arranged in a hierarchy on Earth. When we ponder Christ's exalted attitude emanating from the Gospels, it becomes apparent that at the core of the Christian faith[12] there is no expectation of worshipping or prostrating before God as in the Islamic sense. However, when we turn our attention to a certain verse in the Koran, we get the impression that Allah expects humankind to obey him and to worship only him.

---

  be considered by their creator as "real beings" when they acquired an ego. Before this, the human's ego was only a potential seed.

11 The quintessence of Christ's—the Son's—being constitutes the *principle of love in the cosmos*.

12 Here, *Christianity* is not used in the context of the prevalent forms of Christianity—i.e., it has no relation with any sect, church, or denomination. In the abovementioned Christianity, what is meant is the initial pure form of Christianity imbued by Christ before it turned into an established religion. It also implies the cosmic Christianity that began to unfold after the reappearance of Christ in the etheric.

51:56 *"I have only created jinn¹³ and men that they may serve me. I created humankind only that they might worship me."*

It seems we cannot argue the clear meaning of this verse. Moreover, this particular statement could be the very reason behind the Muslims' strict worship of Allah and the way they prostrate themselves before him. However, we need to consider other factors. Let us briefly contemplate the act of creation from the creator's point of view. In accordance with its divine nature, the original place of a divine being (as a creator) is the spiritual realm, and the intrinsic quality of this dimension is that it is eternal and nonperishable. In contradistinction to this, our human place is the physical plane, which is perishable and temporal—in other words, the quality of "being eternal" is lacking in this dimension. At this point, we must ask Muslims—indeed, everyone—an essential question: Why would any deity who has a divine-spiritual and eternal nature become involved in the incredibly hard and phenomenal task of creating a temporal and perishable physical world, as well as an ephemeral and perishable being such as a human?

We can think of many answers, but we cannot simply answer with this: So that they might worship me. To a deity whose intrinsically divine qualities (such as being eternal) form the foundation of the cosmos, the rituals of worship and prostration of ephemeral beings created by the deity itself would not provide any worthwhile satisfaction. Thus, it is illogical that a deity might create an incredible world and a certain being so that this being prostrates before him. Some very essential factors are undoubtedly lacking in this answer. "I created the human beings only so that they might worship me" should not be a satisfactory answer even for a Muslim. The Koran states that Allah created humankind stage by stage. This means that the creation of the world and humankind, as well as other beings, was a gradual process

---

13 In Arabic lore, *jinn* are certain invisible entities of good or bad natures found in the desert that can influence people in certain ways. For instance, when the Prophet Muhammad began to recite his inspired verses to the people of Mecca, the unbelievers mocked him by saying that his inspirations must have come from the *jinn*. In anthroposophic terms, some of the *jinn* are nature spirits (spirits of fire, air, water, and earth; successively: salamanders, sylphs, undines, and gnomes). Accordingly, luciferic *jinn* and ahrimanic *jinn* also exist.

that required a lot of effort,[14] and surely all this did not happen in a short span of time.

> 71:14 *"Why do you deny the greatness of Allah when he has made you in gradual stages?"*

Let us take as fact the Islamic dogma that "Allah alone was the creator of the cosmos." From a logical perspective, a statement that claims that an eternal divine being has taken all this trouble and done an incredible amount of work all by himself just to achieve the result of "having humankind worship him" does not sound probable or logical at all, because a deity who is capable of such a creation surely would be a deity who is beyond such insignificant and trivial needs. Could any Muslim imagine that Allah is a deity who would indulge in such a simple worldly desire? Surely every Muslim could surmise that Allah is not in need of any kind of worship that may come from beings he himself has created. Then, why does Allah mention "worship" in verse 51:56? Could this verse possibly mean something else? Did Allah actually have some other significant purpose in mind? Could this verse have perhaps been misinterpreted by Muslims?

When we bear in mind what is said at the beginning of 71:14, "Why do you deny the greatness of Allah?" we could suggest that *worship*, in fact, means "acknowledgment of his existence." At the outset of Islam, not every Arab tribe easily accepted the deity proclaimed by the Prophet Muhammad, and this resolute denial continued for a long time. As a consequence, believers in Allah and nonbelievers fought many serious battles. When we remember that most of the verses in the Koran were inspired during the beginnings of Islam, it becomes clear that at those initial stages Allah couldn't have said anything that directly demanded worship of him, because the first and main objective of Muhammad during those times (when people did not yet accept Allah as a divine being) was to establish the existence of Allah as a reality so that every Arab tribe would acknowledge him as the creator of the world and humankind.

---

14 As we recall from anthroposophic elucidations, the beings of the divine–spiritual hierarchy made a lot of sacrifices during the stages of humankind's creation, also.

In the words "Why do you deny the greatness of Allah?" we see that Allah is not yet acknowledged by all Arab tribes as a great deity who encompasses the universe. In the words "I created humankind" (indicating that Allah created humankind), we see an attempt to draw Arab nonbelievers' (idolaters') attention to the fact that it was the deity called *Allah* who created them. Like their relatives (their distant cousins, the Hebrews, who had acknowledged Yahweh as their God in the past), it was necessary that now Arabs, who worshipped idols in pre-Islamic times, also achieve the awareness that they were created by a divine–spiritual being—that is, by Allah.

When Islam came into existence, certain facts and spiritual concepts that Hebrews had already known for several centuries were now revealed to the Arabs. Among other fundamental teachings, Arabs had to learn and understand the fact that idolatry was an iniquitous practice and that they needed to acquire a concept of morality and had to abide by certain rules suggested by Allah—which would also be a guideline in legal matters—and that Allah is the almighty deity who created everything in the world and is the only one who should be acknowledged as a deity. All this had to be achieved and put into practice within a very short period of time. Muhammad's struggle to inaugurate Islamic teachings and establish Allah as the deity of the Arabs lasted twenty-three years. This was indeed a very short span of time to achieve a successful transition from paganism to a monotheist religion. Arabs had difficulty in comprehending and accepting these new teachings and transforming themselves, and many at first strongly refused to accept Muhammad's inspired verses.

When we consider these explanations, it becomes clear that the "problem" at issue actually originates from an erroneous understanding and application of a verse that *had been inspired in accordance with the necessities of the times at the outset of Islam.* Verses 51:56 and 71:14 and many others are related only to certain situations encountered by Muhammad at the emergence of Islam. Now, in the present time, it would be impossible to come across any Arab or Muslim who denies Allah or who does not recognize him as the creator. This is why utterances such as "Why do you deny the greatness of Allah?" and "I created humankind so they might worship me" no longer carry the original mission or meaning that they had 1,400 years ago. However, when such verses are read as if they came from Allah only very recently, they inevitably impose a kind of dogma on the believers, and this creates many problems. In other words, when fundamentalist, radical, or extremist Muslims read such ancient verses in the present time, they believe that the idea of worship inherent in a particular verse must also be imposed on members of other religions, and they expect all non-Muslims to become Muslims and worship Allah.[15]

This brings us to the point where we must again ask the question: Can it be claimed that Allah created human beings so that they would worship him, or could there be some other, more profound reasons behind the creation of the kingdoms of minerals, plants, animals, and human beings? If humanity's true relationship with God (which is clearly explained by the Christ-being) could be considered objectively by Muslims, the quality inherent in this relationship could serve as an indication for them that worshipping God in an Islamic sense[16] is not expected from humanity. Rather, it is expected that humans acquire a more profound understanding of their creator and comprehend what the word *friend* denotes, so as to experience the necessary spiritual transformation to be able to meet their creator in "spiritualized love." They may also realize that at a certain time in the spiritual history of humankind, "an exalted God," whose intrinsic nature is love, *made a profound sacrifice to save them from their entanglement with the material world and to elevate them to his divine–spiritual realm.*

It is necessary to mention another issue that marks a significant difference between the Gospels and the Koran. This has to do with

---

15 This subject will be dealt with in more detail in a later section.

16 In fact, although in three Koranic verses Muslims are advised to do the prayer of *namaz* (prostrating before Allah), in another verse Allah states that "to remember him" or to ponder on him is more important than namaz. This means that it is more important for a Muslim to possess an awareness of Allah's admonitions at all times, providing a continuous guidance for one's thoughts, feelings, and actions. This could be regarded as an initial endeavor for the development of conscience. However, in contradistinction, a jihadist practices the act of namaz but does not strive to acquire any spiritual awareness to develop his or her conscience; in other words, he or she does not "remember Allah."

how the concept of love has been expressed in each. Whereas love is one of the most important messages in the Gospels, there is no emphasis on it in the Koran, nor is there any indication of what love's cosmic mission is and how this mission relates to humanity. In fact, there is hardly any noteworthy mention of it. For instance, in verse 3:31, it is stated that if one loves Allah, then one should follow Muhammad—that is, one should become a Muslim, and then Allah will also love that person. According to this verse, however, one must fulfill "a certain condition" to deserve Allah's love, for Allah does not love unbelievers. In verse 3:32, "loving Allah" is synonymous with "obeying Allah." Allah's love is not an unconditional but depends on the fulfillment of certain conditions. Thus, Allah's love for humankind can be expressed in this way: If you believe in me, this means you love me, and thus I will also love you. This approach is very different from the all-encompassing love that emanates from the Gospels.

> 3:31 "If you love Allah, follow me [Muhammad]."[17] Allah will love you and forgive your sins. Allah is forgiving and merciful.
>
> 3:32 "Obey Allah and the Apostle [Muhammad]." If they [unbelievers] give no heed, then truly, Allah does not love the unbelievers.

Let us compare how love reflects from these verses with the quality of love that reflects from Christ's words in the Gospels.

> I have given them the glory that you gave me, that they may be one as we are one—I in them and you in me—so that they may be brought to complete unity. Then the world will know that you sent me and have loved them even as you have loved me. Father, I want those you have given me to be with me where I am, and to see my glory, the glory you have given me because you loved me before the creation of the world.... I have made you known to them, and will continue to make you known in order that the love you have for me may be in them and that I myself may be in them. (John 17:22–24, 26)

---

17 Brackets are not used in N. J. Dawood's translation of the Koran; all the brackets found in the verses have been added by the author.

St. Paul's words also reveal the sacrificial quality inherent in Christ's love toward humanity: "But God demonstrates his own love for us in this: While we were still sinners, Christ died for us" (Rom. 5:8).

We can see that according to John, the love Christ speaks of is unconditional, transcending the differentiation between God and the being God has created. Moreover, it opens the door for human beings to be united with their creator. When we consider Islam and Christianity from this perspective, a distinct contrast appears between the attitudes of the Islamic God and the Christian God, and this contrast is clear in the Scriptures.

Can we easily conclude, then, that true spiritualized love was not as important for Allah? Could there be some other reason why the concept of love did not make it into the Koran as a central issue? In this context (bearing in mind that Yahweh is very closely related with the Christ and has the same qualities as the Christ, and that it is claimed by Muhammad that Allah is actually Yahweh), it is necessary to ask this: Why has Allah acted differently in his relationship with the Arabian people? During the period when their relationship was founded on "the covenant," Yahweh was not only a strict God, but was also capable of showing his love to the Hebrews. The Jews were able to sense that love, which reflects from the Old Testament.[18] If, after many centuries, Yahweh has now become the Arabs' "Allah," why does he hide or keep his love hidden and not bestow it on the Arabs also?

---

18 It is necessary to point out that Yahweh's love (*hesed*) for the Hebrews came into being as an outcome of having made a special covenant with them. Accordingly, we can see that his love for the Hebrews is affirmed in various chapters of the Old Testament. For example: "I will bow down toward thy holy temple, for thy love and faithfulness I will praise thy name" (Ps. 138:2); "The LORD will accomplish his purpose for me. Thy true love, O LORD, endures forever; leave not thy work unfinished" (Ps. 138:8). Yahweh's love is also mentioned in Jeremiah 9:23–24: "These are the words of the LORD: Let not the wise man boast of his wisdom, nor the valiant of his valor; LORD, let not the rich man boast of his riches; but if any man would boast, let him boast of this, that he understands and knows me. For I am the LORD, I show unfailing love, I do justice and right upon the earth; for on these I have set my heart. This is the very word of the LORD."

Without dispute, according to the Koran, *Allah is the deity who was formerly the Jewish God Yahweh.* Many koranic verses connect Allah with attributes ascribed to Yahweh.[19] In addition, there is a visible attempt throughout the Koran to connect Muhammad's inspired messages with Abraham, Moses, and Yahweh and to bridge the times when each had close relations with Yahweh.

> 45:16 We gave the Scriptures to the Israelites and bestowed on them wisdom and prophet-hood. We provided them with good things and exalted them above the nations.

> 23:49 And we gave Moses the Torah, so that his people will be rightly guided.

Apparently, these verses aim to establish that Allah is the deity formerly known as Yahweh, and now he has chosen a prophet from descendants of Ishmael to deliver additional messages. However, there are many factors that we must consider before we can fully accept this statement as fact. For example, between the time when Yahweh became the Hebrew God and the time when Islam was born, the appearance of Jesus Christ and the birth of Christianity occurred. When we analyze the Koran, it seems the verses conveniently bypass this very important matter—that is, the verses that deal with Jesus and Christianity are composed in such a way that gives the impression that Jesus was not successful in his mission, and that Christianity was born because of a great misunderstanding, and, therefore, it should not have come into existence in the first place. The explanations and arguments postulated in the koranic verses will be dealt with in detail in a later section, but meanwhile let us continue in accordance with the Koran's claim that Yahweh is Allah.

In the Gospels, Jesus Christ was able to speak about love on many different levels and to underline these aspects, because his close circle of disciples and some of his audience were able to understand what he revealed. Rudolf Steiner elucidated that love in its spiritual form, interrelated with the divine–spiritual world, is the result of attaining profound spiritual consciousness—that is, it is a result that follows

---

19 These verses will be mentioned in a later section.

the development of consciousness. Accordingly, Yahweh trained and prepared the Jewish people[20] for several centuries. During that period, they acquired a certain level of consciousness needed to glimpse spiritual love and to understand what Jesus Christ had to say about love. On the other hand, their cousins, the Arabs, did not experience this essential period of training and preparation, nor did they have a chance to acquire this measure of consciousness; thus it was not possible for Allah to draw their attention to concepts related to love. For this reason, the main purpose of the koranic verses—inspired by Allah via the Angel Gabriel and recited by Muhammad—was to establish rapid awareness of certain spiritual issues, so that the Arabs would acknowledge Allah both as a divine deity and as their guide. It was crucial to achieve this result, and, in a sense, there was a concealed deadline for the accomplishment of this task.[21]

The quality and character of the task that had to be accomplished by the Arabs were fundamentally very different from the essence of the former mission of the Jewish people[22]—that is, although acquisition of a certain level of consciousness, conscience, and love was needed by the Hebrews to succeed in their mission, to abide the long period needed to acquire a certain degree of spiritual consciousness and conscience that would have opened the door to acquiring spiritual love was not essential for the Arabs to accomplish their task successfully. This is why Allah was unable to offer Arabs the concept of love directly or to speak of love more often in the verses; for any teaching based on love would have meant nothing to Arabs in those times. Although at a glance one perceives a distinct contrast between Christianity and Islam, at a deeper level it becomes clear that such spiritual facts are not the outcome of random personal choices, but are consequences of the development of cosmic processes. This brings us to other concealed reasons that Allah demanded total submission, obedience, and worship from the

---

20 Yahweh prepared the Jews for the arrival of the Christ impulse, which the Christ-being would bring to the world. Among others, love was the most important influence encompassed by this impulse.

21 The concealed deadline for the accomplishment of this task was the year 666.

22 The tasks of Hebrews and Arabs will be explained in detail in a later section.

Arabs. Within this context, it is initially necessary to ask the following questions: Has Allah actually given Arabian people *sharia* law (similar to that of the Torah) and fettered them within the framework of these particular laws permanently? Is there really no way out of *sharia* for the Muslims, or could it be that koranic verses pointed out certain measures that had to be implemented only during a transitory period? If the latter is the case, might certain verses indicate a way out of *sharia*, which Muslims have somehow overlooked until now?

The visible part of Islam can be likened to an iceberg whose tip is seen but the greater part is immersed in the water and concealed. Obtaining the true answers to these and many other questions and trying to form a clear idea about Islam and its deity is not an easy matter. External history can provide only limited explanations. Thus, in our endeavor to form an understanding of Islam and Allah, we need to move around the main subject and look at Islam from many different angles, while considering in particular the spiritual-historical aspect of this *reemerged Moon religion of Yahweh*. Once we are able to form a clear idea about the reasons why Islam came into being, it will become clear that various negative aspects of Islam that presently confront us are the outcome of its adherents' lack of knowledge concerning the factual reasons behind the existence of Islam.

For the sake of comparison, it is necessary to point out that in the past the same kind of negative development led to Christianity's gradual transformation into an institutionalized dogmatic religion, which manifested, for example, in the oppression and torture of the Inquisition. According to Rudolf Steiner, although the truth regarding the origin of Christianity was known in its early days, this profound knowledge was lost after three or four hundred years, and then Christianity was exposed to luciferic and ahrimanic influences. Following this period of luciferic and ahrimanic influence, it became a dogmatic, terrestrial religion, and certain negative aspects began to manifest in it. By contrast, Islam was exposed to luciferic influences from its outset and became an institutionalized dogmatic religion almost from the very beginning. The founder of Islam did not have an idea about the real esoteric reasons behind the emergence of Islam at the beginning, nor did he know about the true reasons behind the existence of Judaism and Christianity.[23] Moreover, after the Prophet Muhammad's death, the emissaries of Islam—who advanced with organized armies and tried to spread Islam beyond the Arabian Peninsula—had no inkling about the concealed reasons behind the new manifestation of Yahweh's monotheistic Moon religion.

Owing to their misinterpretation of various verses, early Muslims assumed that Allah initially selected the Hebrews and gave them their sacred book and many laws so as to establish the "Jewish religion" and commanded their obedience to him. From time to time, he reiterated his messages by sending new prophets. But the Hebrews failed to take heed of those laws and Allah's admonitions; they diverted from his path—for example, they worshipped a golden bull. Thus, Allah sent Jesus as a prophet, and he conveyed Allah's messages and admonitions to them. But the Jews misunderstood the Prophet Jesus and his teachings and again diverted from Allah's true path and started to believe in false gods, such as the Father, Son, and Holy Spirit. As a consequence of adopting controversial opinions and beliefs, they divided into Jews and Christians. This resulted in Allah sending another prophet to convey his messages and his *sharia* laws, bringing clarity to all the matters that were in conflict, and demanding that descendants of Ishmael and Isaac henceforth become Muslims and gather under the religion of Islam to worship only Allah.

Apparently, according to Muslims, this "last prophet" was Muhammad. In present times, we see that those who have adopted this dogmatic belief—fundamentalist, radical, and extremist Muslims and jihadists—claim they have the right to project it on adherents of other religions with the expectation of transforming them into Muslims. However, more lenient Muslims who do not agree with the

---

23 It is not intended by this statement to imply that the Prophet Muhammad lacked knowledge of spiritual issues. As a matter of fact, the prophet surely acquired much of his knowledge from what was revealed to him by Gabriel, which as a result motivated him to start a great struggle so that Arabians would also acknowledge Allah and attain a certain degree of spiritual consciousness.

extremists and jihadists and who do not identify with these dogmatic opinions do not get involved in such radical claims or acts of violence.

Nonetheless, it seems Muslims who readily adopt such radical and dogmatic beliefs are unaware of a very important issue concerning Allah. Although surely unintentional, their dogmatic opinions give the impression that they are underestimating Allah. At the root of this belief is the implication that Allah made mistakes in the past and that he later tried to compensate for his mistakes. At this point we must ask: Can they imagine it possible that Allah would entangle himself in mistakes concerning his relationships with humankind, the beings he himself created? As Allah is an omnipotent God who created the world, human beings, and all the other creatures, should he not be beyond making mistakes?

"Esmaul Husna"[24] indicates that an attribute of Allah is that he is "all-knowing and beyond making mistakes, thus can never be at fault." If these indications about Allah's nature are taken into consideration, how could Muslims assume that Allah made certain mistakes at the beginning with the Hebrews and, after sending them other prophets, sent Jesus as a solution? And how could he be mistaken about the outcome of sending them Jesus as a prophet? Could he not have anticipated that they would misunderstand Jesus and branch off as Jews and Christians? Is it possible for any Muslim to imagine that *Allah is learning how to deal with human beings by trial and error?* Actually, it is hard to imagine that any Muslim who has common sense would agree with this statement; surely all would sense that an omnipotent deity who is all-knowing and beyond error would not adopt trial-and-error as a method of dealing with the beings he himself created.

Many more reasons must be hidden behind the religions of Judaism, Christianity, and Islam, and certain Muslims' interpretation and evaluation of these facts are not correct. It is also clear that the foregoing Islamic proclamations and dogmatic beliefs are far from reflections of the profound spiritual truths found beneath what can be seen on the surface.

---

24 Esmaul Husna (found in the Koran) explains "the ninety-nine beautiful names," which are also ninety-nine divine merits attributed to Allah.

Reasons concealed behind the emergence of Islam as a new Yahweh Moon religion

To bring more clarity to the aforementioned issues—which actually originate in the past but continuously assert themselves in the present—we need to delve into significant incidents narrated in the Bible and try to reconstruct from an anthroposophic viewpoint the reasons of why and how Islam emerged as a monotheistic religion. This may shed light on certain past developments that were actually preliminaries of profound impulses that were to unfold in sequences in future times. In the Old Testament, Yahweh promised Abraham a son.

> When Abram was ninety-nine years old, the Lord appeared to him and said, "I am God Almighty; walk before me faithfully and be blameless. Then I will make my covenant between me and you and will greatly increase your numbers...this is my covenant with you: You will be the father of many nations. (Gen. 17:1–4)

Although many years passed, Abraham and Sarah did not have a child; as time went by and they grew older, they began to lose hope of ever having a child. To resolve this problem, Sarah suggested that Abraham have a child with Sarah's Egyptian handmaiden, Hagar. Abraham consented to this marital arrangement, taking Hagar as his second wife; thus, Abraham had a son from Hagar. This boy was named Ishmael (Ismail). According to custom, although Hagar was the birth mother, any child conceived belonged to Abraham and Sarah. Yet, Sarah eventually bore their long-awaited son, and they named him Isaac.

Yahweh's promise was now fulfilled, and through Isaac and his descendants the Hebrews (the Israelites) came into being. After some time passed, problems arose between Sarah and Hagar, and it was decided that it would be better if Hagar and Ishmael left the household, which they did. As they were crossing the desert, they ran out of water and found themselves in a perilous situation. When Hagar had lost all hope for their lives and started weeping, the angel of the Lord called from heaven and comforted her. The Lord provided her water and also promised Hagar that "he will make the descendants of Ishmael a great nation"—that is, Ishmael and his descendants would become the Arabian people.

Why did Yahweh give special protection and help to Hagar and Ishmael and promise something similar to what he had promised Abraham? In keeping with the preparations made by the divine spiritual realm, besides Isaac, it was also necessary to have a continuation of Abraham's lineage through Ishmael. When we notice how the Prophet Muhammad, in his inspired verses, often claims that Abraham was also their ancestor and directs Arabs' attention to this historical fact, we can form an idea about why a continuation of Ishmael's lineage parallel to that of Hebrews (although they were totally disconnected from Isaac's lineage) was also necessary. Keeping in mind that Muhammad was a descendant of Ishmael, it is clear that Muhammad's birth in AD 570 was not a random incident. His birth (as a prophet descended from Ishmael who would, for this reason, receive inspired verses in the future revealed by Gabriel) had been previously planned and prepared by the beings of the divine–spiritual world since the birth of his ancestor Ishmael, so that the impulse of Islam could be brought about at a very precise time in the flow of human evolution.

Anthroposophic studies reveal that, in the background of the biblical story and in external history, another, deeper truth also exists and that these two sons of Abraham had been assigned different tasks by the divine–spiritual world. What they had in common was that through their descendants two different lineages of people and many tribes would be generated. In addition to the fact that their tasks were fundamentally different, they also differed from one another in other ways. Isaac's lineage was to form a "threshold" through which a sublime spiritual being could eventually enter the physical world at a certain future time. The lineage of Ishmael—the Arabian people—had the task of deadening, or blunting, Sorath's[25] intervention, which was due in 666, and later to transfer the remnants of that deadened Sorathic wisdom to different parts of the world.

---

25 Sorath is an adverse spiritual being of darkness from the Sun sphere, who had a devious plan of intervention by which he aimed to hinder or even stop the natural development and flow of human evolution.

The birth of Abraham's sons Ishmael and Isaac coincided with the age of Kali Yuga.[26] Steiner often explained that, during Atlantean times, humanity possessed a natural faculty of clairvoyance, enabling them to behold the divine–spiritual world directly and to maintain a connection with the beings of that world. Although the human faculty of clairvoyance gradually diminished, remnants of it continued during the following post-Atlantean civilizations. Nevertheless, the faculty of clairvoyance had to be eliminated completely—first, because human beings had to lose their inner (soul) contact with the divine–spiritual world so that they could unrestrictedly become beings of the physical–material world in every respect. (Actually, this was the predestined consequence of the Fall from Heaven.) Second, instead of the faculty of clairvoyance, humanity had to develop the faculties of thinking, intelligence, and logic. Whereas, during the Atlantean times, humanity was guided by the Atlantean oracles and, later, during the first post-Atlantean civilization—the Old Indian civilization—by the Seven Rishis, human beings eventually had to learn to develop and use their own capacity of thinking and intellect to come to terms with the physical world with no inner guidance from the divine–spiritual world.

At the same time, this was also the route humankind had to traverse on their way to becoming free beings—"free" in the sense that, having severed their connection with the divine world, they would no longer be guided by divine–spiritual beings. These developments were interwoven with the evolution of the human sense of self and the initial implantation of the "I" (or rather, when its seeds first began to unfold) and took place during the period of the fifth Atlantean root race—the Semites. In this context, Abraham's progeny (the Hebrews and the Arabs) were going to be the future representatives of the Semites. Through this race, furthering "terrestrial intellectual

---

26 Kali Yuga, the Dark Age, which started in 3101 BC and ended in AD 1899, was a period during which humankind's spiritual connection or spiritual guidance began to be gradually severed from the divine–spiritual realm. The starting point taken by Rudolf Steiner, 3102 BC (written astronomically as –3101, agrees with the Hindu tradition for the start of Kali Yuga. However, Steiner's elucidation concerning the length of Kali Yuga (5,000 years) is different from the period of 432,000 years given by Hindu sources.

capacities" and developing a faculty for comprehending the material world according to number, measure, mathematical logic, and weight were to be achieved. This could not come to fruition unless humankind lost the last remnants of clairvoyance during the Kali Yuga period. Steiner explains:

> Abraham was a man who possessed the faculty to grasp and comprehend the nature of Yahweh, or Jehovah, as the God who lives and moves in the outer phenomena of the universe. It was now a matter of driving from the particular faculties possessed by the individual man, Abraham, the mission of the whole people. Abraham's spiritual constitution had to be transmitted to the others....
>
> Only by way of physical heredity, within a people linked by blood relationship, could such faculties be transmitted.... A brain capable of understanding Yahweh had to be preserved through physical heredity. Yahweh's covenant with Abraham had also to pass on to his descendants.... The human corporeality which was to propagate itself through the generations and which possessed the faculties necessary for comprehending the world according to number and measure, by mathematical logic—this human corporeality was to be preserved intact and received back as a gift of Yahweh.
>
> However, so that the intrinsic nature of this bodily constitution could remain pure and unalloyed, it was necessary for all old shadowy clairvoyance, all Imaginations and Intuitions, all inflowing revelations such as had poured into the other ancient religions, including those of Chaldea and Egypt, should be renounced.... So that this bodily constitution might be preserved in Isaac, the last clairvoyant gift, the gift of the ram, the two-petaled lotus-flower is sacrificed.... As the mission of the Hebrew people progresses, these Abrahamic faculties are transmitted from generation to generation.[27]

It is necessary to mention that, in addition to the Hebrews, the descendants of Ishmael would acquire the faculties for comprehending the material world according to number, measure, and

---

27 Steiner, *Deeper Secrets of Human History*, lecture 2.

mathematical logic and transmit it to future generations. However, insofar as the Hebrews were concerned, since they were not going to receive further inner spiritual guidance from the divine–spiritual world through clairvoyance, they needed to receive spiritual guidance from an external source to protect them from the dark influences of the Kali Yuga period. Accordingly, they received protection and guidance from Yahweh. Yahweh had clearly informed them that he was their God and made a covenant with them.

> Then God said to Abraham, "As for you, you must keep my covenant, you and your descendants after you for the generations to come. This is my covenant with you and your descendants after you, the covenant you are to keep: Every male among you shall be circumcised. You are to undergo circumcision, and it will be the sign of the covenant between me and you. For the generations to come every male among you who is eight days old must be circumcised.... My covenant in your flesh is to be an everlasting covenant." (Gen. 17:9–13)

Later, as a continuation of this covenant, Moses was given the Decalogue and several other laws that governed even minute details of their life. These laws would be their guide and protect them for several centuries. As they kept their blood ties pure by endogamy and by strictly abided the laws and admonition from Yahweh, Hebrews did not face any serious danger of degeneration of moral values. Keeping the law also helped them develop a profound spiritual consciousness of Yahweh's sacredness—his divine qualities—and of Michael, who was his countenance on Earth at the time. Implementation of Yahweh's law also prepared them for the Advent of the Christ-being, who could have incarnated only in a community not exposed directly to the powerful influences of the Kali Yuga period, and that had not fallen into degeneration of spiritual and moral values. As a result of having been successfully prepared for their mission, the Hebrews were successful in creating a threshold for the entry of the Christ-being. As a result of keeping meticulous track of their descendants, the Hebrews could trace their blood ties all the way back to their father Abraham. Through

Abraham, they sensed that they were connected to Yahweh, which enabled them to perceive Yahweh as their God. Consequently, the spiritual inflow from Yahweh was transmitted through their blood ties from generation to generation since the times of their ancestral father Abraham. However, this transference could be successful only while the Hebrews remained as *a group soul*. From the spiritual aspect, as long as they had a close bond with Yahweh and were continuously guided by him, they did not yet possess full freedom; they would not possess full freedom until Christ brought the "Christ impulse" to the world along with the *"principle of freedom,"* a very important aspect of this impulse.

As time passed during Kali Yuga, descendants of Abraham gradually lost their faculty of clairvoyance, and this slowly reflected in their way of life. In addition, after many centuries, they developed the faculty of comprehending the world according to number, weight, measure, and mathematical logic, and eventually they started perceiving the world from a totally materialistic perspective. However, they did not become completely engulfed in the darkness of the Kali Yuga period, for the spiritual inflow from Yahweh and Michael continued to guide and protect them until the event of the Advent of Christ.

Influences on the descendants of Ishmael during the Kali Yuga period

Once Abraham's first son Ishmael had grown up, his mother arranged for him to marry a woman from Egypt.[28] As time went by, Ishmael's descendants grew in number, and many Arab tribes were generated from them. As mentioned, the two sons of Abraham were assigned different tasks. Therefore, their destinies would unfold in different ways. Although the Hebrews had received special guidance and spiritual protection from Yahweh, the Arab tribes received no guidance, admonitions, or commandments to spiritualize their way of life and to nullify the early degenerative influences brought about by the Kali Yuga period. For example, Muhammad—a descendant of Ishmael—did not receive inspired verses from Gabriel until c. AD 610. Consequently, throughout

---

28 In the Bible, Genesis 25:12–15 indicates that Ishmael had twelve sons, and their names are also given.

those centuries, the soul and spiritual constitution of the Arabs were not protected against the dark and degenerative effects imposed by the Kali Yuga period. This kind of preparation was necessary for their encounter with Allah, which was to take place at a future time. At a very specific time, Arabs did receive admonition and some guidance from Allah, but although Yahweh had made a covenant with the Hebrews, *Allah made no covenant with the descendants of Ishmael.*

The absence of a covenant between Allah and the Arabs signifies a very important issue. Allah did not make a second covenant because, once the Arabs accomplished their mission, the special relationship between them would end and Allah would no longer guide them.

This was because the Islamic impulse was supposed to be short-lived, lasting only so long as it took for the Arabs to accomplish their task (before the year 666). After that time—in fact, since the Advent of Christ—it would have been pointless from the perspective of the divine–spiritual realm to establish a covenant similar to the earlier one known as the Old Testament, and to run a kind of separate guidance parallel to the Christ impulse. To start with, the Christ impulse involves humanity as a whole, with no discrimination; with the arrival of Christ and the Christ impulse, the previous circumstances that shaped the human soul and spirit changed entirely. The old principle (formerly active in the Hebrews) of connection with the divine–spiritual world through pure blood ties while belonging to a group soul was abandoned—or rather, transcended. With the Advent of Christ, connection with the divine–spiritual realm would be formed through humanity's relationship with the Christ-being, and this would no longer be compulsory; now it was up to every single individual to decide whether to be connected to the divine–spiritual world or not. Moreover, there could be no possibility of establishing a covenant between Allah and the Arabs, because they had not meticulously kept their blood ties pure through the centuries as had the Hebrews. Since blood is the manifestation of the "I" (individuality) in the physical body,[29] by maintaining pure blood ties Hebrews were able to receive the spiritual influences that came from Yahweh and be

---

29 The heart, blood, and the blood circulatory system is where the human "I" manifests in the physical body.

imbued by them. It was also possible to transmit these accumulated spiritual values—such as morality and conscience—to future generations through pure blood relationships.[30]

To what extent were the Arabs affected during the Kali Yuga period? To form a better idea of this we may refer to *Tafsir*,[31] a voluminous book by Ibn Kathir.[32] It refers to the times prior to the emergence of Islam and the Koran, and indicates that, even before Muhammad's "call," Arab paganism was beginning to show clear signs of decay. According to Ibn Kathir, the descendants of Ishmael were then worshipping some 360 idols that surrounded the sacred Kaaba building in Mecca. Those idols did not represent divine-spiritual beings but non-divine spiritual beings. Until that time, Arabs had not acquired a concept of a divine God that manifested in the outer worldly phenomena and could be sensed and perceived by them. Apart from the idols in Kaaba, each Arab tribe also had an individual idol. Ibn Kathir's book says that, before Islam, Arabs were going through a period of moral degeneration, which was reflected in manifold ways in their way of life. That "dark" period was later designated as *jahiliyyah* period[33] by Muslim Arabs. Ibn Kathir mentions that Arabs engaged in many unchaste ways of marriage; according to some pre-Islamic traditions, Arab men and women were involved in unchaste sexual relationships, which meant that, unlike Hebrews, they showed no special care in protecting their blood ties. Also during pre-Islamic times, women did not have much value or importance according to Arab men and, therefore, had no legal rights whatsoever. Ibn Kathir indicates that in the *jahiliyyah* period

---

30   The spiritual role and importance of blood as "a very special fluid" can be studied in Steiner's *The Occult Significance of Blood*—an esoteric study.

31   The actual title of Ibn Kathir's book is *Tafsir al-Qur'an al-Azim*. *Tafsir* means "commentaries." So, Ibn Kathir's *Tafsir* is actually "Commentaries on the Koran and the *Hadiths*." *Hadiths* are "sayings of the prophet Mohammad."

32   Hafiz Ismail Ibn Kathir (c. 1300–1373) was a renowned Muslim sage—a *muhaddith*, or narrator.

33   *Jahiliyyah* period: The pre-Islamic period during which Arabian tribes were living in a state of spiritual ignorance. *Jahiliyyah* literally means "ignorance."

Arab men believed women were no more important than the cattle they owned; some Arab tribes even buried their daughters alive, since girls were considered to bring dishonor to the family.[34] The Koran addresses this subject:

> 17:31 *You shall not kill your children for fear of want. We will provide for them and for you. To kill them is a great sin.*
>
> 81:8 *"And when the infant girl, buried alive, is asked, for what sin was she slain?"*

In addition to such disregard for their own daughters, the admonition ordained in 24:33 gives an idea of the degenerate situation for slave girls who belonged to Arab households:

> 24:33 *You shall not force your slave girls into prostitution so that you can make money if they wish to preserve their chastity. If anyone compels them, Allah will be forgiving and merciful to them.*

It is also noted in Ibn Kathir's book that the Arab tribes were constantly battling each other over trivial affairs. The author's unbiased, objective explanations point to the fact that the pagan Arabs' connection to the divine–spiritual world had been completely severed, and that they had been left unattended and with no guidance from the divine realm for several centuries during Kali Yuga. Ibn Kathir relates several other details, describing the Arabs' degenerate way of life was before the emergence of Islam. During Kali Yuga, the Arab way of life prevented them from acquiring the kind of spiritual maturity that would have enabled them to understand consciously the nature of a divine God and his spiritual aspects. Another result of leading an unspiritual and degenerate way of life and not being infused with moral values was that descendants of Ishmael were unable to develop "conscience." This is indeed a very significant point. The fact that descendants of Ishmael were unable to develop conscience before the Islamic impulse had an influence on future Muslims and even on

---

34 Arabs would also bury infant girls because, in their eyes, girls were not as useful as boys in the hard conditions of desert life and were extra mouths to feed.

Christian cultures. *Arabism* was the unavoidable consequence of this lack of conscience and consciousness prior to Islam.[35]

Whereas the descendants of Ishmael were deprived of spiritual guidance and admonition, in another region of the Middle East, Yahweh had guided the descendants of Isaac for many centuries, guaranteeing the development of conscience and morality. The Decalogue and many other laws contained in the Talmud were blended with the law, or principle, of *talion*. In other words, the principle of "life for a life, eye for an eye, and tooth for a tooth" stood firmly at the foundation of Judaic law. In addition to the law of *talion*, moral feelings of fear, shame, and repentance also had an effect during the time when Yahweh was providing spiritual guidance. As a result of the strict spiritual discipline infused with these moral feelings, Hebrews became obedient, and this strict discipline helped them transform into individuals who acquired conscience. Valentin Tomberg wrote:

> By causing the starlight of thinking to oppose the dark current of original sin, Moses gave rise to the moral feelings of fear, shame, and repentance.... Feelings of fear and shame could make those people obedient, because at the time of Moses the link between human thinking and willing had not developed enough for anything higher than obedience. The people of the Old Covenant were beings of obedience. By displaying this sharp contrast through the Law, however, he awakened the first yearning of the human heart for a condition that later the prophets called the condition in which the Law is written in the heart.... The "time wisdom" of Moses is knowledge of the human path through the whole of earthly evolution. That path involves, first, the human organism becoming a victim of sin—becoming a karmic organism—so that it could develop as an *obedience* organism, then as a *conscience* organism, and finally rising to the freedom of a *love* organism.[36]

People of the Old Covenant were obedient, but Arabs who never went through the training of the law of *talion* and never came to

---

35 The subject of Arabism will be discussed in detail in a later section.
36 Tomberg, *Christ and Sophia*, chapter 8, "Moses," pp. 100–101.

know the moral feelings of fear, shame, and repentance before they received Muhammad's messages and started to implement the rules of *sharia* knew nothing of obedience to God. The concept of obedience entered Arab life only after around AD 610. As a consequence, it has not been easy for them to comprehend the meaning of the law that is "written on the heart."[37]

Such a transformation was difficult for them because, to start with, to attain this result one must sense the spiritual necessity of such a transformation and wish to transform one's astral body—and, accordingly, exert a great deal of conscious effort toward achieving it. Even before this stage, one needs a strong desire to transcend the weighty restrictions of the law. Evidently, however, since the outset of Islam, Muslims have had no yearning to transcend *sharia* law. Some people belonging to other religions in the world have to a certain extent achieved the condition by which the law is "written on the heart," but Muslims in particular have been unsuccessful in this. The specific state of becoming a being of immaculate conscience cannot be easily achieved in a short time; it is a goal that can be truly achieved only in a far distant future. For this reason, every human being will go through numerous incarnations and be given numerous opportunities. Continuous implementation of *sharia* law and willful employment of obedience and worship may have helped Arabs (who were previously in the *jahiliyyah* period) gain certain spiritual merits, but their achievement did not help them develop an ability to distinguish between right and wrong. The basic requirement for developing this ability is to stop identifying as a group soul and learn that people can make their own decisions in total freedom as individuals. However, always being told, according to *sharia* law, what to do and what not to do has not helped Muslims in developing the condition whereby the Law is written in the heart. In other words, the three members that constitute the human soul (the sentient, intellectual, and consciousness souls) need to be free so that further spiritualization and transformation can take place within each.

---

37 "Declares the Lord: '*I will put my law in their minds and write it on their hearts*'" (Jer. 31:33). Yahweh's proclamation indicates a future when people will no longer need to be guided by an outer law but be able to distinguish inwardly between right and wrong, good and bad; people will be guided by conscience.

The critical situation 333 years after the coming of Christ

While the Kali Yuga period was running its course, it overlapped with the fourth post-Atlantean epoch, the period of the Greek and Roman civilizations that lasted 2,160 years, from 747 BC to AD 1413. The fourth post-Atlantean epoch was the time when earthly human intellectual capacities were intended to develop. As a result, the human "I" would become freer. However, it was necessary that the constitution of the human astral body experience some very important changes so that further development in this direction could take place. What did this change in the astral body involve? Previously, the upper part of a human astral body had a strong connection to the astral world, but it had to decrease in size. This important change occurred around 333. Steiner elucidates those circumstances:

> This point of time, which in a certain sense signifies the greatest crisis in the whole of human evolution, came approximately 333 years after the Mystery of Golgotha.... Before 333...the greater part of the astral body, the more active part of it, was in the upper human and its less active part in the lower human, the middle human between the two. Because in those ancient times the upper part of the astral body was the more powerful, it was through it that divine–spiritual beings exercised their greatest influence on human beings. In accordance with the plan for humankind, human evolution proceeded in such a way that, until about 3,000 years before Christ [Kali Yuga had already began 102 years prior to this date], those conditions for the astral body held good, but by 1,000 years before Christ, the lower part of the astral body was becoming larger and the upper part relatively smaller, until, in 333, the two parts were equal. This was the critical situation 333 years after the coming of Christ, and since then the upper human astral body has been continuously decreasing. That is the course taken by human evolution.... If human beings had not undergone this decrease in the upper part of the astral body, their "I" would never have been able to gain sufficient influence and could never have become free.[38]

---

38 Steiner, *The Evolution of Consciousness*, lecture 13, pp. 253–254.

According to Steiner's explanations, as a result of this "cosmic operation," which involved a continuous decrease in size of the upper part of the astral body, the human "I" became freer around 333. As a consequence of this change, a more serious crisis occurred that humankind inevitably had to encounter during its ongoing evolutionary period. What was this second crisis, and when was it due? It was the Sorathic intervention that was to take place in 666. Why was the timing of Sorath's intervention planned for the year 666—that is, 333 years after 333? We could find the answer by considering the implications of the significant changes the human soul and spirit experienced during this evolution.

It would not be correct to imagine that the human soul and spiritual configuration remained static throughout all the previous epochs it underwent. In fact, humans went through many considerable changes in their physical, ether, and astral bodies. Accordingly, the astral body was to abide the aforesaid change in the year 333, but it was necessary for Sorath that, after those changes, another change in this direction took place so that he could gain a better opportunity to implement his plan. In fact, the decrease in the size of a person's upper astral body also signified that, as a result of this process, one's connection with divine–spiritual beings would be steadily weakened.[39] Consequentially, human beings would transform and gain the faculty of intelligence and be able to use it instead of relying on guidance from the intelligence and wisdom of the beings of the divine realm. In other words, 333 would be the approximate time when people would lose their inner soul–spiritual relationship to "the spirituality" that had previously flowed from the divine realm to permeate human beings, and as a result of being severed

---

39 Actually, the decline in the soul–spiritual forces of humans had already been noticeable at the time when Christ's incarnation took place. Thus, humankind's situation was going to become even more susceptible in the year 666. In the lecture Steiner held in Cologne on December 17, 1913, "The Fifth Gospel," he conveyed the gist of the conversation Jesus had with his mother in which Jesus speaks of the pain he felt upon his profound realization of humanity's decline in its soul–spiritual forces and upon seeing how luciferic and ahrimanic beings were exerting a powerful influence on humankind. Also, in the lecture he gave in Berlin on May 9, 1917, "Aspects of Human Evolution" (CW 176), Steiner explained the consequences of the human's soul–spiritual decline from a different angle. In these lectures he also made an astounding connection between humanity's gradually decreasing age and Jesus Christ's age and indicated how both of them coincide at the age of thirty-three.

from the divine realm they would become more intelligent but spiritually vulnerable. Thus, a being that had a developed intellectual faculty but not a fully developed spiritual consciousness and conscience would also be easy prey for the adversarial spiritual beings who oppose evolution. Steiner explained the critical situation of humanity:

> At a point as many years in the future as the Mystery of Golgotha was in the past, certain spiritual powers had intended to guide earthly development in a direction very different from the one it took as a result of the occurrence of the Mystery of Golgotha. That is, Tertullian's time, the year 333, the point exactly 333 years after the Mystery of Golgotha, was the midpoint, and the new direction in earthly development was planned for 333 years after that—namely, for the year 666. This is the year the writer of the Book of Revelation speaks of so passionately, and I recommend that you read those passages about the year 666. Certain spiritual powers had intended for certain things to happen to humanity in that year, things that would have happened if the Mystery of Golgotha had not taken place. Those powers wanted to use the descending line of development of the intellectual, or mind, soul that began in 333, the year that this development reached its peak, to steer humanity onto a very different track from the one the divine beings connected with us since the beginning, since the Saturn evolution, had intended for us.[40]

However, the significant change that was to take place in the soul constitution of humans in the year 333 was also not sufficient enough for Sorath to launch his intervention. According to his calculation of "the right time" of the intervention, more time—another 333 years—was required so that human intellectual faculty grew in capacity and capability to be able to receive all that which Sorath intended to send as a deluge. From Sorath's point of view, the other factor that would serve his purpose better during this additional time would be for human beings to identify more deeply with the physical world, becoming materialistic and losing their connection with the divine-spiritual world, leading them to think that they were originally beings

---

40 Steiner, *Death as Metamorphosis of Life*, lecture 7, "How Do I Find Christ?" (p. 136).

of the material world. In other words, 666 would be a time when humanity was deeply engulfed by maya, the great illusion induced by Lucifer and by Ahriman, especially.

Considering Jesus Christ's temptations in the wilderness,[41] and especially Steiner's elucidations about the temptation of turning stones into bread, we see that, at the beginning of our time, humanity had already sunk deeply into the material world. Thus, when we recall various narrations of the Gospels that give information indirectly about the Hebrew way of life, we see that even in Jesus' time, barter (previously used as a more innocent means of trade) had been left behind, and money, Ahriman's most powerful instrument to establish his kingdom on Earth, had been put into use.[42] Jesus taught, "No one can serve two masters. Either you will hate the one and love the other, or you will be devoted to the one and despise the other. You cannot serve both God and money" (Matt. 6:24). Touching especially on the subject of money, it seems Christ wanted to indicate that people had already become entangled in the snares of the material world and warn that we are prone to ahrimanic influences. Accordingly, human intelligence was a product of the material world and had developed in such a way that it would build the capacity and capability to receive Sorath's demonic inspirations; then, later on, people would become totally prone to Sorathic influences. Therefore, this was the "right time" anticipated by Sorath and was probably the reason that the year 666 arose as the time when Sorath's intervention would occur. This intervention would completely alter the flow of human evolution and stop further spiritualization of humanity and the possibility of reaching higher stages of consciousness and conscience. Steiner explains the grave situation humanity would have faced if the Christ-being had not come to the world as our savior 666 years before the Sorathic intervention.

---

41 Accounts of Jesus Christ's temptation in the wilderness are Matt. 4:1–11, Mark 1:12–13, and Luke 4:1–13.

42 It is written that when Jesus went to the temple, he drew out all who were buying and selling in the temple precincts and upset the tables of the money changers (Matt. 21:12–17, Mark 11:15–17, Luke 19:45–48, and John 2:12–22).

> If the beast [Sorath] had gone on stirring up mischief among people from 666 until the fifteenth century, by then he would have gained complete control of what was coming. What was approaching was the grasping of the world through a ghostlike natural science and the unleashing of human instincts. Because the consciousness soul was to grasp a person as a mere ghost, the real person lagged behind; one did not understand oneself. In the age of the consciousness soul, people can become human only by becoming conscious of what they are; otherwise human beings remain as animals and lag behind in human evolution.[43]

Returning to the subject of the Hebrews and the Arabs, as a result of the changes in 333, the Hebrews were also influenced and their astral bodies went through the same kind of changes that the Arabs experienced. Nevertheless, since the Hebrews had been receiving spiritual guidance and protection from Yahweh since long before this critical time, they were more protected from these influences; thus, their moral and spiritual losses were not too serious. Still, as a result of these changes they gradually lost their faculty of clairvoyance, and this led to the development of an earthly intellectual faculty. In fact, Yahweh foresaw precisely all of the previously stated changes that had taken place during the course of the evolution and issues such as when and how the Hebrews would lose their clairvoyant faculty. Thus, Yahweh's wise spiritual guidance and training enabled them to become a threshold for the entry of the Christ-being. At the same time, however—as indicated by Tomberg—the decline in their spiritual aspect was effective to an extent that prevented some of them from conceiving the fact that God's Son had come among them: "The wooden Cross of Golgotha was merely the outer expression of the spiritual fact that Israel had long ago prepared—in the form of rigidified knowledge and morality—a Cross for the Messiah."[44]

When we compare Arabs with Hebrews while bearing in mind Ibn Kathir's explanations, we see that as a result of the aforementioned crucial changes and their further entanglement with the material

---

43 Steiner, *Three Streams in Human Evolution*, lecture 3, "Consciousness Soul and Scientific Thinking, Sorat and 666."

44 *Christ and Sophia*, "Abraham, Isaac, and Jacob," p. 38.

world—permeated with luciferic and ahrimanic influences—with no guidance from the divine realm, the descendants of Ishmael were severely influenced by the effects brought about by Kali Yuga. Thus, shortly before 666, as a result of being fully exposed to the dark influences of the Kali Yuga period, Arabs had formed a mental, soul, and spiritual constitution far different[45] from that of the Hebrews; their innate qualities were in contrast to each other. The Hebrews, had formed a threshold for the entry of a divine being who was coming from the spiritual hierarchy; but, as a result of having gone through a retrogressive preparatory period, Arabs were prepared initially to make a direct interference—and later on an indirect contribution—to Sorath's intervention, which was to take place in 666. Considering the latter, if the Arabs' soul and spirit configuration had not formed in the particular way it had, it would have been impossible for them to absorb part of Sorath's inspired wisdom from the Academy of Gondishapur[46] and to transfer the shadows—the ghost of the gnostic wisdom of Gondishapur[47]—to Europe afterward.

The advent of Christ in relation to the crisis of 333: Lucifer's involvement in blunting the Sorathic intervention

If we consider only the plan of Sorath—and, behind it, that of Ahriman—it may seem as if there was no reason that their strategy should not have succeeded; preparatory stages of the intervention had been meticulously planned and implemented step by step. However, the wise divine guides of human evolution had known this entire devious scheme and certain measures were taken; there was simply too

---

45   This difference in their soul and spiritual constitution later played a great role in how Arabs perceived Yahweh and how they evaluated him when Mohammad introduced him as Allah.

46   Arabians had initially absorbed part of the inspired wisdom of Sorath when they went to destroy the Academy after Mohammad's death. Later, they continued to absorb more of this knowledge when the scholars and teachers from the destroyed Academy of Gondishapur invited them to take part in the famous court of Haroun al Rashid. Thus, the former teachers and scholars of the Academy of Gondishapur through Haroun al Rashid originally gave this impetus to the Arabian culture. (Note: The Arabic name *Haroun* derives from "Aaron"—the brother of Moses.)

47   The Academy of Gondishapur is also known as the Academy of Jundí Sábúr.

much at stake concerning the outcome of human evolution. In this context and in their endeavor to deaden the intervention, the beings of the divine–spiritual hierarchy had made a very important decision that involved sending a sublime divine being from the spiritual hierarchy to the Earth.

Rudolf Steiner referred to this extraordinary macrocosmic operation, which also involved the microcosm, as the *Mystery of Golgotha*. Regarding the microcosm, with the births of the Solomon Jesus child and the Nathan Jesus child respectively (as indicated in the Gospels of St. Matthew and St. Luke), the Mystery of Golgotha began to unfold 333 years before the year 333. Actually, the macrocosmic preparations concerning the births of these two children at a very precise time in Judaic history went all the way back to Abraham. Moreover, as we recall from Steiner's anthroposophic revelations, it goes back even further, to the middle of Lemuria,[48] when a part of the brother–sister soul of humanity remained in the spiritual world and did not take part in the event of the Fall from heaven and in subsequent Earthly incarnations. Later, at the beginning of our time, an embodiment of this pure brother–sister soul of humanity took place in the Nathan Jesus child. At the culmination of these preparations, as expressed by Steiner, this sublime divine–spiritual being threw his substance on the balance of evolution. If this counter-spiritual force had not come from the beings of the divine hierarchy, the balance of human evolution would have been totally upset, seriously endangering the ultimate aims of the evolution intended by the divine hierarchy.

To understand how Lucifer became involved in blunting the Sorathic intervention, we need to consider the quality of Christ's act. The Deed of Christ was implemented to resolve the threat imposed on human progress, but did not involve a direct intervention. *As a matter of fact, what the Christ-being did was a profound sacrifice.* His act was not a direct forceful interference that utilized to the power inherent in the divine–spiritual realm, but was his sacrifice, based on profound divine love, which produced a specific effect, or reaction. As a result, concerning the blunting of Sorath's intervention, help

---

48 Lemuria was the third main epoch, or stage, of the seven main epochs of the Earth evolution.

came from a certain spiritual being in the future—before the year 666. Besides, certain cosmic principles that had been effective since the Christ impulse came to the world did not allow Christ to interfere directly in stopping Sorath's intervention. In other words, certain measures that would have been valid before the Advent of Christ—when Yahweh was the ruling God—were no longer valid, because the spiritual impulse brought by Christ was based on new and different principles that reflect the quintessence of the divine–spiritual realm. These cosmic principles were at the same time cosmic laws that everyone—including divine–spiritual beings—had to abide. If beings of the divine–spiritual hierarchy had resorted to using former forces of the Moon Sphere, in which Father–God's power and will was the ruling principle, this would have contradicted the new impulse Christ had brought and would have inevitably induced an unsolicited retarding influence on evolution. In addition, a direct interference of the divine–spiritual realm would have imposed certain limitations on the sphere of activity or the task of the non-divine spiritual beings such as Ahriman and Sorath; but it was necessary that their activity continued until the end of the Earth evolution. Therefore, this crisis had to be resolved in an indirect way—for example, the necessary help had to come from a source other than the divine–spiritual realm.[49]

In lectures, Rudolf Steiner and Valentin Tomberg both indicate that this aid came from Lucifer. How did Lucifer get involved in

---

49 At this point we need to remember that many unavoidable battles had been fought during Muhammad's struggle to establish Islam, and inevitably weapons were used. But approximately 600 years prior to these battles—in accordance with the principles of the impulse he brought—Jesus Christ indicated that weapons should not be used any longer. "With that, one of Jesus' companions reached for his sword, drew it out, and struck the servant of the high priest, cutting off his ear. 'Put your sword back in its place,' Jesus said to him, 'for all who draw the sword will die by the sword'" (Matt. 26:51–52). Evidently, here, the sword represents all kinds of weapons. Therefore, the former severe means of using weapons that were employed to cope with certain crises prior to the Advent of Christ could no longer be employed after the Christ and the Christ impulse came to the world. Thus, after this specific time, even if it was absolutely necessary to use weapons, this could no longer be prompted by the beings of the divine–spiritual realm but could only be encouraged by so-called retarded spiritual forces that no longer have a place in the divine–spiritual hierarchy but only have a distant relationship with them.

resolving the crisis of deadening the Sorathic intervention? Did the beings of the divine–spiritual hierarchy ask Lucifer to give help? From Tomberg's comments, we understand that the divine–spiritual beings did not ask him for help directly, but Christ's profound sacrifice produced a certain effect, and it resulted in the inward conversion of Lucifer so that he decided to help in resolving this important crisis concerning human evolution. In this excerpt from "Anthroposophic Meditations on the New Testament," Tomberg states:

> The establishment of equilibrium (and with it, human freedom) is not the only result of the Mystery of Golgotha. It was also the beginning of a gradual retrieval of Lucifer's territory. The spirit who had severed this territory from the region of the hierarchies of good now experienced an inner conversion through the Mystery of Golgotha. True, that conversion initially concerned only Lucifer himself and not, say, the luciferic influence in human beings—which is still active in the old direction and can be changed only by human beings themselves. The prince of the luciferic hosts changed his course, however, because of the Mystery of Golgotha. The conversion took place within him when, looking at the Crucifixion on Golgotha, it pierced him with the insight that it was in fact he who should have experienced those sufferings. And now the other [Jesus Christ] was bearing them *in his place*.[50]

Rudolf Steiner also speaks of Lucifer's help in relation to Sorath's intervention:

> The preliminaries for this [Sorath's intervention] were prepared. But the influence that was to go out from Gondishapur was deadened, held back by retarded spiritual forces that were nevertheless connected (though they form a kind of opposition) with the outflow of the Christ impulse. Through the appearance of Muhammad and his visionary religious teaching, there was a deadening of the influence meant to go out from Gondishapur. Above all, in those regions where it was wished to spread the Gnostic wisdom of Gondishapur, Muhammad took the ground from under its feet. He skimmed the cream

---

50 Tomberg, *Christ and Sophia*, "The Mystery of Golgotha," p. 296.

of it, and so the Gondishapur influence was left to trail and could accomplish nothing in the face of what Muhammad had done. Here we can see the wisdom in world history; we come to know the truth about Islam only when, in addition to other things, we know that Islam was destined to deaden the Gnostic wisdom of Gondishapur, to take from it the strong ahrimanically seductive force that would otherwise have been exercised upon humankind.[51]

As expounded by Rudolf Steiner, the main reason for the emergence of the Islamic impulse and its task was to deaden Sorath's intervention. Steiner has also pointed out the role of the "retarding" spiritual forces that played a role in the struggle to deaden this intervention. His phrase, "retarded spiritual forces,"[52] refers to Lucifer and the luciferic hosts. However, it is important to bear in mind that, although the monotheistic religion of Islam came into being as a result of the measure they implemented, the divine–spiritual beings *had not actually intended to establish a monotheistic religion for the second time*. Thus, the reemergence of the Yahweh Moon religion was not an unexpected surprise; it was an unavoidable consequence of those obligatory measures. Lucifer's involvement was therefore also not a surprise, and from the viewpoint of certain cosmic processes, it was necessary and inevitable that luciferic forces became involved in the emergence of Islam and the appearance of the Islamic impulse.

---

51 Steiner, *Three Streams in Human Evolution*, lecture 5, "Free Human Personality by Self-training, Justinian, and the Schools."

52 "The influence that was to have gone out from Jundí Sábúr [Gondishapur] was deadened, held back by retarded spiritual forces, which were nevertheless connected—although they form a kind of opposition—with the outflow of the Christ Impulse. Through the appearance of Mohammed and his visionary religious teaching, there was a deadening of the influence that was meant to go out from Jundí Sábúr" (*Three Streams in Human Evolution*, lecture 5).

2.

SORATH'S INTERVENTION IN AD 666
AND THE ROLE OF ISHMAEL'S DESCENDANTS

How did Sorath intend to implement his plan? What were the step-by-step preparations of the intervention?[1] At first glance, many events in the years before 666 may not seem to have any connection with one another. But those occurrences were not accidental but actually preparations of Sorath's intervention. What inspired the closing of the philosophy schools were the forces of darkness. Similarly, in 489 Emperor Zeno closed the Edessa School, which had been founded in 363. This drove the Nestorians from their school. In 529, Emperor Justinian closed the Greek schools of philosophy, and the philosophers and pupils of these schools were cast out. At that time, Khusrew, the Persian (Sassanid) king and a great admirer of the Greco-Roman culture, offered hospitality and welcomed those philosophers, scholars, and sages. As a result, many of the scholars with well-trained minds (i.e., their intellectual faculties of thought and mathematical logic, which had the opportunity to develop during the age of intellectual soul) took refuge in the Academy of Gondishapur. However, because the development of the human intellectual faculty is closely related to Lucifer (indeed, induced by him), those scholars and teachers were affected by luciferic influences as they worked in the Academy of Gondishapur. Ahriman can be effective on human beings only through the door opened by Lucifer, so these people were also influenced or inspired by Ahriman. This is how Steiner explains these advancements:

---

1   Rudolf Steiner has elaborated on this subject in various lectures. However, to go into all these details is beyond the scope of this book, so only the main and crucial points that are directly related to the subjects analyzed here will be mentioned.

The emperor Justinian was one such puppet of those beings and acted under their influence and direction when he closed the schools of philosophy in Athens in 529. Justinian was a fervent enemy of ancient Greek wisdom and everything connected with it, and by shutting down the schools he expelled the last remnants of Greek learning and Aristotelian–Platonic philosophy and forced scholars and philosophers to flee to Persia. Earlier, in the fifth century, Zeno Isauricus had already expelled other Greek sages from Edessa, and they and Syrian scholars had fled to Nibisi. And there, in Persia, as the year 666 approached, the representatives of the most exquisite and outstanding learning gathered at the Academy of Gondishapur. Most of them had come from Greece and had ignored the Mystery of Golgotha. The faculty at the Academy of Gondishapur was inspired by luciferic–ahrimanic powers.[2]

As these scholars and teachers settled and began working in the Academy of Gondishapur, the circumstances to receive the Sorathic inspirations gradually ripened, and the Sorathic knowledge (or demonic wisdom that actually belonged to a future epoch) was about to stream into the Academy. It is necessary to point out that, although Arabs would become involved in spreading a certain amount of the gnostic wisdom of the Academy of Gondishapur in a deadened form at a later stage, they did not play a direct role in the initial and central preparations of that intervention. While these preparations in the Gondishapur Academy continued, a certain, seemingly insignificant event took place among the Arabs. In addition to the aforementioned ancient preparations that had begun with the birth of Ishmael, this seemingly minor event in 570 was the birth of the Prophet Muhammad, a descendant of Ishmael, ninety-six years before the time of the Sorathic intervention.

Sorath's intention and plan was to transmit the knowledge and know-how that originally belonged to a future time (around 2493) during the epoch of the consciousness soul—or spiritual soul. According to his plan, all the knowledge belonging to that future time would

---

2   Steiner, *Death as a Metamorphosis of Life,* lecture 7, "How Can I Find Christ?" p. 137.

stream into the Academy of Gondishapur without opposition. Consequently, humanity would be inoculated with this Sorathic wisdom. In other words, as Steiner articulated it, the knowledge that people were meant to have in 2493 would have begun to sprout in 666. If Sorath's plan had been fully successful, this would have resulted in an immense development of humanity's abstract scientific (and later technological) intellectual capacity *instead of developing spiritual wisdom* (in relation to the development of the consciousness soul). According to Sorath's plan, after being flooded with this abstract scientific knowledge that would become a purely ahrimanic science in the future, humanity would be permanently fettered to the physical world in the age of the intellectual soul. As a result, they would be prevented from moving on to the following age—that of the consciousness soul—and from developing their own consciousness soul during this age, beginning in the fifteenth century. Humankind would thus become exclusively terrestrial and confined permanently to the earthly plane with no hope of moving on to the dimension of the divine–spiritual realm. Steiner indicates the danger that awaited humanity:

> In this age of consciousness soul, earthly humanity has the choice of striving for the truth, which requires us to confront the spiritual with courage, or avoiding the spiritual, remaining in illusion, and holding to untruth. The Academy of Gondishapur wanted to spare people this effort for the truth and to spare people the trouble of further evolution. Therefore, it wished to reveal to them what it had itself received as an ahrimanic revelation. The Academy of Gondishapur—of which the last shadows, or ghost, remain in today's scientific illusions—wanted to make humans beings entirely earthly.[3]

Things did not work out exactly as Sorath had planned, however. His plan was only partially successful because, prior to 666, the Islamic impulse began to unfold through Muhammad's inspired teachings, which later acted as a counterforce. As a result, the transmission of the main part of the Sorathic inspirations was blocked, and the great impact of the intervention was deadened; it could not

---

3   Steiner, *Three Streams in Human Evolution*, lecture 5.

rain down as the deluge as Sorath had intended. Nevertheless, a part of these Sorathic inspirations managed to infiltrate certain receptive minds that had been well trained at the Academy of Gondishapur as receptacles for what flowed from Sorath.

Although Muhammad's new religion had deadened the main part of Sorath's intervention, later on the Arabs—who by that time had become Muslims and had a well-developed intellectual faculty for comprehending the material world according to number, measure, and mathematical logic—became an instrument for transferring the infiltrated but deadened part of the Sorathically inspired wisdom to Europe. Steiner explained the route of this gnostic wisdom to Europe at a future time and how it spread across Europe.

> It is possible to trace, step by step, decade to decade, how the Gnostic wisdom of Gondishapur (certainly in a deadened form) spread over to southern Europe and Africa to Spain, France, England, and over the Continent by way of monasteries. We can trace how the suprasensory is driven out and only the sense-perceptible retained; we can trace the tendency, or intention, as it were, and what arises from the deadening of the Gnostic wisdom of Gondishapur in Western scientific thinking.[4]

The aftermath of the invasion of the Gondishapur Academy

Not long after the impulse of Islam began to unfold—overwhelmed by the Prophet Muhammad's visionary teachings—the pagan Arabs became Muslims. Remarkably, this conversion was completed in a relatively short time, while the Prophet was still alive. Shortly after Muhammad's death in 632, the period of Arab expansion began. As they began to spread Islam, Muslim Arabs also started expanding their territories. The Sassanid dynasty fell to the Muslim Arab armies in 638. This coincided with the seizure of the Gondishapur Academy and burning down the library. The destruction of the Academy took place twenty-two years before the designated time of Sorath's intervention. These unexpected events altered the course of history. Because of the seizure of the Academy by the Muslim Arabs, Sorath's plan could

---

4   Ibid.

not proceed with the same intensity and produce the intended effect. Therefore, it could be stated that, with the seizure of the Academy of Gondishapur, the first part of the task of Ishmael's descendants was consummated.

The Academy survived the change of rulers and continued as a Muslim institute of higher learning for a while longer. Later, when Baghdad was established in 762, Haroun al-Rashid (766–809) and his minister Ja'far ibn Yahya Barmakid (767–803) sought out scholars. Many scholars and teachers from Gondishapur Academy were drawn to the Abbasid court of Haroun al-Rashid. After the scholars, philosophers, and teachers from Gondishapur gathered in Baghdad, the Abbasid court of Haroun al-Rashid became better organized. Up until the end of his reign Haroun al-Rashid did many things that contributed to the spread of Arabism in the physical world. In his *Karmic Relationships* lecture course Steiner said, "Indeed Arabism had taken on a peculiar form at the court of Haroun al-Rashid."[5]

During the long reign of Haroun al-Rashid, Sorath-inspired wisdom continued to spread among Muslim Arabs. Therefore, it can be said that the second part of the task of Ishmael's descendants began. It entailed spreading the gnostic wisdom of Gondishapur in other parts of the world. Steiner emphasized that, when this deadened wisdom of Gondishapur began to spread in Europe, an ahrimanic, or ahrimanically inspired, natural science began to emerge.

> It is not surprising that, at a time such as this, much can be misunderstood through the aftermath of the Gondishapur Academy above all, and is therefore taken up by natural science, with no desire for a connection with the Mystery of Golgotha. Because of this, natural science becomes a purely ahrimanic science, corresponding to all the ahrimanic needs of humankind and to the state of mind that wants to organize the world according to externals alone.[6]

The result was that a description of an external physical world and cosmos devoid of spirit that arose from Muslim thought permeated

---

5   Steiner, *Karmic Relationships*, vol. 1, lecture 10.
6   Steiner, *Three Streams in Human Evolution*, lecture 6.

with Arabism began to materialize in Europe. This "world description" based on Western scientific thinking was founded solely on measure, number, and weight, and has been continuously supported and protected by ahrimanic inspirations ever since. This scientific description of an external physical world devoid of spirit[7] has gradually become the prevalent worldview around most of the modern world. However, humanity did not realize that this ahrimanic worldview is only maya, or illusion. As they identified and became increasingly entangled with this ahrimanic, materialistic view, their connection with the divine–spiritual world continued to loosen and was finally severed completely.

> Then the final impulse came, plunging human thinking to its lowest point, banished and completely chained to the physical life. This arose through the Arabs and Muslims. Islamic thought is a peculiar episode in Arabic life and thought, which in its passage over to Europe gave the final impulse to logic and what cannot rise to the spiritual.[8]

It can be said that, because of the wisdom of the divine–spiritual hierarchy and the sacrifice of the Christ-being, Sorath's intervention was not wholly successful. He was unable to chain humanity permanently to the era of intellectual soul development (and to the physical world) and to stop the flow of human evolution completely. Evidently, however, his intervention has significantly changed the worldview of humanity in general. Since the human faculty of clairvoyance had been lost, *human beings began to see a world and space devoid of spirit; they were incapable of rising to what is spiritual in this new state of being.* This did not surprise the divine guides of human evolution with whom humans had

---

7 For instance, this ahrimanic materialist description has found expression in the widely accepted and supported Darwin's theory, which basically proclaims that a divine being had nothing to do with humankind's creation. Such an assertion endeavors to nullify the concept of the spirit. When people believe that God had no role in the creation of humans and the world, and that they have evolved from primates—as a result of the rigidified thoughts inspired by Ahriman—their souls identify more with the material world and consequentially cannot establish the necessary and vital connection to the divine–spiritual realm.

8 Steiner, *The Apocalypse of St. John*, lecture 11.

once had a very close connection. On the contrary, they had intended this particular result from the very beginning of humanity's creation.

In keeping with the purposes and aims of our divine guides, at a certain stage during their evolution, human connection with the divine realm had to be severed so that we could gain freedom. People would eventually find themselves in a state whereby they would become free of the overwhelming power and will of the Father–God's cosmos. This stage—when humankind was going to separate from the divine realm and achieve freedom—was the fourth Earth stage of their cosmic evolution.[9] Accordingly, the Garden of Eden (the first half of Lemuria) was humanity's last home in the divine–spiritual world before the Fall from Heaven occurred.

In addition to beings of the divine–spiritual hierarchy, beings of hindrance such as Lucifer, Ahriman, Sorath, and the Asura also had to take part in the Earth phase, so that human beings would be able to gain freedom. Evidently, during the fourth stage of the evolution, the forces and influences of adverse spiritual beings were allowed to participate, but they were not allowed to interfere directly with the evolution prior to this stage. When we bear in mind the spiritual history—the events and preliminaries that have taken place on Earth, and the existence of actors such as the Hebrews and the Arabs, as well as their creeds of Judaism, Christianity, and Islam—we realize that all of this was part of a grand cosmic event, and that *the Mystery of Golgotha was at the fulcrum of this gradually unfolding cosmic event.*

When we consider how Muslims approach and evaluate spiritual issues closely related to Christianity since the beginning of Islam, it must be emphasized that the phenomenal cosmic event that Steiner called the Mystery of Golgotha has always escaped their attention. In addition to the fact that there is no indication of the Mystery of Golgotha in the Koran, we sense that there must be another factor that prevents adherents of Islam from recognizing and understanding this profound cosmic truth that affects all of humanity. Steiner's points to

---

9   As in the three previous evolutionary stages, the fourth evolutionary stage—the Earth—is comprised of seven main periods. See, for example, *An Outline of Esoteric Science*, chapter 6, "Cosmic and Human Evolution, Now and in the Future."

the fact that even the gnostic wisdom of Gondishapur was influenced and made to assume a different form owing to a certain factor before Muslim Arabs brought it to Europe; this factor was *Arabism*. Arabism is the peculiar force that has kept Muslims from comprehending the Mystery of Golgotha and from being permeated by the spirit of the Christ impulse.

Let us consider the beginnings of Islam and analyze further details concerning the newly emerged Yahweh Moon religion. This may help us understand what Arabism really is and how it influences Arabs, the Muslim communities of other nations, and even the Western world.

Yahweh's transformation into Allah:
The beginning of the denial of spirit

From 610 to 623, as inspired messages kept coming, Muhammad made sure that all Arab tribes would become acquainted with Allah. The Prophet's verses introduced Allah to the pagan Arabs as the former God of the Hebrews. Koranic verses also explained that the ancestral Hebrew father Abraham was at the same time the ancestral father of the Arabs. However, since the beginning of Islam, the way Arabs have perceived or imagined Allah and what he means to them has been quite different from the way the Hebrew people have perceived Yahweh and what he means to them. When Arabs acknowledged Yahweh as their God and began to call him Allah, it was as if the former image of Yahweh began to change as well. As time went by, this image indeed changed substantially, and he became a different deity. *Eventually, "Yahweh, the God of Hebrews" transformed into "Allah, the God of Muslim Arabs."* This is why—since the beginning of Islam—Hebrews found it difficult to recognize their God Yahweh when he was presented to them as "Allah" by Muhammad.

One of the main factors that brought about this substantial transformation of Yahweh was the influence of Arabism. It is necessary to emphasize that the God who was introduced to the Arabs as Allah (though it was often emphasized that this was Yahweh) was not perceived by them exactly as Yahweh had been perceived by Hebrews in past centuries. Certain of his qualities that the Hebrews knew well could not be imparted fully to Arabs in this short time. Instead, owing to hereditary characteristics peculiar to Arabs, after receiving Muhammad's messages they attributed other qualities to him and overlooked or did not perceive Yahweh's spiritual qualities. Another reason that Arabs were unable to perceive and understand Yahweh as the Hebrews had was because Arabs previously practiced paganism and idolatry. There were luciferic and ahrimanic beings behind most of the pagan idols they had worshipped. Since they had been worshipping non-sacred beings for a very long period, when Yahweh was introduced to them as Allah they did not yet possess a refined spiritual understanding of what "divine" and "sacred" means.

> 43: 14 *The Arabs of the desert declare: "We are true believers." Say: "You are not. Rather say: 'We profess Islam [or We have become Muslims'*[10]*], for faith has not yet found its way into your hearts."*

This koranic verse clearly indicates the fact that the Arabs' comprehension of Allah had been only superficial. Here, Allah speaks to the Prophet Muhammad and indicates the difference between *barely recognizing Allah and becoming Muslim* and *having a deep faith in Allah*. Arabs are told in this verse that their superficial acceptance of Allah—merely stating that they have become Muslims—is not sufficient; their comprehension should go much deeper, and Allah expects it to come from their hearts. In other words, it should come from the core of their "I"-being, as the heart is the manifestation of the "I" in the physical body. Thus, when we compare "Yahweh, the God of Hebrews" with the Muslim Arab understanding of "Allah," their differences become clearer. It would not be incorrect to suggest that *Allah is the Islamized version of Yahweh, and that this particular Islamized image of Yahweh was formed after it had been permeated by Arabism.*

Today, when we hear Muslims speaking of Allah and Islam, we are likely to receive two different impressions from them about their religion. The first (which will come from almost all Muslims) projects the deeply ingrained conviction that Allah is the God, who belongs only to Muslims and to the religion of Islam, and that Allah excludes anyone who is not a Muslim. This discrimination is

---

10   In the Arabic language, *Muslim* means "one who believes in Allah."

widespread among Muslims, because they generally identify Allah solely with the Islamic culture formed by Islamic teachings, feeling that, being Muslim, they naturally belong to this special religion. These opinions have been a source of pride for them. The second impression we are likely to receive is their feeling of being members of the "latest" or "final" religion, along with the privilege of having been given the last prophet sent by Allah. A sense of superiority often accompanies this feeling. Most Muslims believe that Allah's messages have come for sake of all humanity; therefore, this latest religion deserves to become *the* religion of the whole world. However, there are also some Muslims who do not ascribe to this proud feeling of superiority and do not necessarily subscribe to converting all people to Islam. It may not be easy for members of other religions to perceive it, but the Islamic belief that Islam is the latest and the most correct and true religion inaugurated by Allah—the one that he intended for the whole of humanity—contains a kind of naïve goodwill in it. Muslims are very pleased when others renounce their former religion and adopt Islam; they become very friendly with these people and embrace them. However, many koranic verses contradict these convictions, emphasizing that these verses were sent only to Arabs—that is, not for the whole of humanity.

> 12:1 These are the verses of the Glorious Book. We have revealed the Koran in the Arabic tongue so that you may understand it.
>
> 19:97 We have revealed to you the Koran in your own tongue that you may thereby proclaim good tidings to the upright and give warning to a contentious nation.
>
> 42:7 Thus we have revealed to you an Arabic Koran that you may warn the mother city [Mecca] and those who dwell around it.
>
> 44:58 We have revealed this to you in your own tongue so that they may take heed.
>
> 43:1 We have revealed the Koran in the Arabic tongue that you may grasp its meaning.
>
> 43:5 Should we ignore you [Arabs] because you are a sinful nation?

> 32:3 *It is the truth from your Lord, which he has bestowed upon you so that you [Muhammad] may forewarn, whom none has warned before you [Muhammad], and that they may be rightly guided.*

Evidently, the Koran's verses were sent to Arabs in their own mother tongue so that they would not only be well understood, but also serve as a warning to be heeded. We can see clearly in 32:3 and 43:1 that these verses were sent especially to a certain group of people who had not previously received any admonition and guidance, and who were pagans and practiced idolatry. Verse 43:5 indicates that they were a sinful nation at the time when the Islamic impulse came. (Let us recall that the statements in these two verses are also in accordance with Ibn Kathir's preceding explanations.) Therefore, it becomes apparent that the content of these koranic verses were not composed for Jewish people, who had been trained spiritually by Yahweh for several centuries before the outset of Islam, nor were they meant for Jews who later became Christians. Rather, these verses were specially formulated according to the needs of Arabs—as an emergency measure—aiming to compensate for their lack of morality and spirituality. In other words, the way to address a group of people who have had a very close relationship with Yahweh and the divine realm for several centuries cannot be the same as addressing people who were idolaters and had no concept of the divine realm.

It is thus obvious that the content of the Koran and the religion of Islam are not meant for the whole of humanity.[11] When fundamentalist and extremist Muslims proclaim, "According to the Koran, everyone on Earth should become Muslims and worship Allah," this should be considered unfounded and unreasonable. It is doubtful that any extremist or fundamentalist has ever deeply and seriously studied the Koran, for when it is thoroughly studied word by word it becomes absolutely clear that Allah does not demand that everyone

---

11 According to certain reasons known by our divine–spiritual guides, throughout the last 1,400 years since the outset of Islam, it is likely that it was arranged for some souls who belonged to the Islamic religion in a previous incarnation to incarnate into a different religion. In his lecture series *Karmic Relationships,* Steiner gives many detailed examples of renowned Islamic persons who have incarnated as different persons in different cultures.

on Earth should become Muslims. It also becomes clear that Islam was an impulse that came only for the descendants of Ishmael. When we bear in mind that humankind belongs to the fourth spiritual hierarchy and that the cosmic mission of humanity is to bring freedom,[12] enforcement of any belief—whether Judaism, Christianity, Buddhism, or Islam—works against the "principle of freedom" brought to the world by the Christ impulse.

Regarding the way Muslims have conceived of and understood Allah, we must point out a very important fact: extremist and jihadist Muslim involvement in terrorist activities and their justification ("We wage jihad in the name of Allah") indicates that beings of darkness have a role in *how* radical, extremist, and jihadist Muslims perceive Allah; the influence of the beings of darkness blurs their understanding and perception of Allah. This also indicates that their soul–spiritual configuration is open to the "negative and detrimental wavelength" of the beings of darkness. The image of Allah conceived by radical, extremist, and jihadist Muslims today is not harmonious with the image of Allah reflected by the Koran. Because their distorted and impure understanding has shaped their image of Allah, many qualities that belong to human beings—who are far from perfect and liable to err—inevitably have been attributed to this image of Allah. In this context, in accordance with one's level of consciousness, a person can be a merciless warrior, a soldier of a materialist system, and a killing machine, but it would be tremendously immature to imagine that Allah is thus also a furious warrior who would wish to attack and destroy his enemies on Earth, or that he would continuously assign believers of Islam to destroy other human beings in his name.

Here we must ask this question: Isn't Allah capable of knowing who would oppose or deny him in the physical world and simply not create that person to begin with? It is very difficult to imagine that Allah would take it so seriously when some ephemeral

---

12 "What is lacking in them [the spiritual hierarchies] must be brought into their sphere of existence by humanity. It is the mission of the fourth hierarchy, humankind, to satisfy the essential need of the first, second, and third hierarchies. That need is the freedom that will have achieved its cosmic destiny once it has overcome karma in the universe" (Tomberg, *Christ and Sophia*, p. 134).

human beings (whom he himself created) deny him, and as retribution assign Muslims to launch a jihad to kill in his name. Rather, we must emphasize that Allah—as the reemerged Yahweh—would never give such a command. Even this simple, logical question clearly shows how false it is to imagine that—although he is a creator and a supreme divine being—Allah becomes entangled with the trivial events, sympathies, and antipathies that belong to the fleeting physical world. Consequently, if a Muslim claims to "hear" or receive orders to kill, we must suspect immediately and recognize that such misleading, enticing, and evil inspirations do not come from Allah, but from evil spirit beings of darkness—mainly from *Shaytan*, or *Iblis*—Satan.

> 24:21 You that are true believers, do not walk in the footsteps of Satan. He that walks in Satan's footsteps is incited to indecency and evil.

This verse contains a clear warning about how Satan entices humans and lures them to do evil. In another verse, we see that, during the outset of Islam, even when the Prophet was going through tough times in his struggle—his jihad—against the pagan Arabs, Allah gave them permission only to defend themselves, advising them not to attack first and forbidding aggression.

> 2:190 Fight, for the sake of Allah, those that fight against you, but do not attack them first. Allah does not love the aggressors.

Muslims acknowledge the Koran as their guideline. Would it not be a violation of Islamic rules if a true believer does not heed the admonition "Allah does not love aggressors"? Is this clear warning not valid and applicable today? If Allah is Yahweh as proclaimed by the koranic verses; since numerous verses declare and verify that the Old Testament is a sacred Scripture given to the Jews by Yahweh; and knowing that Yahweh ordered "You shall not kill" in the Ten Commandments—how can we imagine that he would now order extremist and jihadist Muslims to kill in his name? It should be borne in mind that this verse and similar ones that speak of jihad and "fighting for the sake of Allah" were valid only during the initial stages of the outset of Islam. Nevertheless, present-day jihadists believe they are killing in the name of Allah. For this reason, it becomes apparent that the way radical, extremist, and jihadist Muslims understand and depict Yahweh in his new identity as Allah does not reflect the true image of the Hebrew Yahweh. Accordingly, it is also necessary to underline that the way some Muslims currently understand and imagine Allah is not the true image of Allah inherent in the Koran. The influence of certain spiritual beings of darkness has distorted their perception of Allah. Although the circumstantial factors were somewhat different in the times of Muhammad, this was also the case 1,400 years ago. The ones who became the first Muslims were idolaters shortly before the Islamic impulse; they were under the influence of certain adversarial beings, and they worshipped idols of those beings. Allah (or Yahweh) was aware of this fact, which could be one of the reasons that so many koranic verses warn Muslims against the power and influence of Satan. Clearly it was expected and hoped that these verses would serve as an admonition for the Muslims in future times as well.

In addition to the influence of the spirits of darkness, could there be any other reason why Arabs perceived Yahweh differently? Yahweh went through a transformation in the eyes of Muslims and became *Allah*—the deity of Islam—because pagan Arabs lacked understanding of a very important concept before Islam arose, and, indeed, after they became Muslims. What they lacked was the concept of *spirit*. The fact that they have been uninterested in understanding this concept has been one of the factors that have influenced how they perceive Yahweh. Rudolf Steiner pointed to this when he said that *Arab life and thought were incapable of rising to the spiritual*. One can observe this fact in their formal way of worshipping Allah.

Steiner's elucidations also explain why there is no place for an understanding of the *Holy Spirit* or *Christ*, or his divine feminine counterpart *Sophia*, in Islam. When we observe various manifestations of Islamic teachings we see that, under the influence of Arabism, Islam allows Muslims to comprehend only what is external and formal, and it permits them to comprehend only the figure of a single almighty deity who created everything all by himself. In other words, the peculiar force of Arabism has not allowed the concept of *spirit* to flourish and dwell among the defining characteristics of the Islamic religion. Furthermore, in Islam there is no yearning to know what *spirit* implies. Apparently, Muslims seem not to realize that something very essential is missing in this Islamic dogma: "There is only one Allah, and Muhammad is his Prophet." It is as if any thought or concept that could lead them to the spirit is not permitted to sprout within the rigid framework of Islamic beliefs.

In keeping with the foregoing explanations, while examining the Koran we cannot fail to notice that the concept of *spirit* does not radiate from the verses. In fact, this concept does not exist in the Koran. Therefore, it could be alleged that the lack of a spirit concept [13] is one of the most important reasons why Islam has become a religion that is clearly identified with the material world. In Islam, what is truly divine, holy, and spiritual is brought down to the level of the physical plane. In other words, Islam has identified what is truly divine and holy with qualities that belong to the Earth realm and, consequentially, Muslims have not been able to acquire a more rarefied understanding of spirituality.

In this context, according to Muslims, Mecca is a sacred land; the Kaaba building, which Muslims circumambulate during *hajj*, is a consecrated building; the objects in the Kaaba building, including an age-old meteorite, are considered sacred; all mosques are holy; Friday is a sacred day; Ramadan is a holy month; the days of the Islamic celebration, which include animal sacrifices to Allah, are believed to be holy (though this belief is clearly contradicted in the Koran[14]); the Arabic language is a sacred language; the *azan* recited from the minarets is sacred; and so forth. When Muslims assume that such things are holy or sacred, this gives them the impression that they already have a close relation to what is holy. In this case, however, the inner demand to know what is truly spiritual and holy and the wish to establish a genuine contact and relationship with

---

13 This issue of the concept of spirit is discussed in greater detail later.

14 There is no verse in the Koran in which Allah commands that Muslims should sacrifice animals for religious ritual. As a matter of fact, his statement in 22:37 clearly contradicts this practice: "Their flesh and blood does not reach Allah; it is your piety that reaches him."

the divine realm is not engendered in their souls; rather, they are content with what they believe is holy. This is because a true concept of spirit is missing in Islam. In contrast to the Muslim belief that the holy and sacred can be found in the material world, Jesus Christ often emphasized that we can find what is truly holy only in the divine–spiritual realm of the Father, not in the physical world, which is thoroughly permeated by Lucifer and Ahriman. Christ also pointed out that the Holy Spirit would come to the world after he leaves. In this way he emphasized that the truly holy cannot be found in the material world, but remains outside the physical world to be found only in the "Father's realm": "When the Advocate comes, whom I will send to you from the Father—the Spirit of truth who goes out from the Father—he will testify about me" (John 15:26).

Rudolf Steiner explained that the physical world in its present form is "the accomplished work" of the divine–spiritual beings, and that they no longer dwell in the physical world they left behind:

> The divine–spiritual comes to expression in the cosmos in different ways, in succeeding stages: 1) through its own and innermost being; 2) through the manifestation of this being; 3) through the active working, when the being withdraws from the manifestation; 4) through the accomplished work, when in the outwardly apparent universe no longer the Divine itself, but only the forms of the Divine are there.[15]

The misconceived Islamic understanding of what is truly holy has echoes in other religions. In Christianity, churches are believed to be consecrated.[16] In every Christian country, there exist countless religious artifacts believed to be holy; and the concept of holiness has been brought down to the level of ritual and rhetoric. On the other hand, people are free to value whatever they deem sacred— the shrine of Turin or the meteorite in the Kaaba building—but it

---

15 Steiner, *Anthroposophical Leading Thoughts*, Leading Thought 112, p. 85.

16 Actually, the belief that churches are consecrated was true up to the time of the Second Coming of Christ. Now that Christ can be found in the etheric body of the Earth, holiness is not limited to church buildings, for the whole etheric biosphere surrounding the world has become holy.

is not people's beliefs that are in question. What we are discussing is the importance and necessity of seeking what is truly holy and emanates from the divine–spiritual realm—the holy that is the fundamental quality and quintessence of the eternal realm. Therefore, no matter which religious belief we choose, endeavoring to find and sense the truly holy within it would be a more correct approach than getting wrapped up in the material objects or values related with the ephemeral physical world.

The belief that a certain harmony among numbers[17] found in the Koran is a great miracle of the Koran is another consequence of Islam's lack of a spirit concept and of what is truly spiritual. Some Muslims claim that there is a miraculous mathematical system inherent in the structure of the Koran encoded in the verses and in the numerical relationship between the *suwar* (plural of *surah*) and verses. According to them, the key to the miraculous structure of the Koran is the number 19, which is a prime number. Since every Arabic letter and related syllable has a numerical value, by using their numerical value and a procedure of addition or multiplication within certain suwar and verses always gives the result of number 19. For instance, this "miracle of 19" found in the Koran was first discovered in 1974; accordingly, if number 19 (signifying this miracle) is placed in front of 74 (this being the number of the surah in which a verse indicates that there is a miracle concerning the number 19), 1974 is achieved.[18] Another example: The Koran contains altogether 114 suwar, and this number can be found by multiplying 19 and 6. It is also stated that when one counts how many times a particular word (say, the name *Allah*) is used in the Koran, the result will be a multiple of 19. For example, it was found that the word *verse* is used 380 times throughout the Koran, and 380 is 19 times 20. There are

---

17 Let us remember that understanding number, measure, and mathematical logic was necessary for humans to comprehend the physical world. So the form in which they manifest in the physical world cannot be used or cannot be of any help for comprehending the spiritual world or sensing the divine and holy.

18 Indeed, the 30th verse of the 74th surah states: "It is guarded by nineteen keepers."

many more examples, and some Muslims claim that these miraculous mathematical combinations are inherent in the Koran because Allah arranged it.[19]

In addition to those that delve into issues that could hardly be called spiritual, many koranic verses describe Allah as a divine being and emphasize his divine qualities in contrast to the qualities of the non-divine idols formerly venerated by pagan Arabs, promulgating that he is the one who should be venerated instead of these idols. These koranic verses affirm that Allah is sublime, forgiving, merciful, compassionate, helpful, and powerful. Nevertheless, there is a certain ambiguity about his deeper spiritual aspects in the descriptions found in some verses. In other words, compared with the descriptions of Yahweh found in the Bible—in which one can feel the profound spirituality and divine qualities of Yahweh—the corresponding feelings that radiates from the Koran are, so to speak, vague and inconspicuous. For instance, in verses 2:163 and 4:57 Allah, who has been introduced as Yahweh, is depicted as a compassionate, rewarding, and merciful deity:

> 2:163 Your God is one God. There is no God but him. He is the Compassionate, the Merciful.

> 4:57 As for those that have faith and do good work, We shall admit them to gardens watered by running streams, where wedded to chaste virgins they shall abide forever. We shall admit them to a cool shade.

But in other verses he is depicted as a deity who could also be like a temperamental and wrathful sovereign:

> 4:115 He that disobeys the Apostle [Muhammad] after Our guidance has been revealed to him and follows a path other than that of the faithful

---

19 It is also emphasized that this system is inherent in the Koran as long as the present Arabic structure of the Koran remains exactly as it is. That is to say, if any slight alteration is made in the order of the suwar or verses, this would upset the interrelation, the mathematical balance, of the suwar and verses and, consequently, the "miracle of 19" would cease to exist. A noteworthy point is the fact that the Koran was not compiled when the Prophet Muhammad was alive; its compilation was done by transcribers after his death.

[path of a Muslim] *shall be given what he has chosen. We will cast him into Hell: a dismal end.*

4:56 Those that deny Our revelations We will burn in hellfire. No sooner will their skins be consumed than We shall give them other skins, so that they may truly taste Our scourge. Allah is mighty and wise.

Besides the verses that suggest Allah could be an unpredictable and wrathful deity, some koranic descriptions of Allah do not reveal adequately the deeper spiritual aspect of a god who was presented to the Arabs as "Yahweh, God of the Hebrews." Yahweh was an *Eloah* (from the ranks of Exousiai) and was, in fact, one of the seven Elohim.[20] He also belonged to the Pleroma of the Christ-being. Because of the requirements of his cosmic mission, however, Yahweh had to work apart from the hexarchy. It is noteworthy that Yahweh's name, throughout the Koran, is never given as *Yahweh* or *Jehovah*. Although there are many allusions to the God of the Hebrews in the Koran, his name is always *Allah* in the verses. Moreover, throughout the Koran, we never encounter any information that indicates that Allah (often referred to as the God of the Hebrews) is one of the Elohim or that there are other Elohim in the spiritual world other than him. On the contrary, koranic verses inform and emphasize that there is only one Allah and no other deity exists besides him, and that Allah is the creator of the universe, humanity, and every other creature on Earth. While trying to persuade pagan Arabs that they are encountering a deity who is the creator of everything in the universe, koranic verses offer examples, most of which refer to things with which Arabs were familiar. For example, two verses indicate that, among other things, Allah is the creator of ships that sail the ocean:

2:164 In the creation of the heavens and the Earth; in the alteration of night and day; in the ships that sail the ocean with cargoes beneficial to humanity;... surely these are signs for rational humans.

55: 24 His are the ships that sail like banners upon the ocean.

---

20 Elohim: Plural of Eloah. The Seven Elohim are the leaders of the Exousiai, the Form Spirits, who are beings from the second divine–spiritual hierarchy.

The fact that Allah is mentioned as the creator of ships with "cargoes beneficial to humanity" calls to mind certain questions. Can we imagine Yahweh (in the Bible) indicating that *he* is behind the creation of ships with beneficial cargoes? We can certainly relate this statement, "the creation of the heavens and the Earth," with him; but could Yahweh be identified with ships? Obviously, the claim that ships, which belong to the transitory world, are also Allah's creation contradicts the first part of the verse, which is in accordance with what is known about Yahweh from the Bible. When we consider how the triviality of this claim contrasts with the sublimity of Yahweh—who was active as a creator during the three previous stages[21] of the creation and continued working throughout the fourth stage, the Earth stage—we may begin to doubt that this information was indeed inspired by Yahweh-Allah and transmitted by the archangel Gabriel. This kind of assertion does not reflect the kind of profound spiritual wisdom that could come from the divine–spiritual realm. Such text does not illuminate Yahweh's deeper spiritual aspects, but leaves questions in one's mind. (In the Koran, many other verses attribute similar "spiritless divine qualities" to Allah.) Then another question arises: If Yahweh did not inspire these verses, whence did they originate and how did they come to appear the Koran?

In his "Anthroposophic Meditations on the Old Testament,"[22] Tomberg elaborated deeply on the identity of Yahweh Elohim. While addressing his cosmic responsibility, Tomberg showed that Yahweh is the being who has taken "cosmic cross-bearing" upon himself. Steiner's lecture course *Genesis* also provides a profound understanding of Yahweh's spiritual aspect and his overwhelming accomplishments during the creation of humankind, inducing wonder. However, one does not see similar sublime divine qualities projecting from the image of Allah as depicted in the Koran. When we analyze the content of Islamic belief (based, to a certain extent, on the koranic

---

21 The successive stages of ancient Saturn, Sun, and Moon conditions are described in Steiner's *Outline of Esoteric Science* and in numerous lectures on cosmic evolution.

22 This study is contained in *Christ and Sophia*.

verses and the *hadith*),²³ it becomes clear that in Islam the human relationship to Allah is founded on simple faith and an unquestionable obedience—worship and fear of Allah. This is probably because koranic verses were composed with the specific aim of invoking these particular feelings in the believers. It may seem like a contradiction, but when we read other verses in the Koran we may get the impression that Allah is not very insistent on turning everyone into Muslims, and that believing in him is not compelled. In these verses, a certain amount of freedom and choice of not believing in him is given. It can be confusing to readers when encountering verses suggesting that it makes no difference to Allah whether people acknowledge him and take heed of Muhammad's verses, since the unbelievers will suffer the consequences in the end."

As suggested earlier, it is not possible to speak of the exaltedness of a deity if that deity's ultimate purpose of creating a being was to obligate that being to prostrate before him. In this kind of relationship, there would always be an unbridgeable gulf between the creator and the created; they could never come together as "friends" (in the sense uttered by Jesus Christ in the Gospel). Therefore, if Muslims continue their adherence to this prevalent Islamic belief, their destiny may be to remain at an unalterable distance from their God forever. However, contrary to Islamic belief, beings of the divine–spiritual hierarchy did not create human beings with the expectation that they would worship their creator in obedience and fear. In fact, during the creation of human beings, spiritual beings of the divine hierarchy made many sacrifices so that we would be free beings. It was their intention and hope that human beings would take their rightful place in the divine–spiritual world in the distant future *as beings who represent freedom and love*. This fundamental cosmic truth concerning humankind has always evaded Muslims. The Islamic belief that they are required to worship Allah in prostration and in fear of him in no way reflects the truth of humanity's existence and mission on Earth. Could it be that the previous verse gives Muslims a distorted picture

---

23 *Hadith* are collections of reports on the teachings, deeds, and statements of the Prophet Muhammad. It is based on spoken reports in circulation after the death of Muhammad.

of why humankind was created and impels them to worship their God in this particular way?

> 51:56 I have only created jinn and men that they may serve Me. I created humankind only that they might worship Me.

Undoubtedly, the statement in this verse and others that convey similar meanings must have influenced the way Muslims conceive Allah's reason for creating humanity. When we recall the circumstances at the time of the birth of Islam (when Arabs were idolaters), it is quite understandable that they might have interpreted this verse in such a superficial way. However, in later times, when they understood Islamic teachings better and had progressed spiritually, this superficial interpretation should no longer be satisfactory. Many centuries have passed since the outset of Islam, and it seems they should have pondered on this important issue more deeply.[24]

Rudolf Steiner's lectures often mention that, in a far-distant future, human beings will achieve a higher spiritual consciousness; their souls and bodily constitutions will be more spiritualized; and to ensure that this development takes place in the future, Christ made a great sacrifice and gave humanity the example of the *"Son of Man,"* the human being who is totally spiritualized and who has reached ultimate perfection in one's spirit self, life spirit, and spirit body.[25] Christ's act was the outcome of his boundless and immaculate Love for humankind. By contrast, we cannot find a concept similar to *spiritualized love* in traditional Islamic teachings. When we consider the structure and content of Islamic teachings, we may

---

24 In the later centuries, Sufism and their teaching *Tasavvuf* have been the outcome of trying to provide a deeper aspect to humankind's relationship to Allah. *Tasavvuf* speaks of a certain evolution that human beings go through, during which they work for perfection of the self, or *nefs*. The final result of the Sufi journey is to merge with Allah and disappear in him—in a sense, this is also total surrender. This result is very similar to enlightenment, the state attained by pursuing various methods of Eastern teachings. However, from the anthroposophic view, this particular result is not intended as the goal of human evolution by the divine–spiritual beings who created humankind.

25 *Manas, Buddhi,* and *Atma,* respectively; see, for example, Steiner, *Theosophy,* chapter 1, especially pp. 53ff.

ask: To what extent could a religious teaching that does not contain profound concepts such as spirit and spiritualized love and is based solely on simple faith—obedience, fear, and worship of Allah with the expectation of securing a place in his blissful Paradise—provide an understanding of what is *truly spiritual* and help its adherents establish a harmonious relationship with their God? A result of this absence of spirit concept in Islam is *denial of the spirit*. In fact, denial of the spirit has become an unchangeable and permanent part of Islamic teachings.[26] Valentin Tomberg's indication in this context is immensely significant: "Therefore, the philadelphic community of the sixth cultural epoch will consist not of 'saints' but of spiritually minded people, just as 'evil' humanity will consist not of criminals but of those who deny the Spirit."[27]

Superficially, it may seem as if Muslims in general today resist acknowledgment of the spirit. However, we must bear in mind that we are still in the fifth post-Atlantean epoch,[28] and that we still have a long time in front of us; the divine realm will provide many more chances for people to find the spirit. Thus, the fact that Muslims presently ignore the spirit cannot be a final judgment in indicating who will be considered "evil," nor can it be said that every Muslim knowingly denies the spirit. Divine–spiritual beings must surely distinguish between knowingly denying the spirit with ill intention and being unable to recognize the spirit because one has not yet attained the necessary spiritual level to become aware of it. Among them, there may be some whose soul is disturbed even by a small trace of what is truly spiritual and will continue to deny the spirit, whereas many Muslims will certainly be devoted to the spirit later in their present incarnation or in a future incarnation. As noted, we are still in the fifth post-Atlantean cultural epoch, and Tomberg's comment refers to a distant future—the sixth cultural epoch.

---

26 The difficulty of regarding this matter by Muslims has its roots in their denial of the Holy Spirit and the concept of the Trinity.

27 Tomberg, *Christ and Sophia*, p. 84.

28 The fifth post-Atlantean epoch started in 1413 and will continue until 3573 (2,160 years), during which development of human consciousness, or the spiritual soul, will take place.

"The Spirit of truth who goes out from the Father" (John 15:26)—this spirit, who is inseparable from the Father and the Son, has a very significant and vital role in all cosmic spiritual processes. Thus, the spirit's value and what it means for the cosmos is beyond words. Jesus Christ has drawn the attention of humanity to this fact by stating the consequence of adopting a negative attitude toward the spirit:

> Whoever is not with me is against me, and whoever does not gather with me scatters. And so I tell you, every kind of sin and slander can be forgiven, but blasphemy against the Spirit will not be forgiven. Anyone who speaks a word against the Son of Man will be forgiven, but anyone who speaks against the Holy Spirit will not be forgiven, either in this age or in the age to come. (Matt. 12:30–32)

Valentin Tomberg refers to these words of Christ and explains the consequences of denial and denunciation of the spirit:

> It is immensely important to understand that what human beings call "righteousness," even "holiness," is not "righteousness before God." We need only to remember the words of Jesus Christ: "None is good, save one, that is, God" (Luke 18:19). In determining to which of the two karmic tendencies [concerning good or evil] certain people belong, it is not the external faults and virtues that must be considered, but their inner attitude toward the spiritual world. It is not faults that decide the matter, but denial and denunciation of the spirit. The Gospel word is quite literally true that says all sins may be forgiven except sin against the Holy Ghost; and the decision depends on this.[29]

Further considerations on the absence of the concept of spirit in Islam: Confusion of three significant Hebraic terms

The Arabic term *nefs* is often used in koranic verses. Actually, *nefs* stems from the Hebraic term *Nephesch*. In English translations of the Koran, *nefs* is rendered as *soul* (in German as *seele*). But this translation is only partially correct, because *nefs*, which also appears in the

---

29 Tomberg, *Christ and Sophia*, "The Karma of the Israelites," pp. 83–84.

Tasavvuf teachings of the Sufis, is a term that corresponds only to the sentient soul—the least-developed member of the human soul. In other words, it corresponds to the human "I," which manifests only in the human sentient soul. After that era came the period when the human intellectual soul began to develop. The sentient soul (*nefs*) had already been fully developed during the previous Chaldean era and the Egyptian epoch, but the intellectual soul was still unable to find expression in the "I." Therefore, from an anthroposophic point of view, the Arabic term *nefs*, which corresponds only to the sentient soul—since it is the most worldly, therefore, spiritually the least developed member of the human soul—cannot correctly and fully represent what the term *soul* actually implies. The human soul consists not only of the sentient soul, but also of the intellectual and consciousness souls. In the Koran, *nefs* is often related to human transgressions and to the part of a person that succumbs to temptations. Sometimes the word *nefs* is also used when it is needed to refer to the "I." (As we recall, it is a person's sentient soul that succumbs to luciferic temptations and the unconscious wrongdoings that follow them.) Because the intellectual soul had not yet fully developed at the beginning of the seventh century, the human "I" in those times manifested more through the sentient soul, or *nefs*; but, of course, this differed in degrees from person to person and from soul to soul. Koranic verses frequently reflect this fact:

> 12: 83 "*No!" cried their father. "Your souls have tempted you to do evil."*

Here, we can see that the translator has used the term *soul*; the actual Arabic word used in this verse, however, is *nefs*. Therefore, a truer rendering should be, "Your *nefs* [sentient soul] has tempted you to do evil." Steiner spoke of these Hebraic terms and explained that the old Hebrew expressions *nefesh, ruach, neshama* correspond to the spiritual-scientific terms *sentient soul, intellectual soul,* and *consciousness soul*.[30]

In the Arabic Koran, when referring to the spiritual aspect of Allah or Gabriel, the term *ruh* (*ruach* in Hebrew) is used. This is another term the Arabs have borrowed from the Hebrews. But throughout the Koran, this term is used not only when referring to

---

30 Steiner, *Genesis*, p. 144.

Allah, but also to the human soul. Therefore, since the term *ruh* is used in both cases, the differentiation between the human soul and the spiritual aspects of a divinity such as Allah or spiritual being such as Gabriel is not distinct. As Steiner clearly indicated, *ruach* corresponds to the intellectual soul, not to the spirit. Therefore, if we consider the composition of the verses from an anthroposophic viewpoint, we may suggest it that would be more correct if the term *ruh* were limited to representing only the soul (which belongs to human beings) and not also for indications related to spirit or the divine. Nevertheless, since it is impossible to alter the present Arabic Koran or its various translations, such a suggestion is moot. Moreover, we do not encounter the term *neshama* in the Koran or any expression similar to it; evidently, at that time Arabs did not have a term that corresponded to it. The term *consciousness soul* was yet unknown and belonged to a distant time.

We can conclude that, since a term that corresponds to *spirit* or defines it did not exist in the Arabic language at the outset of Islam or during the compilation of the Koran, the only available word, *nefs* (which can only represent the sentient soul), was used when referring to the human soul as well as when describing the divine–spiritual aspect of a deity. Arabs had to adopt this less-than-satisfactory word to resolve this language problem. Arabs had been worshipping human-made idols representing non-divine beings long before the emergence of Islam and never had the opportunity to comprehend the concept of soul or to develop the capacity to understand the spirit—or to rise to an understanding of what is truly spiritual. When they confronted certain problems during the compilation of the Koran, because of their lack of spiritual concepts—as when they referred to spiritual attributes of Allah—they did not have much choice but to use the term *nefs*, which was somehow transformed into *ruh*, while the term *spirit* has been added where needed by modern-day translators. Indeed, the Hebraic terms *nefesh* (*nefs*) and *ruach* did—to a certain extent—serve their purpose in the koranic messages at the beginnings of Islam; but since humankind is now in the epoch of the consciousness soul (the era of human consciousness soul development), the lack of significant terms such as *spirit, spiritual,* and *spirituality* is clearly causing serious confusion among Muslims and limiting their capacity to comprehend important spiritual issues. For instance, according to Muslims, any mention of the profound spiritual concept of a Godhead comprised of three separate divine personalities in one, or speaking of the cosmic principles of Father, Son, and the Holy Spirit as the Trinity, is considered blasphemy.

As we read the English translations of the Koran, we encounter the terms *spirit* and *Holy Spirit*.[31] Consequently, Christian readers who are cognizant of the fact that Muslims deny the Holy Spirit may be surprised to find the terms *Holy Spirit* and *spirit* in the koranic text at all. They would probably wonder how it is possible for Muslims to deny what is clearly stated in the Koran, since they are known to revere their sacred book. It is highly probable that this will pose a contradiction for Christian readers. However, the reason for this seeming contradiction is that translators tend to select certain words according to personal choice and interpretation when translating the Arabic Koran into English or other languages. Contemporary translators, on the other hand, are generally cognizant that the expressions *soul* and *spirit* have different meanings in English. We may deduce, therefore, that when confronted with words such as *nefs* and *ruh* in the Arabic Koran and realized that *ruh* does not convey the meaning inherent in the term *spirit*—and needing a word in keeping with Western terminology—translators take the liberty of introducing the term *spirit* into English translations of the Koran. In their rendering, they might also use *soul* in place of *nefs*. As mentioned, at the time of Muhammad pagan Arabs, who previously did not possess knowledge of Yahweh or Allah, were far from comprehending terms such as *spirit* or *Holy Spirit;* nor did they use such words consciously in their language.

In accordance with their level of consciousness, from the beginning of Islam the idea of the Trinity was regarded as a blasphemy by Muslims; for them, polytheism was inherent in that concept. Therefore, the Arabic version of the Koran does not contain the terms *spirit* or *Holy Spirit*. Those terms were not spoken in Arabic and never

---

31 In various English translations, these terms are used in eighteen verses scattered throughout the Koran.

appeared in the text of the Arabic Koran, simply because they did not exist during the time of Muhammad.

In an English version of the Koran, verse 2:87 states: "To Moses we gave the scriptures and after him we sent other apostles. We gave Jesus the son of Mary veritable signs and strengthened him with the Holy Spirit."[32] Again, when Christian readers read the words *Holy Spirit* in koranic verses (readers already familiar with the concept of the Holy Spirit), they would probably assume that this term is generally known in Islam as it is in Christianity. This would be an incorrect assumption and is very misleading. The actual word translated as Holy Spirit in the original Arabic text is *Ruh-ul Qudus*,[33] is an Arabic name for Gabriel (*Jibrael*). In other words, insofar as the Arabic language and Muslims concept of this name is concerned, *Ruh-ul Qudus* refers to Gabriel in Arabic and certainly not *Holy Spirit*. There are reasons why Gabriel has been given a permanent place in the Islamic culture. Muslims have been familiar with Gabriel's name (*Jibrael* and *Ruh-ul Qudus*) since the beginnings of Islam and have acknowledged him as their official angelic emissary from Allah. They proclaim that Gabriel inspired Muhammad's verses. Two verses also state that Mary became pregnant after Gabriel came to her to herald the birth of Jesus. Muslims believe that it was Gabriel who guided the Prophet during his renowned "night journey."[34] Thus, according to Muslims, Gabriel is indisputably a sacred emissary and a special *ruh*, or soul, assigned by Allah. In the Arabic text of verse 16:102, the phrase "by whom these verses were brought down" actually refers to Ruh-ul Qudus, but the translators have wrongly rendered the name as "Holy Spirit."

> 16:102: "The Holy Spirit brought it down from your Lord in truth to reassure the faithful."

---

32 A German translation renders the word similarly: *Heilige Geist* [Holy Spirit].

33 In Arabic, the root of *Qudus* is *Quds* and means "the sacred and reliable one."

34 According to the alleged account of Muhammad's night journey, Gabriel took the Prophet first to the Aqsa Mosque in Jerusalem (Kudus), and after Muhammad mounted a winged horse named Buraq that was waiting for him at the mosque, he guided the Prophet to the seventh heaven where his meeting with Allah and the former prophets took place.

Because the original name used in the Arabic Koran is *Ruh-ul Qudus*, who is none other than Gabriel, the correct translation of this verse should be: "*Gabriel brought it down from your Lord.*" Moreover, we certainly cannot imagine the Holy Spirit (of the Holy Trinity) bringing verses down to the Prophet Muhammad. Therefore, while reading an English or German translation of the Koran, it might be helpful to bear in mind that, since Gabriel is regarded by Muslims as a sacred *ruh* sent by Allah, the modern-day translators have made a logical assumption that Ruh-ul Kudus should mean Holy Spirit and use "Holy Spirit" for *Ruh-ul Qudus (Jibrael)* in their translations. In addition, the fact that nearly all translators of the Koran are English-speaking Muslims suggests that, by striking such similarities, they probably wished to give Christian readers the impression that the Koran contains similarities with the Gospels.[35]

The confusion and misuse of terms in any language can lead to serious confusion when trying to understand intricate spiritual subjects, and the Arabic language is not exempt from this situation.[36] Perhaps this partially explains, even at present, why Muslims do not sense the missing concept of spirit and do not feel an inner necessity of knowing the Christ, the Holy Spirit, and the divine Sophia, all of whom are divine–spiritual beings. Nevertheless, could there be other reasons why Muslims have closed themselves to any understanding of those divine–spiritual beings? We may get a better idea of the state of mind and soul of the present-day Muslim Arabs by reflecting on the state of the mind and soul of seventh-century pagan Arabs immediately before the impulse of Islam began to unfold.

Until AD 610, Arabs had no idea of the spiritual nature and qualities of Yahweh.[37] As we recall, at that time Arabs worshipped some 360 pagan idols surrounding the Kaaba building in Mecca. Moreover,

---

35 There is no doubt that they have done this with good intentions. However, when the translation of a book like the Koran that can be influential on millions of people is concerned, it is necessary and important that translators remain loyal to the original text.

36 The language of the Koran will be discussed in detail in a later section.

37 Perhaps a small minority who were neighbors of Jewish people had a vague idea that Yahweh is a deity who was revered and worshipped by their neighbors.

each tribe had its own unique venerated idol. By contrast, the Hebrew people had always adhered to the monotheistic faith inaugurated by their ancestral father Abraham.[38] Yahweh had been their one and only God for several centuries, during which deeper spiritual aspects of Yahweh were revealed to them. However, during the spiritually darkened period of Kali Yuga, spiritual facts regarding the Hebrews' monotheistic faith did not mean anything to descendants of Ishmael, and they knew nothing of Yahweh (as Allah) until Muhammad began to spread his message.

A comparison between Christian church fathers and Muslim scholars of today (who rely solely and strictly on the Koran and the *hadith*) may give a better idea of the mind and soul of the Arabian people prior to the introduction of Allah to their culture. Long before the emergence of Islam, church fathers could discuss and deal with profound spiritual subjects, though some of them may have had personal doubts about certain issues. For instance, at the Council of Nicaea held in 325, about 285 years before the emergence of Islam, the spiritual aspect of Jesus Christ was a subject of debate between Athanasius and Arius, along with other members of the council who supported one or the other thesis. Although these theologians presented different theses during the council (for example, Arius was not persuaded that Jesus had a divine–spiritual aspect), unlike Muslim Arabs their intention was not to refute or blindly deny significant spiritual concepts, but to discuss them and form a clearer understanding of them.[39] As for Muslims, although it has now been a long time since they first became aware of Allah's existence, they still do not allow more profound spiritual concepts to flourish in Islamic teachings. In general, it is impossible to discuss or argue about any Islamic dogma

---

38 That is, except in the case when they worshipped the golden calf for a certain period during their history. Some Koranic verses refer to this particular era.

39 However, also being influenced by dark forces during the Kali Yuga period, the church fathers' knowledge of spirit (as far as it was related with humankind) only managed to survive until the year 869, when, in the meeting of the Eighth Ecumenical Council of Constantinople, they agreed on abolishing the human's spiritual aspect. According to their final declaration, humans only consisted of a physical body and a soul but did not have a spiritual aspect in their constitution.

with them—even logical arguments may be considered disrespectful and blasphemous toward Allah and Islamic dogma.[40]

What are the fundamental messages of the Koran?
How did Muhammad's verses influence pagan Arabs?

When the Prophet Muhammad began to receive verses by way of inspiration and proclaimed his visionary teaching, he faced much opposition and hostility. Strong enmity and even disparagement came mainly from pagan Arab tribes. Koranic verses may give us an idea of how difficult it was for the Prophet to get his messages through to pagan Arabs at the beginning:

> *25: 41 Whenever they [unbelievers] see you [Muhammad], they scoff at you, saying: "Is this the man Allah has sent as his apostle? Had we not stood firm he would have turned us away from our deities." 25: 42 But when they face their punishment they shall know who has been more grossly mislead.*
>
> *25: 44 Do you think that they can hear or understand? They are like beasts, and even more misguided.*

Apart from a small group of people who believed in him, most of the Arab tribes did not want to change their old beliefs and pagan worship. Believers fought many battles against unbelievers for several years. When we look at Muhammad's struggle from an anthroposophic perspective (recalling Steiner's lectures *Three Streams in Human Evolution*), it becomes clear that the Prophet had no choice but to persuade all Arabs, and that (although he did not know the deeper reasons behind the guidance he received from Allah) he had the overwhelming feeling that this crucial task had to be accomplished as quickly as possible; the concealed crucial deadline was AD 666, and the Islamic impulse had to be inaugurated before that year. Throughout his struggle, one of his main tactics was to persuade pagan Arabs

---

[40] Although this statement covers the attitude of a large number of Muslims, undoubtedly there are also open-minded Muslims with whom one can discuss certain religious matters. For instance, some Islamic theologians do not condone the hatred, hostility, and aggression that radiates from fundamentalist, extremist, and jihadist Muslims.

to depict a vivid image of an almighty divinity (Allah) who was capable of offering great rewards and at the same time doling out admonishments and potentially severe punishments, which aroused moral feelings of *fear, shame,* and *repentance* in Arabs. Eventually, Muhammad succeeded in persuading the nonbelievers who had persistently opposed him. He achieved this prior to his death in 632. Among those moral feelings, fear of Allah played a significant role in persuading pagan Arabs to embrace Islam. In the Koran, many verses aimed at unbelievers mention the consequence of facing the inescapable wrath of Allah if they refuse to believe in Allah and his Prophet. Those unbelievers were called *kafir* (infidels).[41] Those who declared belief in Allah were called *Mosalmân* (Muslim).

In this context, what does *Muslim* mean? In Arabic, it means literally "one who believes and surrenders completely to Allah." This complete belief and surrender means obedience to the koranic admonitions given by Allah. If we bear in mind Ibn Kathir's explanations concerning the pre-Islamic state of the Arab tribes while analyzing the composition of the koranic verses, it becomes clear that *the admonishment given in the verses corresponds directly to particular transgressions of the pagan Arabs—verses that convey various admonitions do not address any other people, tribe, or race, but only to Arabs.* In other words, these verses point to the Arabs' [former] transgressions and aimed to ameliorate their morally degenerate way of life and lack of spirituality. Some of the verses indicate punishments that correspond to particular wrong actions. For instance, according to the Koran, the punishment for adultery is that "the adulterer and the adulteress shall each be given a hundred lashes." Later, these verses indicating certain wrongdoings and the punishments became the basis of Islamic *sharia*.

Fundamentally, the Koran preaches the oneness of Allah. In a way, this central teaching is already summarized in the principle Islamic maxim: "There is only one Allah; there is no deity other than him." Onto this central teaching must be added "and Muhammad is his

---

41 Koranic verses reveal that the word *infidel* (*kafir*) was initially used in relation with the unbelievers of Muhammad's time. It was actually associated with the Arabs and not with anyone else. At the present time, it is used by fundamentalist and radical Muslims and has been associated with Christians and Jews who refuse conversion to Islam.

Prophet."⁴² In the Koran, many other subjects cover details of Arab life in those times. Several verses are composed of quotations and information from the Bible and other sources, but expressed in the form characterized by the Koran. Rudolf Steiner provides further explanations of the Koran:

> This idea of the one God, however, included much derived from other sources—for instance, from Egypt–Chaldean religion, which yielded very exact knowledge of the connection between events in the starry heavens and earthly events. Thus, thoughts and ideas current among the Egyptians, Chaldeans, Babylonians, and Assyrians appear again in the religion of Muhammad, but suffused by the One God, Yahweh. Speaking [spiritually] scientifically, what we have in Arabism is a kind of collection, or synthesis, of Egyptian and Chaldean priestly wisdom teachings and the ancient Hebraic religion of Yahweh.⁴³

Throughout the Koran, unbelievers, sinners, and those disobedient to Allah are threatened with being thrown into the eternal inferno of Hell to suffer endless torments. On the other hand, for those who choose to become Muslims and obey Allah, a very pleasant paradise of delights is promised.⁴⁴ Evidently, vivid descriptions of Allah's Paradise combined with the threat of being thrown into Hell were very effective in persuading pagan Arabs to become Muslims.

In addition to dealing with pagan Arab unbelievers, Muhammad also had to deal with the "People of the Book."⁴⁵ He had confrontations particularly with the Jewish people. Arabs regarded Jews and Christians as people who already believed in God and had a sacred

---

42 As we recall, this principal Islamic maxim is recited from the minarets five times a day.

43 Steiner, *Background to the Gospel of St. Mark*, lecture 9.

44 47:15: "This is the paradise which the righteous have been promised. There shall flow in it rivers of unpolluted water and rivers of milk forever fresh; rivers of delectable wine and rivers of clearest honey. They shall eat therein of every fruit and receive forgiveness from their Lord. Is this like the lot of those who shall abide in Hell and drink scalding water which will tear their bowels?"

45 Because adherents to Judaism and Christianity had holy books, they are often referred to as "People of the Book" in the Koran.

book. Nevertheless, it was very important to Muhammad that they acknowledge him as the "last Prophet" sent by Allah (or Yahweh, who was initially their God) and believe in his inspired verses. If he could persuade them to acknowledge him as the prophet sent by Allah for all the descendants of Abraham, it would have made his struggle with the pagan Arabs much easier; if People of the Book became Muslims (believers of Allah), Muhammad could have used them as irrefutable, bona fide evidence that God had sent him. In other words, he was experiencing harsh conflicts with the Arab tribes and needed support from the Jews. We understand from the koranic verses that his relationship with the Christians was of secondary importance; forming a bond with the Jews was more important to him, because they were similarly connected to Abraham. Therefore, in the Koran we frequently encounter verses that call on People of the Book to believe in Allah's revelations; we also find verses that reflect Allah's disappointment with Jews and Christians—especially with the former, since they refused to acknowledge Muhammad as their new prophet and did not embrace Islam.[46]

Because the Koran was compiled after Muhammad's death by gathering the scattered verses written on pieces of wood, bones, rocks, papyrus, and from the few Muslims who had memorized them, it is not hard to imagine that the transcribers had a hard time compiling related messages under a specific surah. Apparently, the result was not very successful; in the Koran, the messages often do not follow an orderly pattern in each surah, and some suwar combine many different unrelated subjects. For this reason, the general impression we get is that there is little coherence among the koranic verses. This lack of coherence causes a problem of continuity and makes it hard to understand why unrelated messages follow each other in a surah. Thus, in an effort to provide logical relationship among subjects in the Koran, a basic categorization of related subjects gathered from different suwar under certain topics can be helpful.[47]

---

46 Nonetheless, a small minority of Jews and Christians who were living in close proximity to the Arabs did become Muslim.

47 There are 114 suwar and 6,236 verses (*ayats*) in the Koran.

If we imagine the Koran's messages arranged in concentric circles (according to what the Islamic impulse had aimed to achieve and to the degree of significance of the messages), all the verses that emphasize that Allah is the one and only deity in the universe and that there is no other deity besides him can be placed at the core of these circles. We can place the divine qualities attributed to Allah along with this proclamation, as he is the sublime creator of everything in the cosmos and is merciful, rewarding, and almighty. All the verses that emphasize idolatry as wrong and that Allah will punish idolaters, as well as those that state how he will reward believers, can also be put in the first circle.

In the second circle we can place all the koranic verses that relate Allah to the Old Testament and to the Jewish people, for—being a newly emerged religion—Islam needed a substantial background, and this historical connection with the Hebrews provided the necessary link. The verses found in this circle emphasize that the Jews previously revered Allah, and it was he who gave them the Old Testament and the Torah. Here we can find references to Jewish prophets such as Abraham, Isaac, Jacob, and Moses. Many biblical stories are also narrated in these verses. However, we also see that these stories are now presented in an Islamic way—they are narrated in a form that aims to persuade pagan Arabs to embrace Islam and to strengthen Muslims' faith in Allah during the early days of that faith. The fact that these koranic Bible stories were inconsistent with what was actually stated in the Old Testament later led to the conflict between Muhammad and the Jewish people. At the outset of Islam, Muhammad insisted that these verses were inspired by Allah, who was also their God, Yahweh, but Jews were not persuaded and found it difficult to accept Muhammad's versions of the ancient Bible narrations. In fact, for the Jews, who were steeped in the original Bible stories, certain discrepancies and anachronistic mistakes found in Muhammad's verses were ample indications to avoid Muhammad and reject Islam.[48]

---

48 Muhammad firmly believed that he was the new messenger of Abraham's God, sent forth to confirm previous scriptures. According to the verses he received, Allah had formerly revealed his will to the Jews and Christians through chosen prophets, but they disobeyed Allah's commandments and divided themselves into controversial sects. Koranic verses accuse the

Sorath's Intervention in AD 666 and the Role of Ishmael's Descendants

Because the Koran declares Jesus as a prophet sent by Allah and one who is close to him, the verses that attempt to form a connection between Allah and Jesus and his mother Mary should also be placed in the second circle. In fact, koranic verses do not seem to have any conflict with Jesus; in the Koran he is only a prophet or messenger of Allah—that is, he is presented in a very different way in the Koran from the way he is depicted in the Gospel. In any case, koranic verses place greater emphasis on Allah's relationship with the Jews and with Jewish prophets, whereas, complicated problems exist regarding "the origin of Jesus" and the concept of the Holy Trinity; indeed, the problems relate to the existence of Christianity in general. Nonetheless, several koranic verses mention Jesus, though in a somewhat distorted and inaccurate way.[49] At the outset of Islam, it was necessary to form a firm connection between this newly emerging religion and the existing religions to prove that Islam had deep roots in the past. Accordingly, several verses emphasize that Allah sent the Koran as a confirmation of the Old Testament and the Gospel, and that he assigned all the prophets mentioned in those Scriptures.[50]

> 6:84–85 We gave him Isaac and Jacob and guided them as We guided Noah before them. Among his descendants were David and Solomon, Jacob and

---

Jews of corrupting the Scriptures, and Christians of worshipping Jesus as the Son of God, although Allah had explicitly commanded them to worship none but him. Having thus gone astray, Allah now intended to bring them back to the right path, to the true religion preached by Abraham, which was Islam. However, the Jews refused Muhammad's proclamations, and this led to serious conflicts. Apart from many smaller disputes, three significant events can be mentioned as main conflicts that happened between the Prophet Muhammad and Jewish communities. In a battle in 626 the Jewish tribe of al-Nadhir was defeated and expelled. In 627 the Jewish tribe of Beni Qurayza was raided by Muhammad, and more than 800 men were beheaded. In 629 the Jews of Khaybar were put to the sword. When we delve into these past events, we may find the reasons why there is endless strife today between the Jewish people of Israel and the Muslim people of the Middle East.

49 The way Jesus is presented in the Koran and how Muslims conceive him will be considered in detail in a later section.

50 Although it is stated in the verses that the Koran confirms the former Scriptures, even at its beginnings Islam was somehow positioned "above" the former religions by Muslims, because in their eyes Islam, as the final religion, is the most exalted and sacred religion, specially inculcated by Allah.

Joseph, and Moses and Aaron (thus are the righteous rewarded). Zacharias, John, Jesus, and Elias (all were upright men).

In the third circle, we can place the verses that point out the morally degenerate Arab way of life and underline the fact that they have been a sinful people. Besides pointing out the reasons for their ignorance and wrongdoings, these verses try to ameliorate their sinful ways and firmly call on them to acknowledge Allah by becoming Muslim and henceforth abide his admonishments. As mentioned, some of the verses in this circle form the basis of Islamic *sharia* law.

In the fourth circle are verses that relate the battles that Muhammad and Muslims fought against the unbelievers. These verses emphasize that Muslims actually fought for Allah and his cause,[51] and in them we find the Islamic concept of jihad, as well as Allah's promise of resurrecting those who die in jihad, promising to reward them by placing them in Paradise.

In the fifth circle we may place the verses about Muhammad's family life, which in a way give us clues about the early Arab Islamic lifestyle. Although these verses are placed in the fifth circle, it must be noted that some of them (such as verse 2:223) have strongly influenced the way women are valued in Islamic countries, both in the past and in the present.

In addition to these five circles, we can add a couple more circles that would include other relatively insignificant issues.

Such an organized grouping of verses could be helpful when analyzing the Koran. Nevertheless, it can provide only a limited guide when we wish to delve into the maze of koranic verses. The fact that different subjects (and messages) have been unsystematically placed in the suwar and usually do not follow an orderly sequence has caused a great deal of confusion, even for the Muslims. Readers often come across verses that all of a sudden jump from one subject to another, making it difficult to understand the meaning conveyed by the messages. This has been one of the reasons why *imams* (worship leaders in mosques) and

---

51 In a later section, it will become apparent that the existence of these particular verses is the root cause of present day Muslims' concept of jihad and the hostile attacks of Muslim jihadists, although these verses in no way assert that Muslims should be hostile and conduct terrorizing attacks.

scholars (*'ulemā*)⁵² have been needed to interpret the Koran and to tell Muslims what various verses mean or imply. These interpretations have often become more prominent than the actual meanings inherent in the Koran. Different interpretations and understandings of the Koran are the fundamental reasons for divisions among Islamic sects and groups, each of whom strictly value their own interpretations of the verses. From time to time, a group of scholars may find themselves in a dispute over how a certain verse should be interpreted.⁵³

Uncertainty caused by the unsystematic arrangement of the verses was one of the main reasons that *hadith* have always had a very important place in traditional Islam; they have somehow complemented Islamic teachings. Since ordinary folk had difficulties in grasping the meanings inherent in these verses that issued from a spiritual source and therefore were complicated, they formed an affinity with Muhammad's sayings, since they came from a human being like them. As a consequence, although many verses explicitly indicate that the Prophet Muhammad's task is only to convey Allah's messages and to warn Arabs, he has been given a very prominent role in Islam. Approximately thirty-five verses define Muhammad's task and the limits of his authority. The verses below explain the boundaries of the Prophet's authority:

---

52 *'Ulemā* (singular *'ālim*) is an aggregate of religious leaders who are knowledgeable and well informed in the interpretation of the Koran and *sharia* law, since these leaders are mostly imams and scholars. In another sense, *'ulemā* can act as an organized political body that exercises power in the name of religion in some Islamic countries.

53 Arabic words often have more than one meaning. Therefore, the way one scholar understands a particular word in a verse and interprets that verse may differ entirely from another scholar's interpretation. This has been a problem inevitably faced by translators who attempt to translate the Arabic Koran into English. For example, the following are the renderings of verse 2:32 given by different translators: "And He taught Adam all the names, then He put the objects of these names before the angels" (Sher Ali); "And He taught Adam all the names, then showed them to the angels" (M. M. Pickthall); "And He taught Adam the names of all things; then He placed them before the angels" (A. Yusuf Ali). However, yet another translation of the same verse made directly from the Aramaic Koran gives a totally different meaning: 2:32 "And concealed from Adam all the names, and then the angels were shaken" (Gabriel Sawma). Sawma's elucidations on the Aramaic origin of the Koran is considered further on.

> 25:56 We have sent you [Muhammad] only to proclaim good news and give warning.
>
> 29:50 They [unbelievers] ask: "Why has no sign [miracle] been given him [Muhammad] by his Lord?" Say: "Signs are in the hands of Allah. My mission is only to give plain warning."
>
> 5:99 The duty of the apostle [Muhammad] is only to give warning. Allah knows all that you hide and all that you reveal.
>
> 33:45 Prophet, We have sent you forth as a witness, a bearer of good news, and a warner; one who shall call men to Allah by his leave.
>
> 28:56 You [Muhammad] cannot guide whom you please: it is Allah who guides whom he will. He best knows those who yield to guidance.

The Prophet was given an important task, but his power and the boundaries of his duty were clearly defined by Allah. Allah was the indisputable guide, and Muhammad's role was to deliver his messages. The messages inherent in these verses do not reflect the approach of using force to persuade the unbelievers.

Is the principle of freedom indicated anywhere in the Koran?

Koranic verses convey powerful messages, emphasizing that every Muslim's fate is in Allah's hands and that whatever Allah has decreed about a particular human being is unchangeable, for it is only he who decides the fate of each human being. He is behind every single occurrence on Earth. Rudolf Steiner spoke about how fatalism is integrated in Islamic dogmas.

> When we consider the form in which [Islam] appeared, we find, first and foremost, the uncompromising monotheism, the one, the all-powerful Godhead—a concept of Divinity that is allied with fatalism. The destiny of human beings is predetermined; they must submit to their destiny, or at least recognize their subjugation to it. This attitude is an integral part of the religious life.[54]

A koranic verse verifies Steiner's explanation:

---

54 Steiner, *Karmic Relationships*, vol. 1, lecture 10.

10:107 *If Allah afflicts you with a misfortune, none can remove it but he; and if he bestows on you a favor, none can withhold his bounty. He is bountiful to whom he will.*

Steiner's words also explain why obedience and surrender have become an integral part of the Islamic religious life. As we recall, obedience played an important role in the Jewish way of life, but obedience and surrender were expected of Hebrews for different reasons altogether. Mosaic Law has a quality different from Islamic *sharia*, because its implementation was necessary for the preparation of a very important cosmic event.[55] Those descendants of Abraham needed protection so as not to lose their spiritual virtues—their moral values; they even needed to strengthen them when they were exposed to the influence of the Kali Yuga period. Therefore, "the Law" was given to them at a much earlier stage. Yahweh's timing in bestowing the Mosaic Law was in keeping with the Hebrew soul and spiritual development. By contrast, descendants of Ishmael did not receive guidance at the beginning. They received admonition and some guidance at a much later time, starting in 610, after they had been fully exposed to the dark influences of the Kali Yuga period, when they suffered the loss of moral values and were unable to show any spiritual progress. This resulted in their conscience remaining undeveloped.

Because the first believers of Islam almost immediately began to implement the admonitions conveyed by the verses, they applied Allah's rules while Muhammad was still alive. Thus, they did not feel the need for a separate *sharia* law that would also serve as an Islamic law. However, after the Prophet's death, Muslims formed a separate *sharia* law by putting together certain verses.[56] The self-imposed implementation of *sharia* did not have any purpose other than helping them amend what was morally degenerate and compensate for their spiritual deficiencies. In other words, the task of Islamic *sharia* was to amend the spiritual deterioration caused by having been fully exposed to the

---

55   These preparations concerned the Advent of Christ.
56   The verses that later formed Islamic law—*sharia*—mainly come from those found in surah 4 and surah 5.

Kali Yuga period. It is also necessary to mention that the way Allah addresses Arabs in the koranic verses is not exactly the same as the way Yahweh had addressed Hebrews (in the form of commandments). The koranic verses *were not meant to be strict commandments,* although Muslims have since chosen to evaluate them as such.

Ever since the beginning of Islam, Muslims do not realize that the koranic verses do not have the same uncompromising tone ("You shall..." or "You shall not...") that underlines the strict tone of Yahweh's commandments in the Torah. Verses in the Koran were not meant to impose perpetual, unalterable commandments on Arabs.[57] Rather, Allah conveyed certain flexible messages that would enable Muslims to achieve a higher spiritual understanding in the future. The admonishment given in the verses was meant to guide Arabs only during a transitory period. Although "fear of Allah" was inherent in several verses, many were really just firm suggestions. Some verses warned them about the serious consequences of ignoring Allah's admonishment, but some indicated that believing in Allah was not compulsory.

The fact that koranic messages vary in sternness may seem contradictory, but actually they are not. On the one hand, it was absolutely necessary to form a kind of strong spiritual force that could blunt the Sorathic intervention, and for this to be achieved Arab folk had to become adherents of an uncompromising, monotheistic faith based on obedience and fear of Allah. On the other hand, the new principle of freedom, which had come to the world approximately six hundred years earlier with the Christ impulse, had to be introduced to them somehow. Verses that allude to the freedom of belief show that the principle of freedom is not totally absent in the Koran, although Muslims do not seem be aware of it. For example:

> 4:80 *He that obeys the apostle [Muhammad] obeys Allah himself. As for those that pay no heed to you, know then that We have not sent you [Muhammad] to be their keeper.*

---

57 In contrast, Yahweh's commands found in the Talmud were unalterable. This is why some Jews had difficulties in accepting Jesus Christ and the new principles he had declared in which radical changes were inherent for, as far as they were concerned, accepting these new principles meant denial of Yahweh's laws.

> 50:45 We well know what they say. You shall not use force with them. Admonish with this Koran whoever fears My warning.
>
> 39:41 We have revealed to you the Book with the truth, for the instruction of humankind [Arabs]. He that follows the right path shall follow it to his own advantage; and he that goes astray shall do so at his own peril. You [Muhammad] are not accountable for them.
>
> 10:108 Say: "Men! The truth has come to you from your Lord. He that follows the right path follows it to his own advantage and he that goes astray does so at his own peril. I am not your keeper."
>
> 88:21-22 Therefore give warning. Your duty is only to warn them: You are not their keeper.
>
> 10:99 Had your Lord pleased, all the people of the Earth would have believed in him. Would you [Muhammad] then force faith upon man?

These verses, as well as many others, denote a certain freedom, but they were not given to establish an understanding of freedom at the very beginning of Islam; this is because other matters had priority at the time, and the concept of freedom would have been of no use in deadening Sorath's intervention. Nonetheless, they were given along with the other verses, with the hope that Muslims would evaluate them under the light of a more developed state of consciousness in the future. It is noteworthy that in one of the verses, Jesus speaks of the freedom he has brought for the Hebrews.

> 3:50 [Jesus] I come to confirm the Torah that has already been revealed and to make lawful to you some of the things you are forbidden. I bring you sign from your Lord [Allah]: therefore fear him and obey me.

In this verse, Jesus is addressing the Jewish people, but his message is aimed indirectly at Arabs. However, this verse does not go into further detail concerning the impulse of freedom brought by Jesus but indirectly serves as a call to guide pagan Arabs to believe in Allah. Moreover, this brief statement is not clear enough to illumine the new principle of spiritual freedom brought to the world by Christ. Therefore, because Jesus does not concern them directly, it is doubtful that Muslims will ever wonder what this verse really means and ask: If the Law was given by God Yahweh, how is it possible that Jesus, presented merely as a prophet of Allah in the koranic verses, could make some of the forbidden things lawful? *What is the source of his authority to alter Yahweh's words?*[58]

It will probably take a while longer before Muslims will begin to wonder about the deeper meanings of messages in verses that clearly indicate freedom of belief. As a result of not showing sufficient interest in these issues, the deeper meaning of what Jesus indicates in this verse (and the fact that Jesus Christ is the bringer of the freedom principle and has authority to make radical changes) will probably continue to elude them. Recall that another profound aspect of the freedom principle is *freedom from having to belong to a group soul*, which allows the development of the human "I" and enables people to become free individuals. As a consequence of following *sharia* law, Muslims fail to comprehend this, and they will have to remain part of a group soul. In the long run, this will have a negative effect on the further individualization and spiritualization process of the human soul.

A result of being a perpetual part of a group soul is that a certain concept (greatly valued by Muslims) has formed and has influenced them through many generations. The Arab concept *ummah* (community or nation) clearly reflects an understanding that does not value individualization of the "I" and freedom of the soul as an ultimate goal. *Ummah* is commonly used to mean the collective nation of the whole Arab world. In the Islamic sense, it also means the whole community or larger family of Muslims, believers of Allah, who live all over the world. Therefore, the term *ummah* denotes the whole of the Islamic world. According to the Muslims' common understanding (whether Arabs or people of other ethnicities), all Muslims are "Muhammad's *ummah*"—they are the Prophet's people (as Jews are the children of Abraham). Thus, as an Islamic standard, every Muslim belongs to Muhammad's *ummah*; all adherents

---

58 The result of this inquiry could have led them to the Pleroma of the Christ-being, for all seven Elohim belonged to the Pleroma—although at a later time Yahweh had to work apart from them because of certain cosmic necessities. Therefore, the alteration made by Christ regarding Yahweh's laws was not a contradictory change but actually a complementary amendment.

of Islam are entitled to be in this large group of believers. This community of believers is also open to the adherents of other religions, so all who renounce their former religion and declare that they now believe in Allah and will henceforth abide by Islamic rules are accepted into the community of Islam (*ummah*) without objection or difficulty.

In some Islamic countries ruled by *sharia*, the penalty for renouncing Islam (i.e., stepping outside *ummah*) is death. Belonging to the larger community of Muslims signifies being part of a collective soul. Since renouncing the community of *ummah* is an unthinkable act for virtually all Muslims, they never approach the point of yearning for more freedom and for acquiring a more individualized "I." They are content with the fact that they belong to the *ummah, the group soul of Islam*. Because Muslims willingly open their souls to the forces of the Moon sphere[59] and are not open to receiving the redemptive effect from the Christ impulse (which originally came from the Sun sphere), they are unable to receive the beneficial spiritual forces that emanate from Christ that would enable them to make the transition from being members of a group soul to a more individualized soul. Those who comprehend that one's connection with the divine no longer relies on belonging to a group soul will make an individual effort to be connected to the divine through the spirit—that is, through the Christ and Holy Spirit. In this context, it becomes clearer why Christ said, "No one can come to the Father except through me" (John 14:6).

The concept of *ummah* is a hindrance to individualization of the human "I" and, in the long run, to further spiritualization; *ummah* is not a concept that is in harmony with the Christ impulse. At the present time, this may be the situation Muslims face, but the redeeming effects of the Christ impulse do not disregard any human being. Because it does not differentiate, therefore, it might gradually have an indirect influence on those who, at present, are not open to the inflow of the Christ impulse. For this reason—because the influence

---

59 Opening their souls only to the forces of the Moon sphere also means that they are open to receiving the guidance of a luciferic archangel instead of a progressive folk soul or a progressive archangel.

of the Christ impulse will continue into the future and its intensity will increase as Christ gradually pervades the Earth's etheric body—it would be realistic to expect positive changes.

Sharia law, the rule of retaliation, and the new principle of forgiveness in the Koran

In the aftermath of the battles between the believers and the unbelievers, it gradually dawned on the Arabs that they had been oblivious to Allah's existence and were living a very immoral way of life prior to Muhammad's messages. As mentioned, these messages awakened moral feelings of fear, shame, and repentance in them. The more these three factors affected their souls and guided their way of life, the more they adhered to the inspired verses of the Prophet and eventually formed a permanent law from a selection of verses. This strict law is called *sharia*. Since they were previously without such laws, *sharia* began to function as a Muslim jurisdiction, which is one of the reasons why obedience and strictly keeping within the framework of Islam has become essential for Muslims. When Muhammad was still alive, messages conveyed by the verses had begun to take shape as strict rules of the new religion, but they were not yet imposed on the Arabs as *sharia* laws. This was in part because the Islamic impulse was still quite new; rules that were too strict might have driven away the pagan Arabs, who had not previously implemented any laws or restrictions whatsoever. Perhaps Muhammad also heeded, to a certain degree, the verses that emphasized freedom. Nevertheless, apart from those that suggested freedom, his inspired teachings had the potential of giving rise to *sharia*. It can be seen in several koranic verses how Abraham's monotheistic religion and the fact that Jews were given a law by Allah[60] have been repeatedly used as an example. Concerning Judaism's influence on Islam, Steiner indicates:

> We see, in the first place, that monotheism in a very strict form was instituted by Muhammad. It is a religion that looks up, as

[60] As we recall, Yahweh has never been named or referred to as *Yahweh* in the Koran. He has always been referred to as *Allah*.

did Judaism, to a single Godhead encompassing the universe. "There is one God and Muhammad is his herald"; this is what goes forth from Arabia as a mighty impulse, spreading far into Asia, and passing across Africa and then into Europe by way of Spain.[61]

It is significant that although several verses admonish, there is not a single verse that *commands* Arabs to form or keep a compulsory law such as the Hebrews have. Although Allah clearly demanded that descendants of Ishmael acknowledge him as their one and only deity, and he gave them thousands of verses, it is noteworthy that in none of them did he say anything like this: "These are the laws of your *sharia*; from now on thou shall abide by my commands and be permanently ruled by *sharia*." However, under the influence of the Jewish people, who had followed Yahweh's law for hundreds of years, Arabs somehow felt the need to adopt an unalterable, compulsory, and permanent *sharia* like that of their distant relatives.[62] Just after Muhammad's death, the caliphs succeeding him decided that it was necessary to impose a strict discipline in an established way so that Arab tribes would not revert back to their old pagan ways of worship, and they wanted *sharia* to be a guide for future generations. Ever since then, the Islamic maxims of "believing in Allah" and "fear of Allah" have been effective on Muslims.

However, as we see how extremist Islamic terror manifests today, it becomes necessary to ask this: To what extent do rigid laws and the fear of Allah (suitable for Arabs at the outset of Islam) successfully function as a guide today? It seems that neither Muslims of the past nor those of the present have ever considered that *sharia* cannot (and should not) be enforced forever. None of them was aware of the danger that such an impulse as Islam (meant as an emergency measure in the past against the *beast*) could be in the future as it inevitably

---

61 Steiner, *Karmic Relationships*, vol. 1, lecture 10.
62 Evidently, Allah did not command the Arabians to institute *sharia* law, but the Arabians singled out certain verses—meant to instruct and guide them only for a transitory period—and began implementing them as their code of conduct.

deviates into malicious forms such as terrorist extremists and jihadists when exposed to luciferic and ahrimanic influences.

We must ask this question: If Islamic countries implement strict *sharia*, which should deter Muslims from hostility and terrorism, why is *sharia* unable to stop them from doing evil acts? How is it that some Muslims can be violent and readily engage in terrorism without any remorse? How can they so easily justify their acts of violence by saying they are doing it for Allah?

At this point, the reason becomes clear why *sharia* cannot mitigate the degenerate conduct of fundamentalists, extremists and jihadists. The structure and nature of Arab *sharia* was capable of offering guidance only *to a limited extent and up to a certain time*. After being under the guidance of *sharia* for a certain length of time, another important factor should have started to act as a guide. What was this factor? When analyzed objectively, the fact that Islamic terrorism always aims its attacks at innocent civilian targets—not even sparing women and children—reveals that *sharia* has not played much of a role in helping Muslims acquire *conscience*. It is an undeniable fact that, since the outset of Islam, strict rules of *sharia* have prevented Muslims from certain sins and transgressions, and that it has helped them achieve a certain amount of morality. For instance, as part of their religious practice, almsgiving has assisted them in acquiring a feeling of mercy and helping those in need. Theft is rare in Islamic countries, but since the guidance of *sharia* always acts as an *external voice*, guiding them to do something or not to do something, it prevents Muslims from attaining the individualized faculty and capability of discerning what is right and wrong. For example, if Muslims do not steal because they are afraid that their hand will be cut off—the traditional punishment for stealing under *sharia* law—this means that their inner law, or conscience, has not yet properly developed. It is necessary for each individual to realize that stealing is wrong and thus a sin *without* being told and reminded by an external source; one's independent discernment of right and wrong is a requirement for individual development—throughout one's personal evolution.

Clearly, these statements are not intended to suggest that all Muslims have bypassed the impulse of conscience and have not acquired any conscience at all. Undoubtedly, there are many adherents of Islam who have acquired a certain degree of conscience. However it is necessary to say that this is because *conscience* was brought to the world by Christ, and the development of conscience is brought about through the Christ impulse. Therefore, Muslims who have acquired a sense of conscience have managed to acquire it with Christ's help, despite the hindrance imposed by restrictive *sharia* and certain obstructive Islamic dogmas.

Since Muslims proclaim that they have become like the ancient People of the Book now that they also have a monotheist religion and a holy book, it should be an essential part of their religious duties to consider every single verse and not disregard any of them, and especially to ponder on certain verses in detail that contain significant messages. If members of Islam had methodically done this work throughout the centuries, certain verses (mentioned later) could have guided them in acquiring a higher spiritual consciousness and in developing conscience. Apparently, since the emergence of Islam, they have never wondered why particular verses exist in the Koran, and they simply followed the external guidelines handed down by tradition from generation to generation. Even now it is not too late to do this work; Muslims could still study these verses in depth; pondering the deep meanings inherent in them and adopting the new spiritual principles indicated in them could prompt them to discard certain laws of *sharia* such as retaliation, lapidation (stoning to death), amputation of hands and feet, severe whipping, and even circumcision, which is practiced on women in some Islamic countries.

Not heeding the deep meanings conveyed by these verses is one of the reasons why Arabism has grown as a force independent of *sharia*. In fact, having permeated *sharia* for many centuries, a kind of merciless and degenerate *sharia* has come into being.[63] The overpowering influence of Arabism has created a vicious circle and a maze that imprisoned Muslims, as a result, they cannot find their way out of the labyrinth of *sharia*. However, if they can manage to bring forward a strong yearning to be emancipated from the imprisonment of the

---

63 In many videos found on the Internet, it can be seen how this "merciless and degenerate *sharia*" is implemented, as *sharia* judges keep coming up with new punishments that do not exist in the Koran at all, and the executioners of these punishments inflict undeserved pain and suffering on those who are found guilty.

law, certain verses can show them the way out of this labyrinth and can provide guidance to transform the principle of retaliation into a higher divine principle. What is this higher principle that beings of the divine–spiritual hierarchy have been striving to instill in the Earth stage of human evolution? It is the new principle of *forgiveness*. The higher principle of forgiveness—in contrast to judgment based on the principle of retaliation—was initially brought to Earth by Christ and was announced to humanity in the fifth petition of the Lord's Prayer: "Forgive us our debts, as we also have forgiven our debtors" (Matt. 6:12). "Forgiving," "love," and "freedom" are the fundamental principles of the Christ impulse. What were the new concepts and principles—foreign to the pagan Arabs—that were indicated particularly in the Koran? These were forgiveness, kindness, resisting evil with what is better, doing good, restraining anger, pardoning all people, seeking reconciliation, and remitting retaliation.

> 7:199 *Keep (hold) to forgiveness, and enjoin kindness, and turn away from the ignorant.*
>
> 23:96 *Repel evil with that which is better.*
>
> 4:149 *Whether you do good openly or in private, whether you forgive those that wrong you—Allah is forgiving and all-powerful.*
>
> 41:34 *Nor can Goodness and Evil be equal. Repel Evil with what is better; then he—between whom and thee was enmity—will become as though he was a bosom friend.*
>
> 3:134 *Those who spend (freely), whether in prosperity, or in adversity; who restrains anger, and pardon all men—for Allah loves those who do good.*
>
> 42:40 *Let evil be rewarded with like evil. But he that forgives and seeks reconcilement shall be rewarded by Allah. He does not love the wrongdoers.*
>
> 5:45 *We ordained therein for them [Hebrews]: "Life for life, eye for eye, nose for nose, ear for ear, tooth for tooth, and for wounds retaliation." But if anyone remits the retaliation by way of charity, it is an act of atonement for himself. And if any fail to judge by (the light of) what Allah hath revealed, they are wrongdoers.*

Let us remember that Arabs were not given a law that was similar to Judaic law. Judaic law was based especially on the principle of retaliation. In the Koran, a special verse that commands the practice of retaliation as a law does not exist; this principle was not ordered by Allah in the Koran—and it is noteworthy that it was indicated in verse 5:45 only in an indirect way by attributing it to the Hebrews. It is also significant that in this verse, right after retaliation is cited, the new principle of forgiveness (giving up one's right of retaliation) is also mentioned. Thus, a connection is formed between retaliation and forgiving. When we look at this statement from another angle, we see that Christ's new teaching of not using one's right of reprisal and, in a sense, the new concept of turning the other cheek when slapped on the face is also inherent in this sentence. Furthermore, this verse contains Christ's teaching: "Do not judge."[64]

Although the principle of forgiveness exists in the Koran (though expressed in a different way), it did not exist in the teachings given to the Hebrews—that is, not until Christ entered the physical world and brought the Christ impulse. After the Advent of Christ all the new principles that came with the Christ impulse were included within the content of the New Testament. Besides indicating it in the Lord's Prayer, Jesus Christ also drew attention to forgiving and not judging when he uttered: "Let any one of you who is without sin be the first to throw a stone at her" (John 8:6). Upon hearing these words, the group of people who had brought the woman caught in a sinful act to Jesus Christ realized that actually all of them were sinners in the sight of God. In other words, like the woman who had sinned, they were also in need of asking God's forgiveness for their sins, for this reason they did not have the right to judge the woman and punish her for her sin. Christ's words motivated them to assess the situation at a more conscious level. Until that time, the Hebrews had implemented the penalty of lapidation (stoning to death) without compromise; this punishment was clearly stated in their law.

---

64 "Judge not, that you be not judged. For with what judgment you judge, you will be judged; and with the measure you use, it will be measured back to you" (Matt. 7:1–2).

Receiving spiritual guidance from Yahweh for several centuries had also gradually helped them acquire conscience, which made it possible for them to understand what Christ meant when he said, "Let any one of you who is without sin be the first to throw a stone at her." Christ's statement had activated their conscience and helped them remove the obstruction imposed by the law. Realizing that, as fellow human beings who also had sins, they were not in the position to judge the woman, they forgave her. In their normal state in which their conscience was—as it were—eclipsed, they would not have hesitated to implement the law and stoned her to death. The Jewish people had to wait until Christ came into the world before their conscience—which had already been prepared as a potential—would be activated, enabling them to make the transition from implementing the law in a sleepy state to withholding judgment and forgiving in heightened consciousness.

In contrast to the spiritual acquisitions of the Hebrews, descendants of Ishmael had not been through the same kind of development. Yahweh did not admonish them or give them special spiritual guidance, because, since Christ was not going to come into their midst (Christ was going to enter the world through the threshold of the Hebrews), it was not required of them to keep any laws or commandments, or maintain pure ancestral blood ties. However, although the descendants of Ishmael were not directly involved in the preparations of Christ's Advent, they were not left completely unattended; at a very precise future time they also received admonition, guidance, and help from the divine-spiritual world. In fact, it was absolutely necessary that they did receive help from the divine-spiritual realm because of their crucial role in blunting the Sorathic intervention. Accordingly, these koranic verses refer to the help sent by Allah:

> 43:5 Shall we then take away the message [conveyed by the verses] from you [Arabs] and ignore you, for that you are a people transgressing beyond bounds? [Or: for you are a wanton folk.]

36:5–6 *It is a revelation sent down by him [Allah] exalted in might, most merciful. In order that thou [Muhammad] may admonish a people whose fathers had received no admonition.*

Help and guidance were eventually given to the Arabs, as a result of which they became Muslims. Nearly all of the new principles that came to the world by the Christ impulse found their way into the Koran, but owing to the prevalent circumstances of the time, more emphasis had to be given to other issues. The Arabs bypassed these new principles, because their soul–spiritual configuration was not endowed with the degree of consciousness that would enable them to comprehend the profound meanings of some verses.

Are there any signs of the Christ impulse in the Koran?

If one has never encountered these aforementioned new principles that exist in the koranic verses, one may assume that the reason why some Muslims are being hostile and aggressive is because Muslims had never received the teaching of the new spiritual principles that the Christ impulse brought to the world. But this would not be correct, because the Christ impulse began to be effective everywhere in various ways soon after it came to the world, and some koranic verses reflect its effect. The new cosmic principle of forgiveness and the profound understanding of turning the other cheek (although it is expressed in a different way in the Koran) were not withheld from Muslims, and the Islamic impulse was infused by it to a certain extent.[65] However, besides having had an insufficiently developed soul constitution, one of the main reasons for not understanding the new spiritual principles of the Christ impulse was because, at this time, Arabian folk's intellectual soul was not yet sufficiently developed to comprehend profound spiritual concepts. Let us remember that the era when the impulse of Islam came was at the time of the development of the intellectual soul during human evolution. To be

---

65 The most important aspect of the Christ impulse, which is the impulse of love (spiritualized love), cannot be found in the Koran. To be able to speak of love in the sense inaugurated by Christ, *the original bringer of this impulse, must also be acknowledged and emphasized along with it*. However, Christ does not exist in the Koran.

able to comprehend the deeper meaning of these new principles, it was necessary that Muslims employed the newly developing faculty of their intellectual soul—mainly *thinking*. In the Koran, some verses emphasize that thinking should be used to understand the meanings of Allah's revelations, and these verses also imply that Arabs do not use their faculty of thinking sufficiently:

> 4:82 Will they not ponder on the Koran?
>
> 38:29 We have revealed to you this Book with Our blessing, so that the wise might ponder its revelations and take warning.
>
> 2:242 Thus Allah makes known to you his revelations that you may grow in understanding.

In contrast, there was no emphasis on thinking in the Old Testament. As we recall, Valentin Tomberg indicated: "Feelings of fear and shame could make those people obedient, because at the time of Moses the link between human thinking and willing had not developed enough for anything higher than obedience."[66] In keeping with Tomberg's statement, the people of the old covenant were a people of obedience, but because the human soul constitution had gone through a significant transformation around 333—prior to the introduction of Islam—the link between thinking and willing was able to develop sufficiently prior to the inception of Islam. However, Muslims did not have to remain "people of obedience" for long, though they had to become people of obedience temporarily during the initial stage of Islam. Thus, Muslims could have used their faculty of intellectual comprehension and would have realized that it was necessary to employ these new spiritual principles to comprehend deeper meanings inherent in some verses. In this way, they could have known that to be under the rule of a law such as *sharia* is suitable only for "a people of obedience," at which point their imprisonment under *sharia* could have gradually ended.

Another important point to bear in mind is that the Christ, in his Second Coming, did not appear among any particular group of people or in a physical body (as he had incarnated among the Hebrews

---

66 Tomberg, *Christ and Sophia*, "Moses," pp. 100–101.

2,000 years ago in the physical body of Jesus), but appeared in an ethereal, rarefied form. He can thus be found in the etheric aura of the Earth, and his presence, his healing, his guidance, and his divine spiritual power to redeem are available for every single human being without distinction. In other words, if Muslims choose to acknowledge the Christ, he will be available to them as well. Furthermore, since humanity is now progressing in the epoch of the consciousness soul, Muslims could also use this opportunity to develop their faculty of consciousness. For such a development to take place, however, they would need to revise and reevaluate *sharia* and transform it into a higher spiritual understanding, eventually transcending it.

Today, however, Muslims are content with *sharia*, a remnant of the epoch of the intellectual soul,[67] and adhering to the rigid doctrine of Islam and its formal ways of worship. They do not feel any need for a deeper spiritual inquiry. Insofar as Muslims are concerned, being a devout Muslim is enough for Allah's approval and to open the doors to his Paradise. If Muslims continue implementing punishments such as lapidation, whipping, amputations of hands and feet, and the Hebraic tradition of circumcision (which the Advent of Christ made unnecessary), they face the danger that Arabism might engulf them permanently. We must all be aware of the fact that, after a certain point, being engulfed by Arabism is irrevocable. The influence of Arabism is the most influential factor preventing Muslims from receiving the revelations of the Christ impulse.

How is it that Arabism has been so influential on Muslims? First, Arabism asserts itself in a multitude of ways in Islam and in every aspect of the social life of Islamic cultures. Luciferic morality and certain ahrimanic and brutal applications of *sharia* strengthen Arabism. The more these adverse spiritual beings of darkness assert themselves in the Islamic way of life, the more Arabism manifests as a forceful, independent entity. Consequently, Arabism—kept alive in this way—also prevents Muslims from assessing and understanding spiritual

---

67 Arabian *sharia* could be regarded as a remnant of the concept of law that was prevalent in the epoch of the sentient soul, since the similar Jewish *sharia*—Yahweh's laws and commandments—had first come into being during the development of humankind's sentient soul in their evolution.

matters objectively, and they end up interpreting such subjects as religion, spirituality, and God strictly from an Islamic perspective. It is as though their understanding of spirit is molded and solidified into an unchangeable form, and nothing can penetrate that hard understanding. According to Muslims, for example, one needn't look in any direction other than Islam and the Koran, because Islam offers everything that humanity needs in a religion. Then the question arises: Do people really need to adhere to any religion at this stage of human evolution? Analysis tells us that the influence of Arabism has been effective in molding Islamic beliefs and teachings. Muslims believe beyond a doubt that their religion is holier and more perfect than any other religion, and this makes them feel righteous about their rigid religious beliefs and acts, including waging jihad or expecting members of other religions to adopt Islam. As a result, other deceptive opinions are formed around these erroneous and prejudiced beliefs.

What causes rigidity and the loss of spiritual vitality in one's thinking? Rudolf Steiner indicates that rigid thinking is a consequence of a calcified etheric body. As we recall, calcification of the etheric body became part of human destiny as people gradually lost their connection with the spirit—the divine realm—and became more deeply identified with the material world after the event of the Fall from Heaven. If as a result of rigid thinking Muslims continue to identify with beliefs and convictions devoid of spirit, the result of further calcification of the etheric body will be unavoidable. However, this need not be their destiny; humanity's situation is no longer hopeless. On the contrary, humanity can now receive the redeeming and reviving spiritual forces of Christ so that the process of calcification reverses into a spiritually enlivening process.[68]

According to Steiner, reversal of the etheric body's calcification must start with *thinking*; it requires spiritualized and strengthened thinking. Steiner spoke of this process as putting force and life into thinking through thinking.[69] However, such a reviving and enlivening

---

68   But this process can only be activated if people acknowledge Christ and, with their free will, open their souls to him so that he can permeate them.

69   See, for example, *Intuitive Thinking as a Spiritual Path: A Philosophy of Freedom*, chapter 5, "Knowing the World."

force—spiritualizing thought—is not generally present in Islamic thought. The thinking inherent in rigid Islamic teachings were originally inspired by the Moon sphere and infused with Arabism. Therefore, Islamic thought is firmly closed to the Christ impulse, which originally came from the Sun sphere. Recall that, if humankind had not been under the threat of Sorath's intervention, a revival of Yahweh's monotheistic religion would not have been necessary, for humanity had reached the point of leaving behind spiritual impulses from the Moon sphere and was evolving through the new impulse from the Sun sphere. In human evolution, humanity have reached a point where forces of the Moon and Sun spheres are now polar opposites. This is why Islamic teachings, imbued as they are with rigid thoughts from the Moon sphere, are not open to the influx of vitalizing and redeeming thoughts from the Christ impulse. This issue has been discussed from different points of view, but to understand the details of how Arabism has influenced Yahweh's newly emerged Moon-religion it is necessary to probe even more deeply into the reasons that have moulded the structure and content of Islamic teachings in this particular way.

3.

In What Ways Has Arabism Influenced Islam?

An important reason for the influence of Arabism on Muslims was the lack of a spirit concept in Islam and the refusal to understand it. Human beings can reach higher spiritual stages of their evolution only if their understanding of the spirit continuously deepens—if the consciousness soul continues to develop—and they receive spiritual guidance from divine–spiritual beings. The lack of a concept of spirit and being closed to the guidance of the divine beings will inevitably contribute to further strengthening of Arabism—that is, a more materialistic evaluation and understanding of spiritual subjects. For this very reason, Arabism has grown strong in Islam and, as a result, a vicious circle has been created whereby Muslims refuse anything that has to do with the spirit. Muslims have difficulties in discerning the true divine–spiritual (what manifests as divine–spiritual) because they are under the influence of hindering beings. These influences that stem from luciferic beings and ahrimanic forces connected to the material Earth divert the Muslims' faculty of thinking away from all true revelations of the divine–spiritual. As a result, those who accept only the rigid Islamic doctrines (which are molded under these influences) refuse to understand any other concept connected with the spirit. Steiner spoke of how Arabism has influenced Islam:

> To begin with, humanity was so led by what may be called "providence"—a spiritual guidance that spiritual life was saved in Christendom. Later, Arabism approached Europe from the south and provided the field for external culture. It is capable of comprehending only what is external. Don't we see this in Arabism, which cannot rise to what is living but

has to remain formal? We also see in the mosque how the spirit is, as it were, drained away.[1]

Apparently, this is one of the reasons for the formal means of worship that has become prominent in Islam. Islamic worship is comprised of religious duties that involve a variety of rituals, usually performed in a visible way so that they are witnessed by every other Muslim.[2] When the main concern of a believer is to acquire merit in Allah's sight, the shadow of "bargain" exists behind this kind of worship. Some koranic verses suggest that Allah is not very impressed by this way of worship and approach. The formal and superficial way of worship that many Muslims have adopted is actually a result of the influence of Arabism.[3] As a consequence of adopting a superficial approach in a fixed framework as a way of worshipping Allah, Muslims are unable to become conscious of the need for further spiritualization of the soul.[4] Thus, the prevalent traditional Islamic teachings do not present the concept of the further development or spiritualization of the soul and the "I" during an ongoing evolutionary process. According to traditional Islamic belief, reincarnation does not occur[5];

---

1   Steiner, *The Apocalypse of St. John,* lecture 11.

2   However, in the Sufi tradition, a branch of Islam, the understanding that "worshipping God should be conducted privately and that it should not be done visibly" has more validity.

3   Needless to say, many Muslims have a deeper understanding of spiritual subjects, and the way they worship is more heartfelt. Some verses in the Koran advise believers to adopt a heartfelt way of worship.

4   The formal and superficial way of worship adopted by many Muslims is closely related with their strong disbelief in reincarnation.

5   Some may claim that in Tasavvuf (Sufi) teachings one may encounter the concept of the soul's gradual evolution, which implies reincarnation. In Tasavvuf, this does not mean further development or spiritualization of the soul ("I") through an evolutionary process of several incarnations. As in traditional Islamic teachings, in Tasavvuf the concept of reincarnation does not exist. The gradual evolution of the self (*nefs*) involves only one lifetime and is part of a practice that aims to transcend the sentient soul (*nefs*) and merge with Allah, getting lost in him. The thirteenth century Anatolian mystic Mevlana J. Rumi says, "My God, am I the one who is seeking You or are You the one seeking me? / It is embarrassing to insist on being "me" and not to leave my 'self' behind, / For in that case, I keep on being someone else and You are someone else" (i.e., in that case we remain apart; I will not be able to merge with you).

when one dies, that is the end for that person. However, Muslims believe in the concept of the "last day"—the Day of Resurrection.[6] In this concept is an intermediate stage (*araf*), in which dead people wait until the last day, when Allah makes a final assessment of whether a Muslim was devout or not, whom he then either admits into his Paradise or casts into Hell.

As a consequence of being permeated by a particular form of Islam that was generated by Arabs and well established over the centuries, all Muslims have been influenced by Arabism in various degrees.[7] Certain behavioral patterns formed within Islamic cultures have been governing their soul and way of life. These patterns have also influenced how they perceive the physical world, how they understand what *spiritual* is, and how they relate to the divine realm. However, similar to the divisions or sects that exist in Christianity, there is no standard or fixed way for how Muslims conceive and understand Islam and can vary from one culture to another. For instance, Muslims living in United Arab Emirates and Oman are more liberal than the others. Furthermore, Muslims living in a secularized Islamic country such as Turkey—in which governmental and religious affairs are separate to a considerable extent—have a more liberal and permissive understanding of Islam compared to those living in countries ruled by *sharia*. This is because these patterns, as mentioned above, are actually the outcome of Arab traditions, and, having lived within the framework of these patterns for such a long time, a substantial change in their solidified beliefs may not take place too easily. These statements are not meant to be final judgments, because at the beginning of the fifteenth century—the beginning of the development of the consciousness soul—humanity stopped progressing as a group soul and the era of individual progression began. Therefore, further spiritualization of the soul is henceforth not connected with belonging to a group soul, but it is a matter of spiritualization of the individual, regardless of the religion one belongs to.

---

6   The concept of Resurrection found in Islamic teachings has got nothing to do with the Resurrection of Jesus Christ; it has a totally different connotation. It is actually connected with the concept of the last day. This subject will be explained in a later section.

7   Since Arabism has permeated Arabian Muslims more than other Muslims, they are more prone to the influences of Arabism.

Absence of the concept of spiritual freedom as a result of Arabism

Another factor that strengthens Arabism is the absence of the concept of *spiritual freedom* in Islamic teachings. Muslims who accept *sharia* as their law—and proclaim that Allah ordained these laws—do not seem to have any intention of adopting the concept of freedom and integrating it with Islamic teachings. Although freedom is one of the most important principles brought to the world by the Christ impulse, because of their intrinsic nature Islamic teachings are firmly closed to any understanding that has to do with it. Muslims' unquestioned acceptance and implementation of *sharia* has made a serious contribution to the lack of understanding of freedom in Islam. As a consequence, a significant aspect of spiritual freedom—freedom from the law, which offers humanity the chance to differentiate right from wrong with their own faculties of conscience—has eluded Muslims. Not wishing to gain freedom from the law and, on the contrary, demanding to be ruled by *sharia* is an unavoidable outcome of Arabism. In contrast to these facts regarding *sharia*, in his Letters to the Galatians, St. Paul spoke of the significance of the freedom Christ bestowed:

> The law is not based on faith; on the contrary, it says, "The person who does these things will live by them." Christ redeemed us from the curse of the law by becoming a curse for us, for it is written: "Cursed is everyone who is hung on a pole." He redeemed us in order that the blessing given to Abraham might come to the Gentiles through Jesus Christ, so that by faith we might receive the promise of the Spirit.... Why, then, was the law given at all? It was added because of transgressions until the Seed to whom the promise referred had come. The law was given through angels and entrusted to a mediator. A mediator, however, implies more than one party; but God is One.... Before the coming of this faith, we were held in custody under the law, locked up until the faith that was to come would be revealed. So the law was our guardian until Christ came that we might be justified by faith. Now that this faith has come, we are no longer under a guardian. (Gal. 3:12–14, 19–20, 23–25)

There was a time when Jewish people also did not wish to be free from the law. Although St. Paul was Jewish, after having a close encounter with Christ on the way to Damascus, he realized the law was like a curse and that they were kept under its custody. Before he was permeated and transformed by Christ, St. Paul (formerly known as Saul) was not cognizant of these facts. Judaic law had been organized in such a way that it had the power to lead Hebrews to Christ, for Yahweh originally designed it with the aim of achieving this particular result. Since the Hebrews had to be prepared to function as the threshold through which Christ could enter the Earth sphere, every single law was arranged in such a way that the group soul of the Hebrews would achieve further spiritualization and would not be influenced by the darkness of the Kali Yuga period—at least not to a large extent. In contrast to the nature of Judaic law, laws of Arab *sharia* were not arranged for the aforesaid purpose; they were given for the amelioration of the immoral and non-spiritual way of life of the pagan Arabs so that they would acknowledge Allah as their God. As previously mentioned, Allah did not give Arabs anything similar to the Decalogue, nor did he utter anything like this: Henceforth, this is the *sharia* law by which thou shalt abide. Although it contains fundamental cautions, recommendations, and instructions sent by Allah, the Arabs themselves formed the structure of the existing *sharia*, and they added various rules that do not even exist in the Koran. This is why their *sharia* contains erroneous laws like lapidation and the amputation of hands and feet,[8] which are not in harmony with the Christ impulse at all. As Muslims insistently continue to implement such laws, they become more vulnerable to the influences streaming in from beings of darkness. Contrary to what has been achieved by Judaic law, *the power to lead Muslims away from Christ is inherent in sharia*.

The intent of these statements is not to criticize or be prejudicial against Arabs or other Muslims. On the contrary, these explanations are an endeavor to bring clarity to these unknown matters regarding Islam so that, whatever misunderstanding and difficulty we may face in our encounters with Islam, we may be able to evaluate the situation without any hard feelings or judgment. Further understanding of the

---

8   Steiner emphasized that cutting into live flesh is an ahrimanic practice.

quintessence of Islam is also needed to form a bridge between Christianity and Islam. When we bear in mind that descendants of Ishmael played a very important role in deadening Sorath's intervention, we realize that their confrontation with the Sorathic wisdom and all that was involved in deadening his intervention was—in a way—a sacrifice. It cannot be said that this sacrifice was made at a conscious level or out of free choice, but when we compare how Hebrews were prepared for their mission with how Arabs were prepared for their task, it must be stated that everything that has been lived out by the Arabs was a kind of sacrifice that was in accordance with the requirements of humankind's evolution. However, this sacrifice had many negative consequences, including Muslims coming under the influence of Arabism and eventually becoming representatives of Arabism. Willingly putting themselves under the rule of *sharia* was also one of these consequences. On the other hand, Muslims have been given the chance to renounce *sharia* and transform this regressive spiritual discipline into a spiritualized form of freedom. To be able to do this, they need not go against or contradict their sacred book, for they can bring about this transformation by using the approval the Koran provides. Several verses within the Koran indicate that it confirms the content of the Gospels, as well as the content of the Old Testament.

> 3:3 He [Allah] hath revealed unto thee [Muhammad] the Scripture with truth, confirming that which was (revealed) before it, even as he revealed the Torah and the Gospel.
>
> 2:136 Say (O Muslims): We believe in Allah and that which is revealed unto us and that which was revealed unto Abraham, and Ishmael, and Isaac, and Jacob, and the tribes, and that which Moses and Jesus received, and that which the prophets received from their Lord. We make no distinction between any of them, and unto him [Allah] we have surrendered.
>
> 57:27 After them We sent other apostles, and after those, Jesus son of Mary. We gave him the Gospel and put compassion and mercy in the hearts of his followers.

If some verses indicate that the Koran confirms the truth inherent in the Old and New Testaments, it would be logical to expect

Muslims to take these indications more seriously and, leaving their prejudices aside, make a more conscious evaluation of the content of the Old Testament and the Gospels. Also, if Allah stated that the Gospels were given by him (in 57:27), surely this information should have a special meaning to Muslims. However, it seems both Muslims in the past and those in the present have disregarded the significance of what these and a multitude of similar verses claim. Although koranic verses clearly proclaim that the Koran confirms the truth of the former sacred books, not taking heed of this indication and not adopting ideas that are in accordance with these verses is a contradiction induced by Arabism's influence on Islam. If Muslims had given serious attention to the meanings of these verses, they could have discovered that in the Gospels a profound wisdom concerning the Christ-being is revealed to humanity. Upon studying the Gospels—which are claimed to be given by Allah to Jesus in the Koran—they could also have learned that those who acknowledge the Christ shall be freed from the bondage of the Law.

However, Muslims claim that the content of the Gospels is not authentic, and that the existing Gospels are not those given to Jesus by Allah, for the Jews had corrupted it. Muslims have always refused to accept the fact that the Gospels are "God's Word." They proclaim that four men wrote them, whereas Muhammad received every verse from Allah, via Gabriel. According to them, since the content of the Gospels did not issue from a divine source like Allah, this lessens the value and authenticity of it. Looking at their superficial evaluation, we can see that they do not consider the information provided by the Koran about the existence of the "akasha chronicle" (*Levh-i Mahfouz*,[9] in Arabic). Although it is true that the Gospels were written by four men, Steiner revealed that these four evangelists were initiates who were able to read the akasha chronicle, and therefore

---

9   *Levh-i Mahfouz* is a term found in the Koran and literally means "protected panels." According to the Koranic verses, these protected panels are found in the realm where Allah is, and Allah inscribes or records the deeds of humankind in *Levh-i Mahfouz*. Therefore, it can be said that these protected panels connote the akasha chronicle, which are the eternal etheric records of everything that takes place in the cosmos and are found in the cosmic ether of the divine–spiritual world.

these four accounts were written according to what they read in the akasha chronicle—that is, from the most true and reliable source that exists in the universe. Moreover, Steiner explained that the differences found in these four narrations was due to the inscribers of the Gospels looking at the events of the Advent of Christ and the Mystery of Golgotha from four different perspectives. As a result, they delivered a four-dimensional spiritual revelation for humanity.

In the akasha chronicle, they found all the lively, true, and precise words of the Word. This is why the Gospels are the Word of God and not some incoherent stories arbitrarily written by four men, as Muslims declare. As a consequence of their denial of the authenticity of the Gospels, Muslims were not able to possess any insight of the true identity of Jesus Christ and the cosmic mission of the Christ-being. For this reason, Islam does not acknowledge Christ as God. When we observe how fundamentalist, radical, and extremist Muslims insist on imposing their religious belief on members of other religions, and that in certain countries ruled by *sharia* the punishment for renouncing Islam—and, for example, adhering to another faith like Christianity—is death,[10] we can deduce that Muslims will hold on to their convictions and prejudices for a long time. Consequentially, they will continue to be fettered to *sharia*. Long before the emergence of Islam, St. Paul had a deep insight concerning the descendants of Ishmael and Ishmael's mother, Hagar, and he spoke of this in his Epistles to the Galatians:

---

10   According to news reports, in May 2014 the *sharia* court in Sudan sentenced a pregnant woman named M.I. to a hundred lashes and death, with the accusation that she renounced Islam when she got married to a Christian man and became a Christian herself. M.I. declared she was brought up as a Christian, as her mother was a Christian, and that she did not renounce Islam because she got married to a Christian man, but this did not alter the *sharia* court's decision. The *sharia* judges declared she would not be executed if she accepted Islam, but she said she would rather die than renounce Christianity. M.I. gave birth to her child in prison, and according to the *sharia* court's verdict she will be executed when her child is two years old. It is necessary to underline that in the Koran there is no verse stating that Muslim women cannot be married to Christians or Jews, nor a verse that asserts that they will be sentenced to death if they renounce Islam. Apparently, *sharia* judges are making up inhumane laws that contradict the Koran. Evidently, their dogmatic opinions and approach are in extreme opposition to the principle of freedom.

Islam in Relation to the Christ Impulse

For it is written that Abraham had two sons, one by the slave woman and the other by the free woman. His son by the slave woman was born according to the flesh, but his son by the free woman was born as the result of a divine promise. These things are being taken figuratively: The women represent two covenants. One covenant is from Mount Sinai and bears children who are to be slaves: This is Hagar. Now Hagar stands for Mount Sinai in Arabia and corresponds to the present city of Jerusalem, because she is in slavery with her children. But the Jerusalem that is above is free, and she is our mother.... Now you, brothers and sisters, like Isaac, are children of promise. At that time the son born according to the flesh persecuted the son born by the power of the Spirit. It is the same now. But what does Scripture say? "Get rid of the slave woman and her son, for the slave woman's son will never share in the inheritance with the free woman's son." Therefore, brothers and sisters, we are not children of the slave woman, but of the free woman. (Gal. 4:22–26, 28–31)

Evidently, St. Paul touched upon a significant truth. Muslims who insist on implementing *sharia* as an unchangeable law are putting themselves under the bondage of law and are unknowingly placing a major obstacle between themselves and Christ, who brought the new law of "no law"[11] and freedom from the law. The new principle of no law means that, having gained freedom from being a member of a group soul, humankind's individual consciousness and conscience could now develop in freedom and that their conscience could now function as an inner law. In other words, through the Christ impulse, humans have become free from having to evolve in a group soul, and this enables them to develop their individuality. *Sharia*—being in strong polarity to the principle of freedom brought by Christ—is an infringement on human freedom and has a retarding effect on the individualization and development of the human "I." One can say that Yahweh's laws induced a similar effect, and Hebrews could not develop their individuality because of it. It is true that the spiritual

---

11   The new principle of "no law"—or the law of no law—that Valentin Tomberg indicated will be discussed in detail in a later section.

influences of the Moon sphere were also inherent in Yahweh's law, and because of these influences Hebrews were trained as a group soul. But Islam, which is under the influence of Arabism, is not Judaism, and Yahweh's Moon religion did not appear in Islam in its original form. It appeared in a different form that was very much distorted by Arabism and other factors. Besides, Yahweh's law and guidance covered only the transitory period of leading Hebrews to Christ; therefore, the period under Yahweh's law has to be regarded as a special preparatory period, which was in accordance with a specific cosmic purpose. As human evolution progressed, the training of the human soul by strict and static laws had to be eventually transcended because of the human need to become a free being for the further development of the "I" and, in the long run, to be able to fulfill the goals assigned by the beings of the divine–spiritual realm. For this reason, it is most important that Muslims realize that the freedom brought to the world by Christ was actually a victory over law. If they acknowledge this fact in the future, *it will be a victory over sharia.*

In the following excerpt, Rudolf Steiner comments on the "reality of freedom," indicating that freedom should find expression in external life, and that it is necessary for humans to reach a stage where they feel they can act as free beings—as free spirits.

> The second, longer section of the book deals with the reality of freedom. I was concerned to show how freedom must find expression in external life, how it can become a real driving force of human action and social life. I wanted to show how human beings can arrive at the stage where they feel that they really act as free beings. Moreover, it seems to me that what I wrote twenty years ago could well be understood by people today in view of present circumstances.
>
> What I had advocated first of all was an ethical individualism. I had to show that people cannot become free beings unless their actions have their source in ideas rooted in the intuitions of the single individual. Such ethical individualism recognizes as the final goal of humanity's moral development only what is called the free spirit that struggles free of the constraint of natural laws and the constraint of all conventional moral

norms, which is confident that in an age, when evil tendencies are increasing, people can, if they rise to intuitions, transmute these evil tendencies into what is, for the consciousness soul, destined to become the principle of the good, what is suitable to the dignity of humankind. I wrote therefore at that time, "Only the laws obtained in this way are related to human action as the laws of nature are related to a particular phenomenon. These laws however are in no way identical with the impulses that govern our actions. If we wish to understand how a person's action arises from his or her moral will, we must first study the relation of this will to the action."

I envisaged the idea of a free community life such as I described to you recently from a different angle—a free community life in which not the individual claims freedom only for oneself, but in which, through the reciprocal relationship of people in their social life, freedom as impulse of this life can be realized. Therefore, I unhesitatingly wrote then, "To live in love of our action and to let live in the full understanding of the other's will is the fundamental maxim of free people."

I wanted to demonstrate that the concept of freedom is a universal concept, that people cannot understand and truly feel what freedom is unless they perceive that the human soul is the scene not only of terrestrial forces, but also that the whole cosmic process streams through the human soul and can be apprehended in the human soul. Only when people open themselves to this cosmic process, when they consciously experience it in their inner life—only when they recognize that their inner life is of a cosmic nature, will it be possible to arrive at a philosophy of freedom.[12]

As Steiner elucidated, the concept of freedom is a universal concept—that is, it originated from the quintessence of the divine–spiritual realm out of vital cosmic necessity. Rejection of this universal concept and implementation of a different concept (for example, a terrestrial law such as *sharia*) will inevitably lead humankind into contradicting *that which is true and real in the cosmos,* and, as a result of this, a polarity to the divine consciousness of the cosmos will

---

12 *From Symptom to Reality in Modern History,* lecture 6.

be formed. Moreover, this will pose a hindrance against the development Steiner indicated above: people can transmute these evil tendencies into what, for the consciousness soul, is destined to become the principle of the good. When we observe the manifestations of Islamic *sharia* and the insistence of some Muslims on forcing Islamic religious belief onto other peoples; how Islamic religious practices have become obligatory in Islamic countries[13]; and how, in almost every Islamic community, women are oppressed in diverse ways—forced to cover themselves, and not allowed to go out on the street alone, drive a car, or have any contact with men within the normal framework of communal life—we see no trace of the universal concept of freedom or the reality of freedom at the foundation of Islam.

Absence of a concept of reincarnation

It was earlier discussed that in the prevalent Islamic teachings, the further development or spiritualization of the soul as an ongoing evolutionary process is a foreign concept. Another reason why Muslims remain under the influence of Arabism is the absence of the concepts of reincarnation and karma, and lack of the fundamental knowledge that they are interconnected. In traditional Islamic understanding, the concept of karma prevails in a somewhat different and fatalistic way that does not reflect the truth of the cosmic law of karma. As for rebirth, most Muslims do not believe in the phenomenon of reincarnation. They believe that every person lives only once on Earth, and since their fate is in the hands of Allah, he will decide each Muslim's fate on the "last day"—the Islamic understanding of Resurrection Day. In other words, they do not possess the insight that the core of

---

13 According to news reports in July 2014, a Christian man was sentenced to have his lips burned with a cigarette for violating the Muslim holy month of Ramadan, a time when every Muslim is supposed to fast. The man was subjected to the punishment in a public square in the city of Kermanshah in Iran. Five other Muslim men were given seventy lashes each for not fasting during Ramadan. These harsh punishments are unfounded, for they are not ordained by Allah and do not exist in the Koran. It is noteworthy that although Sudan and Iran are geographically thousands of miles apart and are not directly able to influence each other, their implementation of *sharia* laws that do not exist in the Koran is the same. We can surmise that this is the effect of luciferic influences and Arabism.

the astral body and the "I" of a human being goes through several incarnations in accordance with the laws of human evolution. Since Muslims do not accept reincarnation as a spiritual fact—and even try to refute it—we may wonder if the koranic verses also reject this concept. The analysis of certain verses indicates that the Koran does not directly oppose or deny reincarnation. On the contrary, several verses—at first glance—give the impression that they refer to reincarnation. Although a specific word corresponding to the term *reincarnation* is never used in these verses, the phrasing—the way these verses are composed—and the meanings they convey seem to imply reincarnation. For example:

> 2:28 How can you deny Allah? Did he not give you life when you were dead, and will he not cause you to die and then restore you to life? Will you not return to him at last?

The end of this verse refers to a person's meeting with Allah on the last day. Illustrated throughout the verse are a person's different states of being. Initially, it points to the state when one is dead. Logic tells us that before one is dead, one must have been alive. Then it states that Allah will cause a person to die and again restore that person to life. Eventually, a person will encounter Allah on the last day. Multiple translations have similar renderings of this particular verse, so we can assume that its composition is correct. Therefore, we may say it attests to reincarnation. Others also indicate reincarnation.

> 10:31 Who brings forth the living from the dead, and the dead from the living? Who ordains all things?

> 22:66 It is he who has given your life, and he who will cause you to die and make you live again. Surely man is ungrateful.

Again, these verses emphasize successive states of being that alternate from being dead to being alive and so on. Although the composition of the verses seems to point to the phenomenon of reincarnation, as do many other verses that convey similar meanings, Muslims insistently ignore and deny these seemingly obvious indications. Furthermore, Muslims regard the concept of reincarnation as a degenerate idea, and some even feel it blasphemous. As far as conservative, fundamentalist, and radical Islamic belief is concerned, the only time when the dead will be brought back to life is on Judgment Day.[14] When this time comes, Allah shall judge everybody and will send them either to Paradise or to Hell according to their good or bad deeds on Earth. Whether or not they believe in Allah will also be a decisive factor. (According to Muslims, Jews and Christians do not have any chance at entering Allah's Paradise, as they do not acknowledge Allah as their God.) The Islamic belief is that human beings do not come back to life (to the world) again after they die; they live only once on Earth and never go through further incarnations. Muslims not only avoid acquiring a deeper insight into the meanings conveyed by these koranic verses, they also refuse to take into consideration any other information concerning reincarnation that can be found in other sources. As a consequence, their denial of reincarnation strengthens the power of Arabism and prevents Muslims from gaining any insight into the mystery of birth and death, and humankind's sojourn on Earth.

Since so many verses in their sacred book cite reincarnation, isn't it paradoxical that Arabs have not acquired insight into the reality of reincarnation in all this time? Why do they refuse and refute this concept? Could some other reason be preventing them from gaining an understanding of it? Or could it be that the koranic verses do not actually imply reincarnation in the sense elucidated by anthroposophic wisdom? We might be able to form a clearer picture if we differentiate between reincarnation as it is explained in Anthroposophy and what the koranic verses imply when they say that Allah will bring the dead back to life. As we recall, at the beginning of Islam,

---

[14] The "Day of Judgment," the last day, or the concept of the Day of Resurrection: It is most probable that this *Islamized version of resurrection* has been inspired by Jesus Christ's explanations found in the canonical Gospels, for example: "For my Father's will is that everyone who looks to the Son and believes in him shall have eternal life, and I will raise them up at the last day" (John: 6:40); "There is a judge for the one who rejects me and does not accept my words; the very words I have spoken will condemn them at the last day (John 13:48); "Jesus said to her, 'Your brother will rise again.' Martha answered, 'I know he will rise again in the Resurrection at the last day'" (John 11:23–24).

believers—Muslims—had to fight against unbelievers, and these battles went on for several years. During these battles, believers often died and many were wounded; therefore, Muhammad's followers were not always very willing to fight and needed persuading to go to battle. For this reason, several verses emphasize that they were fighting for Allah and for his cause in order to persuade them to continue fighting. Verses also emphasize that they should not be discouraged in fighting for Allah's cause due to the fear of dying, but in fact should not worry, for everything is in the hands of Allah. Some of these verses indicate different states of being, as in verse 2:28, and guarantees that Allah will definitely revive the dead.

> 2:154 Do not say that those who are killed in Allah's Cause (in the way of Allah) are dead. On the contrary, they are alive but you are not aware of it.

Other verses support this assurance with the further promise that if a believer died for Allah's cause, he or she would be to be brought back to life and admitted to Allah's Paradise.

> 6:4 Allah loves those who fight for his cause in ranks as firm as a mighty edifice.

> 61:11 That you believe in Allah and his messenger, and carry out jihad [holy war] for His cause with your wealth and in persons. That is much better for you—if you but knew it!

> 61:12 [If you do so] Allah will forgive your sins and admit you into Paradise wherein streams flow, and you will live in the lofty mansions of the Garden of Eden. This is indeed the greatest triumph.

When we examine what is conveyed or promised by these verses, it becomes apparent that this particular form of revival narrated in the Koran has a connotation different from what is actually involved in reincarnation as a cosmic principle. Another aspect that differentiates Allah's promise of bringing his believers back to life from the phenomenon of reincarnation is that the believers who Allah revived were admitted to his Paradise without any delay (as soon as they died). Therefore, Allah's promise of revival of the dead—or bringing them back to life—also means that life in Allah's Paradise is, in a way, going to be very similar to life on Earth, but much more pleasant in comparison. The way of life in Allah's Paradise as presented in these verses also denotes *deathlessness*. According to Allah's promise, dying on Earth for his cause grants the enjoyment of a deathless life in addition to opening the doors of Paradise. In contrast, what Jesus Christ promised in the Gospels is not deathlessness in a delightful paradise but the concept of *"eternal life,"* in which the "son of man"[15] is spiritually united with Christ and the divine–spiritual realm, and consciously works with them to achieve their cosmic purposes and aims. Rudolf Steiner often emphasized that eternal life has a very different connotation compared to deathlessness.

While analyzing the verses that seem to imply reincarnation, it is also necessary to distinguish between the believers who will have immediate access to Allah's Paradise[16] if they die in a holy war and those who will go through an ordinary death and have to wait until the last day in a transitory stage (*araf*) and be admitted to Paradise after being judged by Allah.[17] When these verses are examined with this in mind, a certain differentiation becomes apparent. Verses that are similar to 2:28 and present different states of being—being dead, being revived by Allah, then dying, and so on—clearly connote reincarnation, whereas verses that are similar to 61:11 and 61:12 clearly point to a different procedure of revival that is only related to dying in a jihad. Thus, since the verses that indicate the phenomenon of reincarnation actually have a connotation different from the others, there is no reason why pagan Arabs and those who later became Muslim should not have formed a clear concept of reincarnation rather than only relating rebirth with being reborn in Paradise after dying in a jihad. Not regarding the meanings inherent in the verses below and many others not cited was a mistake that misled Muslims into refusing the existence of reincarnation.

---

15 *Son of man:* the transformed future form of today's humankind.

16 As seen in 61:12, Allah will forgive the sins of those who die in jihad.

17 According to Islamic teachings, human evolution comes to an end at the end of the Earth stage (the last day), when everyone ends up in Allah's Paradise, or in Hell; it does not continue any further. In the Koran, there is no indication of the following stages of Jupiter, Venus, and Vulcan.

We can sense the influence of Arabism in the clouds cast over the true phenomenon of reincarnation.

> 17:49 What! They [ones who do not believe in rebirth] say: "When we are turned into bones and dust, shall we be restored to life?"

> 16:38 They solemnly swear by Allah that he will never raise the dead to life, but Allah's promise shall be surely fulfilled, though most men may not know it.

> 26:81 The Lord of Creation [Allah] will cause me to die and bring me back to life hereafter.

> 6:122 Can the dead man whom We raised to life, and gave a light [guidance of Allah's verses] with which he may be guided among man, be compared to him who blunders about in darkness from which he will never emerge?

> 36:12 It is We who bring back the dead to life. We record the deeds of man and the marks they leave behind: We note all things in a glorious book.[18]

Although the verses we have been discussing are directly related to the jihadists of Muhammad's time, Allah's promise of revival and immediate admittance into a blissful paradise must be influencing present-day suicide-bombers' decisions when declaring jihad and blowing up a bus or an aircraft. Likewise, when a group of Muslims decides to wage jihad on members of other religions or members of their own religion, they are under the impression that if they die for their cause they will surely end up in Paradise. They do not realize that the ambiguous promise of Paradise only involved the jihadists of Muhammad's time.

---

18 Verse 36:12 is one of the rare examples in which a kind of recording reminiscent of the Akasha Chronicle is indicated ("We note all things in a glorious book"). As we recall, the Akasha Chronicle is the etheric recording of everything that takes place in the cosmos. Rudolf Steiner explained that the Akasha Chronicle is found in three layers, and that these "etheric scriptures" are under the protection of the divine–spiritual beings. The Akasha Chronicle is also mentioned in 85:22: "Surely this is a glorious Koran inscribed on the preserved panel (*Levh-i Mahfouz*)."

Absence of the concept of karma and confined to the fatalistic concept of qadar

In Islam, rejection of the concept of reincarnation is accompanied by rejection of the concept of karma. Muslims do not acknowledge the fact that karma functions as a cosmic law that is interconnected with reincarnation. As a result, they confine themselves to the fatalistic concept of *qadar*. Similar to what fate or destiny implies, Muslims believe the *qadar* (fate) of each person is predetermined, unchangeable, and that Allah actually determines every detail of it. Thus, each person must submit to the *qadar* Allah inscribed for him or her. This belief has its roots in the Islamic concept of surrendering to Allah. Trying to change one's destiny is unthinkable, and this fatalistic attitude is one of the main characteristics of Islam. In this context, everything concerning one's life on Earth is assessed from the point of view that people are helpless against Allah's will and what he decrees. Accordingly, when a misfortune befalls them, Muslims claim that it came from Allah and try to accept it and come to terms with it; all the same, some may complain about their misfortune in a sentimental way. So in Islamic tradition, instead of the concept of karma, which is the objective consequence of one's good or bad deeds from one's past life, Muslims have adopted the concept of *qadar*: "I am a victim of *qadar*" or "One is a victim of *qadar*" is often heard in Islamic countries. Precisely because Allah has inscribed on the brow of each human being his or her fate, Muslims do not question why everybody has a different *qadar* or ask vital questions such as: Why do some people face many misfortunes while others do not? Why does each human being have a different *qadar*? What are the meanings of accidents, diseases, and illnesses? Why do some people suffer from illness while others are healthy? Is every person's destiny randomly chosen by Allah without taking into consideration one's worldly deeds? The fatalistic attitude of *qadar*—rejecting responsibility for one's actions and leaving everything in the hands of an outer authority—is another result of Arabism's influence.

When a person does not comprehend the cosmic role of reincarnation and karma at a conscious level, this inevitably influences her or his thinking, feeling, and will. Not taking into consideration the significance and deeper meaning of the law of karma and how it functions together with reincarnation at a conscious level inevitably gives way to unconscious deeds such as wrongdoings and sins. As a consequence of these unconscious deeds, more wrongdoings and future karma are created. Also, people with fatalistically disposed attitudes will be passive and uninterested in putting an effort into achieving positive changes in their karma. As opposed to the understanding of *qadar*—according to anthroposophic elucidations—one's karma is not fixed or unalterable. When one begins to wake up in one's thinking, feeling, and will, one creates the possibility to change one's destiny. In other words, a person is not stuck with that which is written on one's brow, and our creators have given us the ability and allowance to change our karma. As a matter of fact, if a person succeeds in changing one's fate, this is a development that is in harmony with the aims of human evolution, since we are expected to awaken and become more conscious in our thinking, feeling, and will. At this point, we realize the importance of the principle of freedom brought by the Christ impulse. Achieving an understanding of the principle of freedom and adopting it will help to overcome the impediments imposed by fatalism. A deep understanding of the function of the law of karma will also help us to free ourselves eventually from the law of karma, whereas adopting the fatalistic attitude of *qadar* will hinder one's spiritual development. Let us recall what Rudolf Steiner indicates concerning fatalism:

> When we consider the form in which Islam made its appearance, we find, first and foremost, the uncompromising monotheism, the one, all-powerful Godhead—a concept of Divinity that is allied with fatalism. The destiny of humans is predetermined; we must submit to this destiny or at least recognize our subjection to it. This attitude is an integral part of the religious life.[19]

Valentin Tomberg drew attention to another important aspect of fatalism. According to him, this fatalistic attitude would cause a serious danger to appear in the future. What Tomberg illustrates is very significant:

---

19 Steiner, Karmic Relationships, vol. 1, lect. 10.

In the present epoch, only the false Holy Spirit and false Son—Lucifer and Ahriman—function as antichrists. In the karmic future, however, those who in the present epoch tend to be fatalistic will fall victim to the third hostile power. For fatalism is the fruit of partiality toward the Father principle; it is the expression of a complete inner passivity toward the world. Such passivity, however, will one day become a tremendous danger once the false Father begins to function in the world. A time will come when *Asura*[20] will appear as the karma of Ahriman, just as Ahriman appeared as the karma of Lucifer. The three dangers of spiritual one-sidedness can be avoided only by conceiving the universal deity as "Three in One." The Trinity of eternal goodness is a unity, and the human soul must think of it as a unity. If this unity is disintegrated, it falls under the power of evil trinity.[21]

When we look at Islamic dogmas and manifestations of Islam projected by the extremists and present-day jihadists under the light of Tomberg's elucidations, we can see Islam is under the influence of one-sided emphasis on the Father principle. We can also see that in the determined terrorizing attacks and other deeds of fanatical jihadists, Asura has already gained a foothold—a sphere of action—in the physical world. Apparently, by way of Arabism, a passageway has been formed through which this demonic being has already begun to assert its power on certain human beings.[22] Another reason why this has

---

20 *Sorath:* A demonic being from the Sun sphere who aims to cut the human bond with the Father–God.

21 *Christ and Sophia,* "Abraham, Isaac, and Jacob," p. 28.

22 Let us remember how in 2014 and 2015, during the battles that took place between governmental forces and Islamic jihadists of a certain religious faction in Iraq, the jihadists mercilessly executed hundreds of captives who were also Muslim and beheaded captives, even playing football with the head of a beheaded soldier. (This was their way of protesting the 2014 World Cup football games.) We may also remember that in Syria an Islamic militant ripped out the heart of his captive and ate it. Although they are Muslim, these fanatical jihadists have blown up age-old mosques because they belong to the Shiite sect. I am aware that these examples sound appalling, but it is precisely through such examples that we may form a clear idea about Asura's influence on fanatical Muslims, which even exceeds ahrimanic influences in diverse ways.

happened is because radical, extremist, and jihadist Muslims are in a deep sleep in their thoughts, feelings, and especially their will. At this stage of humankind's evolution—when we are constantly encountering demonic beings such as Lucifer, Ahriman, Sorath, and Asura—we must endeavor to be more awake in these three forces of our "I," particularly in the will, otherwise Asura can easily take hold of it. The unavoidable consequence of this shall be that Asuric influences will fortify and bring forward humankind's ahrimanic sub-nature. Then "true evil" shall be able to manifest on Earth through certain human beings who have regressed to this nature.

Besides having created a fatalistic attitude in Islam, denial of reincarnation and karma has also created the wrong idea about the role of God in the terrestrial affairs of humankind. It was mentioned that, according to Islamic belief, Allah is responsible for everything that happens to humankind—that is, Allah is behind every misfortune, illness, and suffering; in short, everything that befalls humanity is believed to be decreed by Allah. However, this misconceived fatalistic Islamic conviction does not reflect the truth and contradicts the reality concerning the role of God. It also contradicts the petitions of the Lord's Prayer imparted by Christ. The profound meanings conveyed in the petitions of this prayer clearly indicate that the Father-God does not interfere with worldly affairs, thus he cannot be held responsible for the tribulations, affliction, and suffering experienced by humankind.

Christ's words in Matthew 6:10, "Your Kingdom come," means that God's kingdom has not been yet established on Earth. By saying this petition of the prayer we—being members of the spiritual hierarchy whose sphere of existence is the physical world—wish for God's kingdom to come to the physical world. When we say, "Your Will be done, on Earth as it is in heaven" this indicates that at the present time God's will is not yet prevalent and effective in the material world, and for this reason we wish that our Father's will shall also be established in the physical world. If it had been effective—that is, if God had been active and effective in every minute detail of humankind's life on Earth, as Muslims believe—there would not have been any evil, natural disasters, suffering, illness, or wars on Earth.

It is essential to understand that the last time humans lived in a state in which there was no misfortune, no suffering, no illness, nor even death was when humankind was still in Heaven. When humanity was in Heaven, God's will and power was still in effect. Accordingly, suffering, misfortunes, illness, and tribulations started when humankind gradually became earthly beings and began to generate karma. Therefore, by holding Allah responsible for all kinds of misfortune and suffering, Muslims unconsciously avoid coming to terms with the fact that human beings must assume responsibility for their own acts and even their thoughts, and that it is actually people who are responsible for every manifestation of evil on Earth and all that causes them suffering.[23] Consequentially, their refusal of these spiritual facts prevents Muslims from comprehending the reality of karma and reincarnation at a conscious level. In other words, as a result of being under the influence of Arabism, their faculty of spiritual comprehension is confined within the rigid framework of the fatalistic belief of *qadar*. This belief functions as an invisible barrier that stops the influx of spiritual intuitions from the divine–spiritual world, which could have enabled them to achieve a higher consciousness concerning reincarnation and karma, and other important spiritual facts related to them.

Should the Koran be held totally responsible for Muslims' misconceived concept of *qadar*? Are there no verses that explain or indicate that human beings are subjected to the cosmic law of karma and that—since Muslims have acquired an individual "I" (self) during evolution—they will be held responsible for their deeds? Although presented in an Islamic manner, indeed some verses scattered throughout the Koran give sufficient information and warning about generating karma and being responsible for this karma. For example, the verses below as well as many others basically indicate that one will be held responsible for one's deeds and that there will be consequences for one's wrongdoings.

> 28:84 *He that does good shall be rewarded with what is better. But he that does evil shall be requited with evil.*

---

23 In this context, the influence of the devil/Satan (Lucifer and Ahriman) on humankind in connection with Islam will be discussed in a later section.

45:15 *He that does what is right does it to his own advantage; and he that commits evil does so at his own peril. To your Lord you shall all return.*

59:18 *Believers, have fear of Allah. Let every soul look into what it offers for the morrow. Fear Allah, for he is cognizant of all your actions.*

However, some other verses, which at first glance may appear to convey similar meanings as the above verses, actually have another connotation. For instance:

39:70 *Every soul shall be paid back according to its deeds, for Allah knows of all their actions.*

When evaluated by itself, this verse may seem to have a similar meaning to the verses stated above. However, when we analyze it together with the following verses, it becomes clear that in verse 39:70 *karma* (understood in an anthroposophic sense) is not implied, and that the meaning inherent in it is actually related to the final judgment that is to take place on the Day of Resurrection.

39:67 *They underrate the might of Allah. But on the Day of Resurrection he will hold the entire Earth in his grasp and fold up the heavens in his right hand. Glory be to him! Exalted be he above their idols.*

39:69 *The prophets and witnesses shall be brought in and all shall be judged with fairness: none shall be wronged. 70 Every soul shall be paid back according to its deeds, for Allah knows of all their actions.*

Therefore, many verses do exist that denote creating karma through one's own wrong deeds during one's life on Earth, but others attest to the Day of Resurrection. The verses found in the latter category point to the inescapable event of the final judgment of humankind's deeds that will take place on the Day of Resurrection. In both cases, the Koran (in its own style) gives ample explanations and warnings regarding creating karma. However, Muslims in general do not seem to take these warnings and facts seriously, which could have guided them to acquire a correct and beneficial evaluation of the concept of karma. Instead, they have adopted the misleading fatalistic concept of *qadar*. This is probably because traditionally transmitted teachings, which vary a lot from sect to sect, are so dominant in Islam that Muslims do not feel the necessity of studying the Koran for themselves. From childhood onward, they readily accept whatever is conveyed to them by the community in which they are born. This becomes a factor that prevents them from crossing the boundaries of their group soul.

There is another significant issue related to the consequences of adopting a belief in *qadar*. When a person explains away one's misfortunes, illness, and sufferings from the fatalistic aspect of *qadar*, seeing a deity's unalterable "will" and decree in effect, the only thing left for this person to do is to accept this fate. This is exactly how Muslims react. But what is really lacking is the understanding of *why* these misfortunes have particularly befallen that person. When one has no real idea about the actual effective factor behind the misfortune, illness, and suffering that happens in one's life, and if the only explanation is that "this has happened because it has been decreed by Allah," then one has no reason to look into oneself and analyze one's own character and deeds. In other words, one does not come close to the reality that it is actually one's own self—the "I"—that is responsible for the misfortune and suffering, and that God is, as it were, acting as a mirror and reflecting the consequences of a person's wrongdoings back on oneself. When a person has no inkling that one's self is actually responsible for everything that happens, one will not feel the necessity of evaluating one's character and deeds to spot where one is actually going wrong. If a person does not face one's own wrongdoings objectively, one will not be able to develop the ability to discern right from wrong—and good from bad. Since the development of conscience is directly related to one's ability to distinguish between right and wrong, it follows that if one's sense of right and wrong is not developed, the development of conscience will be hindered. This is the danger that some Muslims face if they do not realize that the belief in *qadar* does not convey the truth and is very misleading, and that reincarnation and karma are significant cosmic laws that work together and influence humankind's spiritual development in countless ways.

Clearly, these explanations draw attention to various potential dangers but do not intend to generalize all Muslims, for obviously many have well-developed consciences, kindness, and compassion and disapprove the activities of the extremist and fanatical jihadist Muslims.

ISLAM IN RELATION TO THE CHRIST IMPULSE

Confusing Islam today with incidents and verses related only to Muhammad's time

The fact that fundamentalist and radical Muslims confuse present-day Islam with the Islam that existed at the time of the Prophet by projecting the events and verses that belong particularly to those times into the present time is another factor induced by Arabism. Influenced by the negative aspects, like jihad, inherent in certain verses that only belong to Islam's beginnings and implementing them in the present is a degenerate behavior incited by Arabism—actions that in turn strengthen the power of Arabism. How does this vicious circle function?

Approximately 1,400 years ago, when the Prophet began his struggle, he encountered much opposition. As a result, many battles had to be fought against the unbelievers. Members of the Arab tribes who refused to believe in Allah and battled against the Prophet were called *kafir*, which means "one who does not believe in Allah." In English translations, kafir is rendered as "infidel." The "holy war" waged by Muslims against the kafirs was called *jihad*. These holy wars fought in the name of Allah were part of a very long struggle against pagan Arabs. In a way, it was a struggle of life-or-death, for the believers were under constant threat and had to protect themselves against the attacks of the unbelievers. Therefore, waging jihad against unbelievers could be considered a counterattack, but with the intention of transforming the unbelievers into believers. For instance, verse 8:39 states that believers should fight against the unbelievers until idolatry is ended:

> 8:39 Make war on them [kafirs] until idolatry is no more and Allah's religion [Islam] reigns supreme. If they desist Allah is cognizant of all their actions; but if they give no heed, know then that Allah will protect you. He is the noblest Helper and Protector.

Since Jews and Christians were not involved in idolatry at those times, it is evident that this verse did not concern People of the Book. The same is also valid for the Jews and Christians of today—that is, the traditional Judaic religion still continues, and Christians have Jesus Christ and the Holy Trinity to venerate. Thus, since neither practices idolatry, fundamentalist and radical Muslims' insistence on converting them into Muslims is totally unfounded. Verse 4:56 conveys a blunt message concerning unbelievers:

> 4:56 Those that deny Our revelations We will burn in hellfire. No sooner will their skins be consumed then We shall give them other skins, so that they may truly taste Our scourge. Allah is mighty and wise.

When reading this verse in relation to the foregoing verses and those following, it becomes evident that its message is also only meant for pagan Arabs. Actually, in none of the verses concerning Muhammad's jihads is there mention of waging jihad or taking action against Jews or Christians in the future; these messages only refer to the incidents taking place at the outset of Islam. Nonetheless, strife between Muhammad and the Jewish people at the time was unavoidable. As previously mentioned, it was very important for Muhammad to persuade the Jews that he was the latest prophet sent by their God, Yahweh/Allah, for this would have supported his claims and strengthened his position. But the Jews did not believe in him or his messages, which in many ways were not in accord with the accounts of the Old Testament. Therefore, Muhammad did not get the support he had hoped to receive. In the koranic verses, it can be seen that Muhammad kept on renewing his call to the People of the Book—especially to the Jews—and for a while he did not lose hope about converting them; this can be understood from the tone inherent in certain verses.

> 2:40 Children of Israel, remember the favors I have bestowed upon you. Keep your covenant, and I will be true to Mine. Revere Me. Have faith in My revelations [sent to Muhammad], which confirm your scriptures, and do not be the first to deny them.

But Jewish people kept on refusing his calls. Consequently, this disappointed and angered Allah, and for this reason in verse 5:61 the Jews are called *infidels*. Before reading 5:61, we must also read 5:59 and 60, as it might give us a better idea of how Muhammad arrived at the point of calling the Jews infidels.

> 5:59 Say: "People of the Book, do you hate us for any reason other than that we believe in Allah and in what has been revealed to us and others before us, and that most of you are evildoers?"

5:60 Say: "Shall I tell you who will receive the worst reward from Allah? Those on whom Allah laid his curse and with whom he has been angry, transforming them into apes and swine, and those who worship false gods [like Jesus as the Son of God]. Worse is the plight of these, and they have strayed from the right path."

5:61 When they come to you they said: "We are believers." Indeed, infidels they came and infidels they departed. Allah knew their secret thoughts.

Many other verses give clues about Muhammad's encounters with Jewish and Christian people, and they clearly reveal that there was strife between them. However, although Muhammad and the People of the Book experienced conflict from time to time, and though Allah's reproaches concerning the People of the Book can be read in the verses, Muhammad never went as far as declaring the People of the Book permanent enemies of Islam or waged jihad against them, for his main task was to convert his own people to Islam. Therefore, it must be underlined that these historical incidents only belong to the past, to the history of emerging Islam, *and there is no indication in the Koran that these verses should be regarded by Muslims as Allah's orders that extend far into the future to be used as excuses to attack Jews and Christians who live at the present time.*

At present, extremist and jihadist Muslims—who do not take heed of the fact that these are only bygone incidents—regard Jews and Christians as unbelievers or deniers of Allah and enemies of Islam, and they call them *kafirs* (infidels). They are also under the impression that they have the right—given to them by the Koran and Allah—to wage jihad against those who do not choose to be adherents of Islam. It is as if what transpired between Arab believers and unbelievers, and the conflicts Muhammad had with the Jews, is projected into the present time, but now in a twisted and degenerate way. Radical, extremist, and jihadist Muslims identify the former expression of *kafir* with Christians of the present day. Extremist and jihadist Muslims do not seem to be aware that *jihad was required only at the initial stage of Islam under those special circumstances,* nor that they are doing great harm to the image of Islam by reviving the "spirit of jihad" after 1,400 years. Obviously these fanatical Muslims take no heed or are unaware of a certain verse that was inspired at a later stage of Muhammad's struggle. It clearly explains that there may have been a time when weapons were needed in their struggle, but jihad was not meant to be always fought with weapons:

> 25:52 Do not yield to the unbelievers, but fight them strenuously with this Koran.[24]

Apparently, in this verse, Allah advises the Prophet to employ another method in his struggle—by using the teachings inherent in the inspired verses. The verse also draws attention to the fact that the unending fighting between Arab tribes must come to an end and the Koran should be the basis of reconciliation. Since it is apparent that the Koran's messages do not encourage or motivate Muslims to carry their struggle into the future or wage jihad to adherents of other religions, who have no intention of becoming Muslims, fundamentalist and radical Muslims are seriously mistaken in believing that to make a "call" to members of other religions and impose Islam upon them is "a right" given to them by the Koran. They do not realize that to impose their belief on people who are not Muslim and expect these people to yield to this call is an unfounded and arrogant demand, because they have been confusing what happened in Islamic history with the reality of the present time. It is thus essential that they study the Koran with the awareness that these incidents only belong to the past and realize it is a serious, anachronistic mistake to imagine that

---

24 The meaning inherent in 25:52 is noteworthy. We can see that Allah is not ordering Muslims to fiercely attack and kill the unbelievers mercilessly; he is not encouraging them to be aggressive or violent. Instead of using brutal force, he ordains that rather than fighting the unbelievers with weapons they should make use of the wisdom that can be found in the Koran. In the Islamic tradition, it is known that instead of dashing into fights that bring pain and death, the Prophet always initially tried to approach unbelievers peacefully, to discuss and debate matters with them. However, in the present, extremists and jihadists do not take into consideration Allah's advice of making a peaceful jihad using the Koranic verses, inspired by Muhammad at the emergence of Islam. Moreover, they are not aware that the time of declaring jihad is over and that it is no longer necessary, as it only belonged to the time of Muhammad. If they studied the Koran, they would realize that its verses do not give anybody else but the Prophet Muhammad the authority to declare jihad.

these verses are also applicable to the present day. Their erroneous convictions and degenerate attitude toward members of other religions and cultures is a result of the influence of Arabism. When they act as a group soul under the effect of Arabism, Arabism gains even more power.

The noteworthy example below can give us a clear idea about the inconceivable and unacceptable demands of radical Muslims. According to a news report in Britain from November 2009, a radical Islamic group, whose members lived in England, demanded from the British prime minister that Islamic *sharia* laws be implemented in Britain. The spokesperson of this group said that he expected *sharia* laws would begin to be implemented in Britain in ten or fifteen years, and that all women should then cover themselves up according to Islamic rules. The spokesperson also stated that they would like to see the Queen covered according to Islamic rules for dressing. This radical group also put up on their Internet site a photograph of Buckingham Palace transformed into a mosque. We can dismiss such an example as immature fantasies not to be taken seriously. Indeed, such fantasies shall never be actualized. Yet, these people conceive such irrational and arrogant ideas and believe that their demands are fully justified. They present their wishes and expectations not as mere fantasies but as very real and serious demands. Failing to consider other people's right of freedom of belief, they insist on imposing Islamic dogmas, hoping that one day they will succeed in converting others to Islam. However, from what source do they receive these biased and degenerate inspirations, which totally disregard the principle of freedom and make them feel their demands are justified? What kind of spiritual influence is motivating them?

It is noteworthy that when the radical group discussed above gathered for a certain occasion, on some of the posters they carried was written: "Islam will dominate the world; freedom can go to hell." What their declaration implies—or rather, openly asserts—cannot be compared with the effort of Christian missionaries who try to persuade others to become Christian, for Christian missionaries at least respect people's freedom and do not try to forcibly impose Christianity on anyone.²⁵ Thus we cannot easily dismiss this kind of arrogance as an innocent and childish fantasy of radical Muslims but need to take it seriously. It is through such arrogant and degenerate ideas that Arabism is widening its sphere of action in the Christian world. How was Arabism initially able to infiltrate into the Christianized Europe? Tomberg addresses this in his "Anthroposophic Meditations on the Old Testament."

> After the influence of Gondishapur had been blunted by the tide of Islamism in the seventh century, it made its way slowly through the centuries by the roundabout path of Arabism into the Christian world, until in the nineteenth century it celebrated its triumphal progress over to the Earth in the external form of materialism.²⁶

As explained by Tomberg, the initial effect of Arabism on the Christian world was through materialism—that is, quickening the transition of European cultures from their religious inclinations to material inclinations. After many centuries, when *Islamism*—manifesting in the Islamic understanding of fundamentalist, radical, and extremist Muslims—managed to get a foothold in the European countries, its second influence began to assert itself as a rigid religious doctrine that is far from comprehending the principle of freedom. Arabism has shaped this doctrine and been influential in generating confusion of the present with events that only belong to Islamic history.

Why do radical and extremist Muslims wish to convert members of other religions to Islam? Why are they so insistent upon this arrogant demand? We may find clues to this answer if we reference Rudolf Steiner and Valentin Tomberg, who discussed how the Sorathic intervention was deadened. As Steiner and Tomberg were shedding light on different aspects of this important event in the spiritual history of humankind, they specifically indicated that Sorath's intervention was deadened with Lucifer's help. Let us remember that since Lucifer was a fallen and retarded spiritual being, his

---

25 When we evaluate the activities of Christian missionaries from the point of view of freedom of religious belief, even the practice of trying gently to persuade people to believe in their doctrine or denomination is not in harmony with the quality of the freedom inherent in the Christ impulse.

26 Tomberg, *Christ and Sophia*, "The Karma of the Israelites," p. 82.

involvement in the affairs of human beings has always brought certain consequences along with it.

Humankind's close relationship with Lucifer in the middle of the Lemurian epoch resulted in humanity's Fall from Heaven. At that time the human being did not yet possess an individual "I." Therefore, Lucifer was able to influence only the human astral body, which was merely at the stage of a group soul. But when the Islamic impulse began to unfold (c. AD 610, coinciding with the epoch of the development of humankind's intellectual or mind soul), the human being had an individualized astral body and a relatively developed "I." Thus, from this time onward, Lucifer was able to influence the human being's "I" through his or her individualized astral body—that is, through the "I" that manifested in the human's sentient soul. In their lectures, Steiner and Tomberg indicated that anger, pride, and haughtiness are characteristics that belong to Lucifer. Accordingly, it can be seen how these luciferic traits manifest in the angry behavior and reactions, in the haughty and prejudiced convictions, and in the arrogant demands of fundamentalist, radical, and extremist Muslims. Arabism acts as an eclipse on these Muslims, but since they have been under its influence for a very long time and because Arabism has been effective on their thinking, feeling, and will, they do not realize that they are under the influence of a kind of demonic force,[27] and since it is the mission of demonic forces to tempt and lure human beings into wrongdoing, this force perpetually affects them in diverse ways. It is essential for them to realize that the only way to dissipate and neutralize this adverse force is to become aware of how and why it influences them.

What is Arabism? How are we to define it?

We have discussed various aspects of Arabism and elucidated how it influences people. Still, more can be said about Arabism. It was influential on Arabs even before Islam began and is still affecting the Muslims of today. It has also begun to influence Western cultures and even Christianity. So how are we to define Arabism? To start with, although

---

27 Demonic force—in the sense that Arabism is not a force that emanates from the good forces of the divine–spiritual hierarchy. Any force that originates from outside the divine realm and is not in harmony with the consciousness and aims of the divine realm can be categorized as demonic.

the term Arabism stems from the word *Arab*, it is not a force or influence that has been knowingly instituted by members of Arab tribes or communities. This force in which multidimensional influences are inherent is fundamentally connected with Arabs, but we cannot claim it was consciously devised by Arabs; therefore, we cannot hold them directly responsible for the influences that derive from Arabism. It would be more correct to say that Arabs have only been a vehicle for the emergence and manifestation of this force. In other words, if we assume for a moment that the roles of the Arabs and the Hebrews were switched, and now Yahweh had guided the Arabs from the beginning, while the Hebrews were given the task of deadening Sorath's intervention, in this case the term *Hebraism* would have substituted for *Arabism*. Thus, the term *Arabism* often used by Steiner is indeed accurate and is not being used in a judgmental way.

The foregoing explanations indicates the influence and relationship of Arabism to various issues concerning Muslims' spiritual development. But what is actually the most significant aspect of Arabism according to Steiner and Tomberg? Steiner asserts that Arab life and thought was not capable of rising to what is spiritual, and that, under the influence of Arabism, Islam only allows Muslims to comprehend what is external and formal—that is, they are not able to sense the spirit of truth that issues from the Father. Steiner also maintained that Arabism provided the field for external culture and that it is only capable of comprehending what is external. This can be seen in the Arabesque, which is incapable of rising to what is living, but has to remain formal. Furthermore, he explained that we can see in the mosque how the spirit is, as it were, drained away. He also drew our attention to the Islamic conception of divinity, a conception that is allied with fatalism. Likewise, Tomberg showed how Islam made its way slowly through the centuries by the roundabout path of Arabism into the Christian world, until in the nineteenth century it celebrated its triumphal progress over the Earth *in the external form of materialism.*

When we ponder Steiner's and Tomberg's various elucidations on this subject, they relate Arabism and manifestations of Arabism fundamentally with *materialism*. So evidently, the main factor that forms the essence of Arabism—well blended with Islam—is that it has no genuine connection with what is truly spiritual, and all kinds of values that originate from the material world are inherent within it. This is why Arab life and thought are incapable of rising to what is spiritual and is only capable of comprehending what is external and formal. This is also the reason why their conception of divinity is allied with fatalism. Let us remember that descendants of Ishmael were exposed to all kinds of materialistic influences while they went through the Kali Yuga period, without any guidance and admonition from the divine realm. This does not mean that they did not receive any spiritual guidance at all. Throughout the centuries before they received the Islamic impulse, folk souls—or folk spirits—guided the Arab tribes. However, *these folk spirits were retarded luciferic archangels.*

When we bear in mind that the archangel who guided the Hebrew people as an emissary of Yahweh was Michael, apparently these retarded archangels were not similarly able to permeate the Arabs with true divine-spiritual impulses. This is the reason why they had completely lost their concept of the divine-spiritual, and this is the factor that quickened their passage into materialism and the adoption of material values. Consequentially, Arabs started practicing idolatry. Instead of forming a deep understanding of what is spiritual, they began to worship carved and chiseled figures of several non-sacred deities. Since they had lost their connection with the divine realm, and the faculty that enabled them to sense the divine had, so to speak, calcified during this period, they were only capable of apprehending what is external and material—the solid. Therefore, the deities they began to worship were also solidified images of certain spiritual beings, and none of the spiritual beings who inspired these carved figures was from the divine-spiritual realm. Since a folk spirit guides the chosen people while affecting their etheric bodies, all the information gathered in the people's etheric bodies in time transfers to future generations through heredity. Accordingly, since retarded luciferic folk souls had guided Arabs as a group soul for several centuries, their association with these folk souls created a certain formation of a group-soul character trait that came into being. This formation, united with their group soul, became more substantial and powerful as time went by. Since these character traits were associated with Arabs and were fed and kept alive by their group soul, this spectral force is termed *Arabism*.

During the flow of human evolution, the impulse of Islam eventually inculcated monotheism—similar to Mosaic monotheism—within the Arab community. Islamic teachings emphasized that Arabs should stop worshipping the idols of several deities and acknowledge a single deity encompassing the universe as their God. This deity, Allah, happened to be Yahweh, the God of their distant relatives, the Hebrews. Although Arabs managed to adopt the new monotheist concept of a single deity, and the religion of Islam emerged, this development was not able to dissipate the specter of Arabism; it was very much alive and effective in the background. Therefore, Arabism inevitably infused into the teachings of Islam. This is why Islam religion, which came into being as a result of the amalgamation of Arabism and Islamic teachings, is not a religion that truly reflects the precise spiritual meanings inherent in Allah's messages, but rather reflects teachings that are permeated with Arabism. In one of his lectures, Steiner indicates that Arabism never died out and explains how it influenced European culture and Christianity:

> Observation of history in its purely external aspect might lead us to the conclusion that Arabism had been beaten back by the European peoples. Battles were fought such as that of Tours and Poitiers, and there were many others. The Arabs were also defeated from the side of Constantinople, and it might easily be thought that Arabism had disappeared from the arena of world-history. On the other hand, when we think deeply about the impulses that were at work in the sciences, and in many respects in the field of art in European culture, we find Arabism still in evidence—but as if it had secretly poured into Christianity, had been secretly inculcated into it. How has this come about? You must realize, my dear friends, that in spiritual life events do not take the form in which they reveal themselves in external history. The really significant streams run their course beneath the surface of ordinary history, and in these streams the individualities of the people who have worked in one epoch appear again, born into communities speaking an entirely different language, with altogether different tendencies of thought, yet working still with the same fundamental impulse.... Arabism most assuredly did not die out; far rather

was it that individuals who were firmly rooted in Arabism lived in European civilization and influenced it strongly, in a way that was possible in Europe in that later epoch.[28]

Steiner also explained that when a person reincarnates after death, it is not only the individuality of a person that incarnates. A reincarnation of thoughts also occurs, and it is the continuation of thoughts from one life to another that makes it possible for these individuals to work within the same fundamental impulse. In this case, the impulse is Islam, and within it Arabism transfers from generation to generation and into the future. There is no external method of dispelling or deadening Arabism, for it has infiltrated into religious teachings and beliefs, and into the background of almost every detail of thought—such as certain philosophies, sciences, and theories such as Darwinism, which principally deny the spirit and the divine, and instead furnish materialistic explanations regarding humankind's existence in the universe. The only way to protect ourselves from Arabism's influence is to understand what kind of influence it really is and how it spreads and becomes effective in our daily life and culture. And the only way to neutralize Arabism is by becoming more conscious. To be able to encounter Arabism with an objective attitude, it would be helpful to bear in mind that Arabs did not choose to be the generators and transmitters of Arabism. Concerning manifestations of Arabism, we must remember that we are encountering an aspect of cosmic processes that is taking place in the earthly sphere.

What does Islam mean for Muslims, and how do they regard other religions?

Muslims, in general, are proud of being adherents of Islam. They believe that Islam came into existence as a religion because Allah especially decreed it. They evaluate Islam from an exoteric point of view and regard it as a religion comprised of certain teachings, beliefs, prayers, and a set of rituals that serve to venerate Allah. Like present-day Muslims, Muhammad and the early Muslims supposed that Judaism was founded solely as a religion, and that Abraham's unshakable faith in

---

28 Steiner, *Karmic Relationships*, vol. 1, lecture 10.

Allah at its beginnings was at the foundation of this religion. Muslims had the chance to probe into Judaism only much later (c. AD 610), and at that stage of Judaism they got the impression that Judaism had always been a formal and established religion. Thus, they never realized that what appeared to them as purely a Jewish religion was actually the remnants of what had transpired as a very important cosmic event,[29] implemented by the beings of the divine–spiritual hierarchy. They had no idea that *the content of the Bible was the narration of the preparatory stages of this incredible, multidimensional cosmic operation known as the Mystery of Golgotha.*[30] They regarded Christianity, likewise, solely as a religion. But Muhammad and his believers were persuaded that a religion such as Christianity was not supposed to exist in the first place, for it had come into being because some number of Jews had misunderstood and misinterpreted Allah's messages, conveyed by Jesus. In the Koran, verse 3:51 explains how Jesus tries to persuade Jews to believe in Allah: "Allah is my God and your God: therefore serve him. That is the straight path." Verse 3:59 emphasizes that Jesus has no spiritual or divine quality and is just an ordinary human being created from the minerals of the Earth: "Jesus is like Adam[31] in sight of Allah. He created him of dust[32] and said to him, 'Be,' and he was."

According to these verses, the emergence of Christianity was the result of a great misunderstanding. Since this was how they conceived Christianity and the role of Jesus, many verses try to give a truer version—that is, from an Islamic point of view—regarding Jesus' role. These koranic messages clearly show that whoever inspired them did not intend to reveal the truth concerning Jesus Christ and Christianity to the Arabs. Nothing in the Koran indicates that Christianity was the outcome of a profound spiritual impulse brought to the world by Christ. On the contrary, it becomes apparent that Allah does

---

29 The very important cosmic event was the Advent of the Christ.

30 Steiner named this cosmic operation the Mystery of Golgotha.

31 The Koran does not mention the three former stages of humankind's creation—Old Saturn, Old Sun, and Old Moon. According to the Koran, Allah created the first man, Adam, in the physical world.

32 When we consider the term *dust* in relation to other verses that refer to how Allah created humankind, it becomes apparent that it is used in the sense of minerals or soil of the Earth.

not even approve of Christianity as a religion. The Islamic impulse circumvented the implications of the Christ impulse entirely. Apparently, Muslims have failed to recognize, both in the past and in the present, that what they conceive of as merely religions that emerged on Earth successively actually have roots in completely different spiritual realities. Likewise, they are unaware that the ultimate purpose of the divine-spiritual beings was not to inculcate rigid monotheistic religions into the physical world one after the other. Nevertheless, the Prophet and Muslims firmly believed that Allah[33] established Islam as the last true religion, and that this is in harmony with Abraham's faith.

> 2:130 Who but a foolish man would renounce the faith of Abraham? We [Allah] chose him in this world, and in the world to come he shall dwell among the righteous. When his Lord [Allah] said to him: "Submit," he answered: "I have submitted to the Lord of the Creation [Allah]."
>
> 2:133 When death came to Jacob, he said to his children: "What will you worship when I am gone?" They replied: "We will worship your God and the God of your forefathers Abraham, Ishmael, and Isaac: The one God [Allah]. To him we will surrender ourselves."
>
> 2:135 They [Jews and Christians] say: "Accept the Jewish or the Christian faith and you shall be rightly guided." Say: "By no means! We believe in the faith of Abraham, the upright one. He was no idolater."[34]

The Koran, various suwar, and several verses emphasize that, although the descendants of Abraham, Isaac and Jacob (the Jews as well as those who later became Christians) were supposed to follow the faith of their ancestral father Abraham, but they were unsuccessful in fulfilling this expectation. Therefore, Allah continuously sent prophets to proclaim his messages, Jesus being one of them. Muslims are also under the impression that Allah never properly actualized his wish to establish the perfect religion (of faith and obedience) on

---

33 As we recall, only the name *Allah* is used in the Koran; Yahweh's name (as Yahweh or Jehovah) is never mentioned.

34 In this verse, "idolater" actually refers to the Christians who—in contrast with Islam's monotheistic faith—believe in the three Gods of the Holy Trinity. According to Islamic dogma, believing in more than one God (Allah) is equal to creating idols, and this is, therefore, blasphemy and idolatry.

Earth, because the Hebrews strayed from the right path, and some of them even became Christians, believing in blasphemous ideas. As a result, they had all transgressed. In the following verses, Allah indirectly reveals that he was the God whom they formerly venerated and reminds them to adhere to the covenant that he had made with them:

> 2:40 Children of Israel, remember the favors I have bestowed upon you. Keep your covenant, and I will be true to Mine. Revere Me. Have faith in my revelations [those given to Muhammad] which confirm your scriptures, and do not be first to deny them.[35]

> 2:122 Children of Israel, remember that I have bestowed upon you and exalted you above the nations. Fear the day when every soul shall stand alone: when neither intercession nor ransom shall be accepted from it, nor any help be given it.

Evidently, the Jews had taken no heed of Allah's recent messages, which were intended to remind them of their covenant and persuade them to believe in Muhammad. The following verses, inspired by Muhammad, again state that, according to Allah, the Jewish people had not properly understood Abraham's faith, had deviated from their covenant, and now they were denying Allah's revelations. These verses also indicate that Christians are mistaken in their belief that Jesus is God's Son. They urge the People of the Book to stop denying Allah's revelations and to take heed of Muhammad's messages.

> 3:65 People of the Book, why do you argue about Abraham when both the Torah and the Gospel were not revealed till after him? Have you no sense?

> 3:66 Indeed, you have argued about things you have some knowledge. Must you now argue about that of which you know nothing at all? Allah knows but you do not.

> 3:67 Abraham was neither Jew nor Christian. He was an upright man, who had surrendered himself to Allah. He was no idolater [i.e., Abraham did not place mortals—like Jesus and his mother—as Gods beside Allah].

---

35 Bearing in mind the information that anthroposophic wisdom imparts concerning Yahweh, it hardly seems feasible that Yahweh, who belonged to the Pleroma of the Christ-being and prepared Hebrews for the Advent of Christ, later asks Jews to take heed of Muhammad's messages and become Muslims.

> Surely the men who are nearest to Abraham are those who follow him [the Prophet Muhammad and the ones who believe in him is implied]. Some of the People of the Book wish to mislead you; but they mislead none but themselves, though they may not perceive it.
>
> 3:70 People of the Book! Why do you deny Allah's revelations [conveyed by Muhammad] when you know that they are true?[36]
>
> 3:71 People of the Book! Why do you confound the true with the false, and knowingly hide the truth?
>
> 3:98 Say: "People of the Book, Why do you deny the revelations of Allah? He bears witness to all your actions."

These verses assert that the People of the Book were reluctant to heed the revelations Allah sent via Muhammad. To acquire a clearer idea of how Muslims evaluate Jesus, let us delve further into the "acts of Jesus" in the Koran. According to Islamic belief, upon seeing that his former messengers were not successful in persuading Hebrews to believe in and surrender to him, Allah sent Jesus, his Prophet, to them to proclaim Allah's messages and establish his perfect religion. Jesus—not *Jesus Christ*, but Jesus, the son of Mary—was also not successful in establishing the kind of religion that Allah demanded, because Jews took no heed of Jesus and Allah's messages. The following verses depict Jesus as having a difficult time trying to persuade the Hebrews to believe in Allah. In 3:52 he asks for help from his disciples. This is how Jesus speaks in the Koran:

> 3:50–52 "I bring you a sign from your Lord: therefore fear him and obey me. Allah is my Lord and your Lord: therefore serve him. That is the straight path." When Jesus observed that they [Jewish people] had no faith, he said: "Who will help me in the cause of Allah?" The disciples replied: "We are helpers of Allah. We believe in him. Bear witness that we have surrendered ourselves to him." [Some translators render the latter as: "Bear witness that we have become Muslims."[37]]

---

36 It is not hard to deduce that when extremist or jihadist Muslims read verses like 3:70 and 3:98 today and turn their gaze toward Jews and Christians, they see people who insist on denying Allah's revelations.

37 It is noteworthy that in this verse, the Apostles surrender to Allah—or become Muslims. *Muslim* literally means "the one who believes in Allah."

In What Ways Has Arabism Influenced Islam?

As we recall, the Prophet's task was to persuade Arabs, who were formerly idolaters with no concept of monotheism, to acknowledge Allah as their deity. So why the insistence on persuading Jews to become Muslim when they had already been venerating Yahweh for several centuries?[38] When we study the Koran, we see that Muhammad was having difficulties persuading Arabs to believe in Allah, and verse 3:52 reverts to the times of Jesus to adduce a similarity between Muhammad and Jesus. The main message in this verse is: the Prophet Jesus also faced many difficulties while trying to persuade the Jews to believe in Allah and surrender to him. Evidently, the hope was that this indirect likening would help to affirm and strengthen Muhammad's position as the chosen Prophet. However, it does not reflect the truth concerning the actual identity and role of Jesus—that is, Jesus Christ. According to the Islamic narrations given in the Koran, some Jews became Christians, but since they had not rightfully understood Jesus' messages, they adopted blasphemous convictions, among which was the belief in the Trinity and that Jesus is God's Son.

In Muhammad's time, the prevalent understanding of the Holy Trinity among some Christians[39] comprised God as the Father, Jesus as his Son, and Mary as the mother. In this concept of the Holy Trinity, a divine being and two ephemeral beings are affiliated. Muhammad's objection to this association was justifiable, but he was also rejecting the existence of three Gods. Muhammad was trying to establish a strict monotheistic religion. His verses conveyed messages emphasizing that a concept such as *Father, Mother, and Son* within the basic idea of a Trinity is erroneous and blasphemous, because Allah is the one and only creator of the universe and cannot possibly be any part of a Trinity. Moreover, Allah was far removed from having a wife and a son. Surah 3:64 was directed toward Christians who were claiming Jesus as the Son of God, and that Jesus himself was also a God. This verse is apparently meant to serve as both admonishment and a call to worship Allah solely.

---

38 This subject was discussed in an earlier section, but it is necessary to mention it again within a different context.

39 Christians who were neighbors of pagan Arabians were Nestorians and Christianized Arabs.

> 3:64 Say: "People of the Book, let us come to an agreement: that we will worship none but Allah, that we will associate none [i.e., Jesus and the Trinity] with him, and that none of us shall set up mortals [such as Jesus and his mother] as gods besides him." If they refuse, say: "Bear witness that we have surrendered ourselves to Allah."

According to the koranic verses, Christianity and its false concepts—like the Holy Trinity and Jesus being God's Son—came into being because the Jews had disputed over certain issues. In this context, verse 27:76 tells the Jewish people that Muhammad's verses clearly explain the issues they previously disputed—for example, whether or not Jesus was the Jews' new prophet.

> 27:76 This Koran [Muhammad's verses] expounds to the Children of Israel most of the matters over which they disagree.

But in verse 3:98, we see that Muhammad's inspired verses were not successful in persuading the Jews and Christians:

> 3:98 Say: "People of the Book, why do you deny the revelations of Allah? He bears witness to all your actions."

In another verse, Allah is disappointed with the People of the Book:

> 5:51 Believers [Muslims] take neither Jews nor Christians for your friends. They are friends with one another. He among you who takes them for friends is (one) of them. Allah does not guide wrongdoers.

4.

MUHAMMAD AS THE LAST PROPHET SENT BY ALLAH: LUCIFER'S INVOLVEMENT IN ISLAM

To form a clearer picture of Islamic beliefs and convictions, it was necessary to analyze both how Muslims conceive Islam and how they regard other religions. The previous chapter delved into this subject, and we recall that as a result of former unsuccessful attempts at establishing the kind of religion or faith that he decreed, Allah decided to send another—and final—prophet. According to Muslims, this was precisely why the Prophet Muhammad and Islam exists. In accordance with this conviction, two verses in the Koran indirectly predicted Muhammad's role as the last prophet sent by Allah. We can surmise that these predictions were placed within the Koran because it was necessary to indicate that Muhammad belonged to the lineage of Ishmael to persuade both the Arab tribes and the People of the Book of Muhammad's role as the new prophet. One of these predictions referred to the time of Abraham. In the verse below, Abraham built the sacred Kaaba building with his son Ishmael, and then he beseeched Allah to send forth a prophet from the lineage of Ishmael.

> 2:127 Abraham and Ishmael built the House [Kaaba][1] and dedicated it saying: Accept this from us Lord [Allah]. You hear all and you know all. Lord, make us submissive to You; make our descendants a nation

---

[1] According to tradition, Ishmael and his father built the Kaaba or, actually, rebuilt it, because the great flood destroyed the original building. Rudolf Frieling states in his book *Christianity and Islam*: "From a historical point of view, it is highly unlikely that Abraham was ever in Mecca. But the possibility that the roving Ishmael found his way there cannot be excluded." Nevertheless, in the Medina period Muhammad still gave great emphasis to the Abraham–Ishmael tradition and its connection with Mecca and Kaaba.

that will submit to You. Teach us our rites of worship and turn to us mercifully; You are forgiving and merciful. Lord, send forth to them [to future descendants of Ishmael] an apostle of their own who shall declare them Your revelations and instruct them in the Scriptures and in wisdom and purify them of sin.

In another verse in the Koran, Jesus predicts the arrival of a prophet named Ahmad (a derivative of the name Muhammad), as we shall later see. According to Muslims, Islam is the last religion founded by Allah—who is the actual force behind Muhammad—Muhammad is the last prophet sent by Allah, and Islam—in comparison with the other religions—is the most perfect and sacred religion as well as Allah's most favored religion. Muslims also believe that as descendants of Ishmael, it is now the Arabs' turn to be Allah's chosen people, for the descendants of Ishmael are now truly representing the original faith of Abraham, and it was through them that Allah's perfect religion arose.

> 4:125 And who has a nobler religion than the man who surrenders himself to Allah, does what is right, and follows the faith of saintly Abraham, whom Allah himself chose to be his friend?

Another verse gives full support to these Islamic convictions:

> 3:19 The only true faith in Allah's sight is Islam. Those to whom the Scriptures were given [Jews and Christians] disagreed among themselves through jealousy only after knowledge has been given to them. He that denies Allah's revelations [teachings proclaimed by Muhammad] should know that he [Allah] is swift in reckoning.

At this point, let us recall how radical and extremist Muslims are insistently trying to impose their belief on members of other religions. They believe they are justified in imposing Islam on other people owing to the influence of these verses and others in which Allah

---

The Kaaba, and worship within the Kaaba, were wholly identified with Abraham and Ishmael, for example in the following verse:

> 2:125 We made the House [Kaaba] a resort and a sanctuary for humankind, saying: "Make the place where Abraham stood a house of worship." We enjoined Abraham and Ishmael to cleanse Our House for those who walk around it, who meditate in it, and who kneel and prostrate themselves.

decreed, "The only true faith in Allah's sight is Islam." As Allah has been clear that Islam is the religion he approves—or, shall we say, favors—some Muslims have no doubt whatsoever concerning their dogmatic convictions and harsh deeds.

Following the example of the Hebrews, Muslims formed *sharia* by selecting certain verses from various suwar. Indeed, the koranic verses provided with guidance, instruction, and regulations that they had previously lacked, but once they adopted the Judaic practice of lapidation and instituted the amputation of hands and feet as a form of punishment, an undeniably brutal element crept into *sharia*. Muslims also adopted the Hebrew tradition of circumcision and turned it into an Islamic hallmark.[2] They used a Bible story specifically for the Hebrews that had been enacted as the result of a specific divine–spiritual purpose into something different for their own purposes. This is one of the reasons why Islam is designated as the newly emerged Moon religion of Yahweh. This new religion, which has adopted the *crescent* as its symbol, was founded on uncompromising and strict monotheism.[3]

We can we detect luciferic influences and characteristics in all of the prejudicial and haughty convictions of the Muslims. Lucifer indeed helped in deadening the Sorathic intervention, but certain luciferic influences inevitably infiltrated into Islam during that period. Therefore, we can suggest that Lucifer played a role in the aggrandizement of Arabism's power and its unceasing influence

---

[2] Although not a single Koranic verse exists in which Allah enjoined circumcision, Muslims used Abraham and the Jews as their example and implemented this tradition as an Islamic precept. However, what St. Paul wrote to the Romans about circumcision is noteworthy here: "Blessed is the one whose sin the Lord will never count against them. Is this blessedness only for the circumcised, or also for the uncircumcised? We have been saying that Abraham's faith was credited to him as righteousness. Under what circumstances was it credited? Was it after he was circumcised, or before? It was not after, but before! And he received circumcision as a sign, a seal of the righteousness that he had by faith while he was still uncircumcised. So then, he is the father of all who believe but have not been circumcised, in order that righteousness might be credited to them. And he is then also the father of the circumcised who not only are circumcised but who also follow in the footsteps of the faith that our father Abraham had before he was circumcised" (Rom. 4:8–12).

[3] It is noteworthy that the crescent symbol exists in one form or other on the flag of almost every Islamic country.

on Arabs. We can also deduce that some of Muhammad's inspired verses later appeared in the Koran in a misleading form because of luciferic influences, and, consequently, the truth pertaining to Jesus Christ was also distorted and totally obscured. As we have seen, many verses depict Jesus in disparate ways, and this inaccurate portrayal reveals how the luciferic influence has infiltrated these verses. As long as Muslims refuse to accept the truth revealed by the Gospel and allow their conception of Jesus to be dependent only on the information conveyed by such verses, how will they ever acquire a true insight of Jesus Christ and the Christ impulse? A riddle remains concerning Lucifer's assistance. Although Lucifer willingly helped the Christ forces to solve the approaching crisis of 666, why did he both stir many contradictions in the Koran and create the serious confusion surrounding the true identity of Jesus Christ? We may find the answer to this question in Valentin Tomberg's "Meditations on the New Testament":

> Lucifer has the pride of opposition in common with Ahriman, and he has love in common with the hierarchies of good. Lucifer is a Janus-like character: with one side of his nature he loves the Christ, while with the other he has affinity with Ahriman. Because of this, both sides have the possibility of winning the whole field of his activity; the spiritual hierarchies hope to acquire it for love, and Ahriman hopes to incorporate it into his dominion.[4]

In accordance with Tomberg's elucidation, we can deduce that because Lucifer loved the Christ, when he saw Jesus Christ-being crucified, he experienced an intense realization, and this was the moment when his conversion began. Lucifer then decided to help the hierarchies of good, but because of his pride of opposition and his affinity with Ahriman, the baser side of his character intervened and he could not help causing serious confusion about the true identity of Jesus—as the Christ—in the Koran. When we look at the *results* of his influence on the Islamic impulse—approximately 600 years after having witnessed the Crucifixion—it becomes evident

---

4   Tomberg, *Christ and Sophia*, part 2, chapter 11, "The Mystery of Golgotha."

that the process of "his conversion" was yet not complete at that time, and he was not yet able to be freed of his affinity with Ahriman. Throughout the Koran, it can be seen that the verses acknowledge Jesus (although in a distorted and inaccurate way), but they never acknowledge the Christ-being or mention anything about Christ's incarnation in the physical body of Jesus. Lucifer's contradictory approach, which obstructs the truth pertaining to Jesus and the Christ-being, was pointed out by Steiner when he elucidated Lucifer's role in connection with Gondishapur and Islam: "The influence that was to have gone out from Gondishapur was deadened, held back by retarded spiritual forces, which were nevertheless connected—although they form a kind of opposition—with the outflow of the Christ Impulse."[5] Tomberg, too, pointed out that Lucifer's manner of conduct manifests in contradictory ways and forms a polarity within itself in the excerpt above.

Lucifer's role in Arabism's increase in power: The influence of luciferic morality on Islam

One of the main and most important reasons why Arabism has been influential on Muslims of the past and present is because Muslims, in general, have not taken heed of Allah's admonitions concerning Satan's powerful influence over humankind. In the Koran, several verses draw attention to the existence of the devil—Satan—and explain that he is an adversary of Allah. In fact, his role as an enticer is explained in a fairly detailed way and many verses warn Muslims that the devil can harm them because he is capable of enticing them:

> 4:117 Allah has laid his curse on the devil, for he had said: "I shall entice a number of your servants and lead them astray."

> 4: 120 "He [the devil] makes promises and stirs up in them [mankind] vain desires; he makes promises only to deceive them.'"

Since these verses depict the devil as a "tempter," this gives the impression that the devil in question is Lucifer. Some verses also state

---

5   See Steiner, *Three Streams in Human Evolution,* lecture 5.

that Allah gave his permission to the devil to entice humankind until the Day of Resurrection. Certain verses emphasize that Muslims should be well aware and protect themselves against him, because they may be thrown into the eternal fire of Hell if they sin as a consequence of falling into the devil's traps. However, there is not a clear distinction between Lucifer and Ahriman in the koranic verses. In the Koran, the image of the devil is as both a tempter and a being that imposes evil on humankind. Some translators interpret the Arabic word *shaytan* as the "devil," others as "Satan," so these names are used synonymously in the Koran. Nevertheless, ample information is given concerning the devil for Muslims to understand that they ought to be very careful about his devious schemes. However, when we observe how Arabism has been so effective on Islam, while bearing in mind the terrible deeds of the radical, extremist, and jihadist Muslims, it becomes apparent that some Muslims take no heed of the warnings concerning the devil's power over humankind. Muslims may be abiding certain rules imposed by *sharia*, and they may not be worshipping the old pagan idols anymore, but a kind of spiritual sleep induced by Arabism inhibits Muslims from gaining an insight of the devil's (Lucifer's and Ahriman's) strong influence on the development of the human "I" and consciousness. Therefore—generally speaking—the Muslims' idea of repulsing the devil does not go any further than saying prayers and asking Allah to protect them against any evil that could come from the devil, as well as taking part in the ritual of symbolically throwing stones at the devil during their pilgrimage (*hajj*) in Mecca. In the verses below, a dialogue between Allah and Satan sheds some light on why Satan rebelled against Allah and began enticing humankind:

> 7:11–18 *We created you and gave you form. Then We said to the angels: "Prostrate yourselves before Adam." They all prostrated themselves except Satan, who refused. "Why did you not prostrate yourself?" Allah asked. "I am nobler than Adam," he replied. "You created me of fire and him of clay." He said: "Begone from paradise! This is no place for your contemptuous pride. Away with you! Henceforth you shall be humble." Satan replied: "Reprieve me till the Day of Resurrection. "You are reprieved," said he. "Because You have led me into sin," said Satan, "I will waylay Your servants*

> [humankind] as they walk on your straight path, And spring upon them from the front and from the rear, from their right and from their left. Then you shall find the greater part of them ungrateful." "Begone!" said Allah. "A despicable outcast you shall henceforth be. With those that follow you I shall fill the pit of Hell."

In addition to this detailed dialogue, very similar dialogues held between Allah and Satan can be found in suwar 38:73–83, 15:30–42, and 17:61–65.

Morality is another subject in which we see that luciferic influence has penetrated into Islam. How does Islamic morality manifest in the Islamic way of life, and how might Lucifer influence it? In Islamic countries, an understanding of this luciferic-based morality can be observed mainly at the foundation of the relationship between men and women in the social order. As a rule—especially in Islamic countries ruled by *sharia*—men and women are not allowed to share an ordinary communal life. That is to say, men and women do not mix in public but lead their lives in two distinctly separate communities, except in their private and closed family life at home. Socializing is restricted to gatherings of one gender or the other. When a man and woman do meet, shaking hands is not permissible, for the rules of Islamic morality (permeated by luciferic influence) deem that this as a sinful act. Another example is that, although Muslim men and women are members of the same religion and perform the same kind of rituals regarding prayer, they are restricted from praying next to each other in a mosque,[6] as do Christians who pray together in a church. Women have to pray and prostrate in a secluded area allocated for them—away from the sight of men. This seems to intimate that men can only focus on their prayer when women are not around. (Contrary to this practice, one can indeed transcend the perception of gender, and all thoughts and urges concerning sexuality can disappear when one is in deep meditation or prayer.) In some countries ruled by *sharia*, women are also not allowed to drive a car or even go out to shop, or go for a walk alone. Talking to men other than members of their family is

---

6   This is a Sunna and Shiite rule. However, this rule is not applied in the Alawi sect.

strictly forbidden. Evidently, Islamic moral norms—that is, luciferic Islamic morality—confine women and impose great limitations on their freedom in numerous ways.

It is noteworthy that in a country like Turkey, where a mixture of laicism and Islam is adopted—the aforementioned rule that forbids praying next to each other in a mosque is retained—most of these religious rules and restrictions concerning the socializing of men and women are not applied, and, therefore, their relationships are similar to those of men and women in Western cultures. (Still, since it is up to personal choice whether to apply Islamic rules, some believers implement them privately.) In the *Alawi* sect of Islam—found mostly in Turkey but also in other parts of the Middle East—men and women can join together in prayer, for people who belong to this sect do not go to a mosque like the Sunni Muslims do. To pray, they gather in informal and modest buildings called *Cemevi*.[7]

The fact that Islamic rules dictate that Muslim women have to cover their heads with shawls or scarves is another example of the influence of luciferic morality on Islam. In some Islamic countries, women are expected to cover their whole body—for example, by wearing a *burqa*. Is there a koranic verse in which Allah clearly and directly commands that women should be always covered? Apart from two verses that mention putting on a shawl (or a cloak), such a command does not exist within the Koran. Moreover, in both of these verses, "covering" has different connotations. In verse 33:59, it can be clearly seen that women covering themselves (or drawing on a cloak/shawl) is only associated with Muhammad's time, when much trouble brewed between believers and nonbelievers. In this verse, it is apparent that wearing a cloak was suggested as a measure of security, and it only concerned Muhammad's wives and daughters, and the wives of believers. Thus, this verse is only relevant to Arabs who had become Muslims in Muhammad's time—and, in fact, is more relevant to those who were close to Muhammad himself. The way this verse is composed reveals that *it does not refer to Muslims in the future*—that is, those who would become adherents of Islam thereafter.

---

7 *Cemevi*: A Turkish word that means "house of gathering" (for prayer).

> 33:59 O Prophet tell your wives, and thy daughters, and the women of the believers to draw their cloaks close around them (when they go abroad). That will be better, so that they may be recognized and not annoyed [another rendering: "not molested"]. Allah is ever forgiving and merciful.

The expression "that will be better"—followed by the reason for why it is so—indicates that these words are meant only as advice, not as a strict order. The second verse, also regarded by Muslims as a strict edict that women cover themselves, is 24:31. However, after careful analysis, it becomes apparent that its message particularly refers to Arab women who had newly become Muslim but had not changed their pre-pagan Arab ways of dressing—which was hardly an inhibited style considering the hot climate of the Arabian Peninsula. For this reason, this message also cannot be interpreted as a strict rule expected to be implemented by all Muslim women into the future.

> 24:31 And tell the believing women to lower their gaze and be modest, and to display of their adornment only that which is apparent, and to draw their veils over their bosoms, and not to reveal their adornment save to their own husbands and fathers or husband's fathers, or their sons or their husband's sons, or their brothers or their brother's sisters, or their women, or their slaves, or male attendants who lack vigor, or children who know naught of women's nakedness. And let them not stamp their feet so as to reveal what they hide of their adornment. And turn to Allah together, O believers, so that you may succeed.

Apparently, the moral code demanding that women cover themselves arose out of the erroneous evaluation of verses 33:59 and 24:31, and this was a consequence of the influence of luciferic morality. Another factor has also contributed to the misunderstanding and misinterpretation of these verses. If Muslim interpreters of the Koran (who are usually learned men) had not singled out these two verses and focused solely on this message but had tried to make a connection with the meanings of former verses—that is, if they went back to the beginning of the surah in question—they would have become aware of some significant factors influencing the messages inherent in verses 33:59 and 24:31. When we look into some of the verses that come before 33:59 (especially 33:28–33 and 36), we see that the Prophet was having problems establishing discipline among his wives and within his household. As far as we can understand it, his wives had strong objections to Muhammad's latest marriage—with Aisha. Therefore, the aim of the verses was a means of enacting more discipline toward his wives in counterbalance to their objections. In short, Muhammad's other wives had objected to his latest marriage. Some verses in the 33rd surah attempt to nullify these objections by stating that the marriage was decreed by Allah (and, in fact, another verse approves this marriage). Since Allah approved the Prophet's latest marriage, further objection could not be raised; everybody was obliged to agree with Allah's decision. As it follows, the unbelievers (Muhammad's enemies) took advantage of this upheaval in Muhammad's household and tried to harm him by gossiping about him. During these troubled times Muhammad tried to protect his wives, daughters, and the women of other believers against their common enemies by telling them to cover themselves whenever they left the house. Verse 33:59 was inspired in accordance with the circumstances and necessities of that time.

Just so, when we analyze the verses preceding 24:31, we see that many of them have to do with a certain incident involving Muhammad's favorite wife, Aisha. As the story goes, Aisha got lost in the desert during a journey, but a Bedouin Muslim later found and saved her. After this incident, gossip about Aisha and the man who found her sprung up among the unbelievers and spread even among some believers, with the intention of damaging him. The gossip went so far as to claim that Aisha had deceived Muhammad. Needless to say, the Prophet was very upset. Finally, with the help of some inspired verses, it became clear that Aisha was innocent. But as a result of this incident, more inspired verses were given with admonitions concerning how "believing women" should behave and dress. Verse 24:31 is one of these. In the centuries that followed, unfortunately, this verse caused Muslim women to recede more into the background within the social order.

When this verse is carefully analyzed, it can be seen that it does not instruct women to cover their heads or the entire body, yet Islamic moral norms that have formed over time have transformed the advice found in this verse into a mandate that Muslim women cover themselves. Luciferic morality is inherent in both the rule that forbids men and women from shaking hands—though no verse forbids this—and in the one that directs women to cover themselves. But take a look at verse 24:30, which appears to be a warning for "believing men." It is very likely that 24:30 was inspired to balance 24:31 by instructing that men should also become more aware concerning their behavior regarding their relationship with women. These verses follow each other and are thus closely related. Therefore, it becomes apparent that these rules did not focus on women exclusively but were given as instructions with the intention of amending former behavioral defects of both men and women.

> 24:30 And tell the believing men to turn their eyes away from temptation and to restrain their carnal desires. This will make their lives purer. Allah has knowledge of all their actions.

It is evident in these particular verses that behind the Islamic rule they convey are incidents that are actually related to the private family life of the Prophet. Evidently, Allah has not specifically ordered Muslim women to cover their heads or to cover themselves from head to toe—or that Muslim men should impose such a rule on their wives or daughters. It's clear that—under the influence of luciferic morality (and Arabism)—conservative Muslims have been implementing the Islamic rule of women covering themselves in public as a result of their misunderstanding and misevaluation of these verses, but this rule has no true basis in the Koran. However, it is understandable that at the outset of Islam certain rules were needed. As we recall from Ibn Kathir's narrations concerning the pre-Islamic pagan way of life, marital relations had become extremely decadent because of the absence of moral rules and guidance, so amelioration of this way of life was necessary. Allah's admonishments to the Arabs were therefore justified. However, why were these rules then exaggerated and rigidified, to include the infliction of brutal physical pain?

After receiving the necessary admonishments from Allah, Arabs turned Allah's guidelines into rigid and inflexible moral laws and strict religious prohibitions. Since they had been under the influence of Arabism even before the outset of Islam, luciferic morality easily infused their newly formed understanding of morality, and as a consequence they ended up implementing distorted rules and laws that deviated from what the koranic verses originally indicated. As centuries went by, luciferic morality became deeply ingrained in the Islamic morality norms of Muslim communities. Note that in the following verse the punishment for gay people is clearly stated, and the punishment is not death.

> 4:16 *If two men among you commit indecency punish them both. If they repent and mend their ways, let them be. Allah is forgiving and merciful.*

Those who have sinned are given the chance to "repent and mend their ways." The Koran also states: "Let them be." Yet, in Iran gay people are severely flogged and then hanged in front of a crowd. The punishment for adultery implemented today in Islamic countries is also very cruel. Muslims take no notice of what has been indicated in the Koran. They ignore what Allah actually decreed and implement other punishments that he has not ordained. The punishment for adultery illustrated in the Koran is not death, but rather that "the adulterer and the adulteress shall each be given a hundred lashes."[8] In countries ruled by *sharia*, though, this verse is not taken into consideration, and a woman who is found guilty of adultery is stoned to death. Another verse verifies that lapidation is not a punishment decreed by Allah:

> 4:14 *If any of your women commit fornication call in four witnesses from among yourselves against them; if they testify to their guilt confine them to their houses till death overtakes them or till Allah finds another way for them.*

There is no mention of the punishment of lapidation in this verse (or in any other verse in the Koran). Therefore, the implementation of stoning is a clear contradiction to the admonishment and guidelines given by Allah. When we consider these explanations, a significant question arises: If the punishment of stoning is not commanded (or even hinted at) by Allah in any koranic verse, then how can Muslims

---

8   24:2 "The adulterer and the adulteress shall each be given a hundred lashes. Let no pity for them cause you to disobey Allah if you truly believe in Allah and the Last Day; and let their punishment be witnessed by a number of believers."

justify it? Surely none among them assume that they have the authority to contradict what Allah has conveyed in verse 4:14. They certainly do not think that Allah merely forgot to mention the punishment of stoning to death in his messages. So what impelled them to adopt this practice? It could be said that it was because Arabs wanted to imitate Judaic law, but the actual reason why this punishment has found acceptance in the Arab culture is due to the influence of luciferic morality. Consequentially, they ended up with a peculiar and impure understanding of morality that hinders the development of conscience.

Besides lapidation, many other examples of unfounded *sharia* laws exist. Accordingly, it is probable that as a result of perpetually implementing these laws—permeated with luciferic morality—Muslims will not be able to transform their present understanding of morality into a higher form of *spiritualized morality*. However, since human evolution is flowing toward more spiritualized future stages, it is essential that people engender a higher spiritualized form of morality that is to become a permanent spiritual quality of their souls. As humankind's evolution keeps on moving toward these future stages, the influence of the Christ impulse will become more effective. In one of his lectures, Steiner made a significant statement: "The future evolution of humanity will take place through the cooperation of human moral impulses with the Christ impulse."[9]

For the benefit of their spiritual development, it is very important that Muslims imbibe everything offered by the Christ impulse. However, when we observe how the prevalent Islamic understanding of morality manifests, it becomes evident that it is not in agreement with the Christ impulse or harmonious with the purposes and aims of the divine–spiritual beings. Therefore, as long as Islamic morality is based on fear of punishment—thus lacking freedom—and remains an *imposed luciferic morality*, it cannot have any role in engendering a higher form of morality. In fact, its nature and how it manifests within Islam contradicts the qualities inherent in spiritualized higher morality. In its present state, Islamic morality is functioning as a hindrance to the development of a higher form of morality. As we recall, anthroposophic wisdom refers to this higher (spiritualized) form of

---

9   Steiner, *The Spiritual Foundation of Morality*, lecture 3.

morality as *"moral ether,"* and humanity will gradually engender moral ether when the Christ impulse thoroughly permeates human moral impulses in the future. As it stands, it seems unlikely that the Islamic concept of morality will be able to make any contribution toward engendering moral ether.

In news reports, we often hear about incidents that give us an idea about the nature of Islamic morality. For instance, in December 2010, a woman in Sudan was flogged simply because she wore jeans (although she was covered with a shawl). In May 2014, an Iranian actress from an award-winning film was reported to the country's courts by activists who demanded a public flogging as punishment for violating Islamic laws. What was her sin? She was condemned for greeting the Cannes festival president with a kiss on the cheek, an act regarded by Iranians as an insult to womanhood. An incident from 2001 may give us an even better idea about how Arabism has permeated luciferic morality, which in turn has influenced the norms of Islamic morality. A serious fire started in a girls' school in Saudi Arabia, and fifteen girls were trapped in the school building. Firefighters arrived quickly. But *sharia* guards appeared at the scene of fire at the same time. The firefighters wanted to go into the building to save the girls, but the *sharia* guards did not allow them to go in because *sharia* law forbids men to go near girls (or women) who were not properly covered. (Because it was a girls-only school, students were not required to wear headscarves or *burqa*s within the school precincts.) Meanwhile, the girls tried fleeing the building but were beaten with sticks by the *sharia* guards and pushed back toward the flames for this same Islamic idea of morality stated above. All of the girls died. Later, the government provided minimal compensation to their families.

The fact that such an incident happened in an Islamic country clearly shows how luciferic morality permeated with Arabism has impaired the development of conscience in Islam. It also indicates that the prevalent Islamic morality is not harmonious with the aims of human evolution. In this example, we see how the Islamic understanding of morality and conscience are placed in contradictory positions. If the *sharia* guards had a developed conscience and could have been guided by it at the scene of the fire, it would have neutralized Islamic morality, and a higher kind of morality imbued with compassion would have become effective. As a result, the girls could have been saved. But the *sharia* guards were motivated by rigid and inflexible rules and acted as a group soul, sleeping and dreaming in their thought, feeling, and will. According to their understanding, if the girls had been saved by the firefighters while they were not properly covered, this would have been a violation of Islamic law. But, as a matter of fact, morality and conscience cannot possibly contradict each other. If they clash, it is an indication of retrogression. Certain koranic verses try drawing Arabs' attention to the necessity of acquiring conscience.

Two specific koranic verses indicate that it is wrong to bury one's own daughter alive for trivial reasons. One cannot expect pagan Arabs to have had a developed conscience in the pre-Islamic times when they were passing through the Kali Yuga period and were exposed to very strong influences radiating from adverse beings of darkness; this is why "they knew not what they were doing" when they buried their daughters alive. Therefore, in accordance with those circumstances at the outset of Islam, these verses were given as an admonishment to draw their attention to the spiritual faculty of conscience formerly unknown by them.

Since these verses were particularly associated with not burying their girls alive, Arab Muslims did put an end to this practice. However, the fact that such an incident occurred approximately 1,400 years later shows that the spiritual faculty of conscience did not develop well in some Muslims, for conscience can only function if it finds a permanent place in the depths of a person's soul *and becomes that person's inner law.* If the children in the school had been boys instead of girls, they undoubtedly would have been saved. The deeper meaning of these two verses could be: "Your daughters are as valuable as your sons, for they are both created by Allah; therefore, you should not differentiate between them and should give them the same value. Never treat your daughters in a way that would result in their death." The fact that these girls suffered a horrible death because the *sharia* guards' degenerate understanding of morality forbade their rescue shows that some Muslims have misunderstood the deeper meaning of the koranic message "do not bury your daughters alive," or they would not have allowed their daughters to be burned alive.

In this incident, we can see that compassion was lacking. Compassion awakens as a result of the conscious development of one's conscience. It is essential that Muslims properly interpret the Koran and realize that morality and conscience cannot be put in contradictory positions. In the long run, it is also necessary for Muslims to comprehend that when conscience and compassion permeate morality, moral ether is generated. In this way, luciferic morality[10]—which has a retrogressive effect on Islamic morality—could be neutralized, purified, and transformed into a more spiritualized morality that is in harmony with the Christ impulse.

Other reasons why the Koran has been misunderstood and misinterpreted

Besides the misunderstanding and misinterpretation owing to Arabism's influence on a number of Muslims, could there be other reasons why the Koran has been misunderstood and misjudged? Gabriel Sawma's book, *The Qur'an: Misinterpreted, Mistranslated and Misread: The Aramaic Translation of the Koran*, provides further reasons and explanations from a different aspect. According to Gabriel Sawma,[11] the inspired verses of Muhammad that were later compiled in the sacred book, the Koran, were not originally recorded in the Arabic language but in *Aramaic*—or more precisely in *Eastern Syriac*, a dialect of Aramaic. In his book, Sawma explains that Classical Arabic is an altered form of the Syro-Aramaic language and—although Arabic was a spoken language—the codices of the koranic verses were originally recorded in Syro-Aramaic because Arabic was very rarely used for writing prior to Islam. Examples of Arabic in written form dated before the seventh century are very uncommon.[12] He also points out

---

10 Luciferic morality is more effective in countries ruled by *sharia*, in comparison with countries like Turkey where Islam is blended with a certain amount of democracy and laicism.

11 Gabriel Sawma is a renowned linguist and theologian.

12 The first recorded text in the Arabic alphabet was written in AD 512. This was a trilingual dedication in Greek, Syriac, and Arabic found at Zabad in Syria.

that no Arabic manuscripts or literature exist that would indicate it had been frequently used for writing until Caliph Utman decided to gather all the codices of the inspired verses and compile them in a book after Muhammad's death. The golden age of the Aramaic—and Syriac—language covers all the fields of study: philosophy, logic, medicine, mathematics, astronomy, alchemy, history, theology, linguistics, and literature. Aramaic, a Semitic language with documents dating from as early as the ninth century BC, was originally the speech of the Aramaeans. Hebrews learned to speak Aramaic when they were in captivity in Babylon. The Aramaic language replaced Hebrew to a large extent after the Babylonian captivity—for example, in the Book of Daniel several chapters were written in Aramaic and Syriac. This continued through the time of Jesus Christ, and it is likely that the language Jesus frequently used was the common Aramaic.

Sawma also points out that, when they attempted to translate the codices (originally inscribed on papyrus, shoulder blades, pieces of wood, stones, and parchments) into Arabic during the initial compilation of the Koran, the scribes faced much difficulty. In seventh-century Arabic, certain vowels, vowel signs, and diacriticals corresponding to Syriac did not exist. For instance, the discovery of koranic manuscripts—known as Sana'a Manuscripts—in Yemen in 1972 was an important development in the study of the Koran, for the Sana'a Manuscripts represented the early form of the Koran and did not have the vowel signs or the diacriticals necessary to render vocalization to the Koran. According to Gabriel's Sawma, the Arabic alphabet developed out of a form of the Aramaic alphabet, which had twenty-two letters. Arab transcribers were faced with the dilemma of having to write their language with twenty-two consonants, meaning they had to write without the dots on top or under the letters. This is why the early manuscripts of the Koran did not have diacritics or vowel signs. Sawma also indicates that the process of transcribing the modern Koran from the early manuscripts resulted in numerous scribal errors, which later caused the misreading and misinterpretation of the verses. In his book, Sawma analyzes many verses in light of the Aramaic language and deals with several erroneous interpretations given by present-day Muslim commentators on the Koran and the consequences of those erroneous interpretations. Below is an excerpt from Sawma's book:

> There is nowhere in the history of religion that a religious book is misunderstood by its followers as the Qur'an is.... Muslim commentators do not possess the necessary qualifications that are necessary to render correct interpretation, because they do not speak, read or write Aramaic or Syriac (or any of its dialects). Without such knowledge, the Qur'an could never be understood.... Erroneous interpretations of the Qur'an have resulted in the appearance of extreme ideologies that do not represent the true meaning of the text. The suicide bomber whose mission is to kill people so that they may go to heaven to meet virgins is absolutely erroneous. The Qur'an does not say so; it is the Muslim commentators who misunderstood the Aramaic language of the Qur'an that made them render such false interpretation. For example, the Qur'anic verse 44:55 does not tell the believers of Islam that they will be joined in heaven with "fair maidens, having wide beautiful eyes" as interpreted by Muslim commentators.[13]

After going into detailed linguistic explanations, Sawma gives the correct translation (from Syriac) of this verse:

> 44:55–56 In their dwelling place (spring of water), we have provided them with zugo—i.e., white raisins. In that dwelling place (water spring), they will eat all kinds of fruits.

Apparently, this verse does not say "fair maidens," but only speaks of fruits like white raisins. As we recall, suicide bombers are confident that if they wage jihad on non-Muslims (or to the so-called enemies of Islam) and die for their cause, their reward will be a secure place in Allah's Paradise where virginal maidens wait for them. But when we consider Sawma's explanations, it becomes apparent that suicide bombers, who believe they will go directly to Paradise, are seriously deluded.

---

13   Sawma, *The Qur'an*, pp. 18–20. One translation of 44:51–54 reads: "Indeed, the righteous will be in a secure place; within gardens and springs, wearing fine silk and brocade, facing each other thus. And We will marry them to fair women with large eyes."

It makes one wonder if these suicide bombers knew the correct meaning of this particular verse, would they still volunteer for such a fate?

Sawma is not the only scholar who claims that the Koran's original language is Syro-Aramaic. A book written by Christoph Luxenberg titled *The Syro-Aramaic Reading of the Qur'an* also deals with the subject of the Koran's language. Luxenberg's work, based on the earliest copies of the Koran, maintains that parts of Islam's holy book are derived from preexisting Christian Aramaic texts[14] that were misinterpreted by later Islamic scholars who prepared the editions of the Koran commonly read today. Luxenberg argues that many of the difficulties and confusions inherent in the koranic text can be clarified when its close relation to Aramaic is brought to light. Touching upon it only briefly will not do justice to Luxenberg's important work, but it is not within the scope of this book to go into its details. A short excerpt will be sufficient to underline once again the concealed truth that the earliest copies of the Koran were written in Syro-Aramaic during its compilation.

> For more than a millennium Aramaic was the lingua franca in the entire Middle Eastern region before being gradually displaced by Arabic beginning in the seventh century.... The fact, namely, that Syro-Aramaic was the most important written and cultural language in the region in whose sphere the Koran emerged, at a time Arabic was not a written language yet and in which learned Arabs used Aramaic as a written language, suggests that the initiators of the Arabic written language had acquired their knowledge and training in the Syro-Aramaic cultural milieu. When we consider, moreover, that these Arabs were for the most part Christianized and that a large portion of them took part in the Christian Syrian liturgy, then nothing would be more obvious than that they would have naturally introduced elements of their Syro-Aramaic cult and cultural language into Arabic. To indicate the extent to which this is the case in the Koran is the task this study has set for itself. The samples contained herein may be considered as a representative of a particularly attainable

---

14 Christian Aramaic texts: the Aramaic texts of the Koran that Christianized Arabs wrote.

deciphering—via Syro-Aramaic (that is, Syriac and in part other Aramaic dialects)—of the language of the Koran.[15]

Besides conveying the results of his own study and investigation, Luxenberg delves into seven other scholars' research concerning Aramaic influences on the Arabic language and on the language of the Koran, and he also gives explanations about the content of their books and how their work relates to one another. When one considers all the intricate and substantial clarifications presented by Luxenberg and these scholars, one realizes that the reason for the many contradictions in the Koran—impeding one from achieving a clear understanding of its content—and why present-day translators of the Koran are often faced with various possibilities of interpreting a certain word and end up with different renderings[16] is because the original language of the Koran was not Arabic but Syro-Aramaic. This situation inevitably gave way to much confusion. As a result of mistranslations, the meanings of the verses differed and were distorted to a great extent. Consequently, Muslim scholars and commentators on the Koran later made many wrong interpretations since they had relied on these wrongly translated verses. Most crucial and important of all, these mistranslated verses have been permanently placed in the canonical Koran, and, generation after generation, they have continued to cause confusion and have negatively influenced a number of Muslims. Lately, the results of this negative influence has been hostility, violence, and terrorist attacks of extremist, radical, and jihadist Muslims. However, since Muslims believe that all koranic verses in their present form are Allah's words delivered in Arabic, we can deduce they will not consider revising and making certain fundamental alterations to the Koran by taking into consideration the results of the objective research carried out on its language. Still, many Muslims have consciously ignored the negativism inherent in certain verses and are good-willed, friendly, and gentle, and we embrace them as our

---

15 Luxenberg, *The Syro-Aramaic Reading of the Koran*, pp. 9–11; Luxenberg is a German scholar of ancient Semitic languages.

16 Recall the example given in the footnote on page 79, which showed different translator's versions of verse 2:32. Sawma's translation directly from the Aramaic presents an entirely different meaning.

friends. They may or may not know that the reason why some verses radiate negativism is because they have been mistranslated, but their common sense and conscience tell them that to be in a continuous state of hatred and hostility against members of non-Muslim cultures is nonsensical and contradictory to the koranic verses, which instruct them to choose peace and goodness. Maybe non-Muslims and Muslims who are not Islamic theologians will not attempt to alter these mistranslated and misinterpreted verses, but perhaps by discussing their accuracy they may amend them to a certain degree.

Although some Muslims and Christians are able to embrace each other as friends and kin, we shall continue to face certain difficulties and problems that are manifestations of the misinterpreted, mistranslated, and misread Koran. When so many spiritual issues of importance are misunderstood in Islam, it is inevitable that some Muslims drift away from spiritual truths. Could luciferic influence exist behind the mistranslation of the Koran? As we recall, Lucifer was closely involved with the Arabs while the Islamic impulse unfolded. Lucifer has a permanent seat in the human astral body, but we might suggest that his help and involvement with the Arabs was misguided. Since Lucifer is a fallen and retrogressive spiritual being, should we expect that he arranged his help rightfully—that is, in a way that would be in harmony with the intentions of the divine–spiritual hierarchy? Actually, he was a retarded spiritual being, thus an unavoidable quality of imperfection and deficiency was inherent in the help he gave. For this reason, it was not possible for him to perform his task in an optimum way and achieve a result that did not deviate from the intrinsic *truth* of the divine realm. In contradistinction to this, when we consider the immensity of the Deed of Christ, it can definitely be stated that Christ conducted his cosmic mission immaculately. The same cannot be said about Lucifer's help; Lucifer's involvement meant that inevitably some untruth, deficiency, and deceit had to show up somewhere in the intricate event of the Islamic impulse. Remember, Lucifer is able to influence a person's astral body directly, and we can perceive how a certain degree of luciferic tampering took place in how the verses were mistranslated and placed in the Koran, and how they have been misread and misunderstood. On the other hand, it is not difficult to see that if the beings of the divine–spiritual hierarchy wanted to achieve a faultless result, they would have taken other measures to ensure this. Thus, it would not be wrong to state that the Islamic impulse had to unfold in this particular way, and the divine realm anticipated that Lucifer's help would bring such consequences. We might ask: Would it not have been better for humanity and human evolution if the divine–spiritual beings had directly implemented the Islamic impulse themselves instead of allocating this task to Lucifer, so that it was handled in an immaculate way? There is no doubt that beings of the divine realm could have achieved an immaculate result, but whether their involvement would have been much better for humanity and human evolution is debatable. If we look at the emergence of the Islamic impulse from the perspective of cosmic processes—and also remember that Lucifer became a fallen angel as a result of the sacrifice he made in the Old Moon stage of human evolution—we see that his involvement was going to change him considerably during his process of conversion. On the other hand, continuation of his role as the tempter of human beings and as an intermediary between the divine realm and adverse beings like Ahriman was still necessary in the long run. As mentioned in a former section, nearly six hundred years after having inaugurated the Christ impulse, it was not possible for the beings of the divine–spiritual hierarchy to revert back to using forces related to the Moon sphere. Therefore, Lucifer—who was still connected to the Moon sphere—was more suitable for this task than those in the divine realm.

Influence of apocryphal gospels on koranic verses and Islam: The influence of folk souls

Since Lucifer and the Islamic impulse are closely connected, we may detect some traces of luciferic influence in the koranic verses also. When we study the Koran, we might be surprised to come across two of Jesus' miracles that none of the canonical Gospels mention, and we might wonder if the writers of the Gospels forgot to do so. The way these two koranic verses are composed gives the impression that Jesus performed them as an adult. But according to the original source, the first miracle took place when Jesus was yet a baby in the cradle and the other one when he was a child. When we recall that Christ's ministry began when Jesus was thirty years old and he had not performed any miracles until that age,[17] we might be curious to know why this source reports these miracles as if baby Jesus and child Jesus performed them. First, however, let us see how they are written in the koranic verses:

> 19:29–34 She [Mary] made a sign to them, pointing to the baby. They said: "How can we talk to one who is a child in the cradle?" Whereupon he [baby Jesus] spoke and said: "I am indeed a servant of Allah. He has given me the Gospel and made me a prophet. And his blessing is upon me wherever I go, and he had commanded me to be steadfast on prayer and give alms to the poor as long as I live; He [Allah] hath made me kind to my mother, and not overbearing or miserable. So peace be on me the day I was born, the day that I die, and the day I shall be raised up to life." Such was Jesus, son of Mary; it is a statement of truth, about which they vainly dispute. [Or, that is the whole truth, which they are unwilling to accept.]

> 3:49 And appoint him [Jesus] an apostle to the children of Israel (with this message): "I bring you a sign from your Lord. From clay I will make for you the likeness of a bird. I shall breathe into it, and it shall become a living bird by Allah's leave."

Considering 3:49, the way it is written in this koranic verse leaves no doubt that Jesus performed this miracle as an adult. Why do these unusual verses about Jesus and Christianity exist in the Koran? The answer to this puzzle can be found in an apocryphal Gospel called "The First Gospel of the Infancy of Jesus Christ," which probably dates back to the second century and is believed to be written by Thomas the Israelite Philosopher. This Gospel is also known by the name "Arabic Gospel of the Infancy of the Savior." This apocryphal Gospel narrated fictitious incidents from the childhood of Jesus and was read by Christianized Arabs and Nestorian Christians. Arabs who had become Muslims in the seventh century also knew of its existence. In the book *The Lost Books of the Bible and Forgotten Books of Eden*, which analyzes some of the existing apocryphal Gospels, it is stated:

---

17 As we recall, Jesus started performing miracles only after the baptism in the Jordan River—that is, after the Christ-being incarnated in the physical body of Jesus, and he was not supposed to show any miracles prior to this event.

"A Mohammedan divine Ahmet Ebu Idris says, 'This Gospel [of the Infancy of Jesus Christ] was used by some Christians in common with the other four [canonical] Gospels.... Therefore, it has been supposed that Muhammad and his successors used it in compiling the Koran.'"

The following represent two miracles from the "First Gospel of the Infancy of Jesus Christ" that correspond to the miracles mentioned in the koranic verses 19:29–34 and 3:49:

> The following accounts we found in the book of Joseph the high priest, called by some "Caiaphas." He relates that Jesus spoke even when he was in the cradle, and said to his mother: "Mary, I am Jesus the Son of God, that word which thou didst bring forth according to the declaration of the angel Gabriel to thee, and my father hath sent me for the salvation of the world."
>
> Then he [child Jesus] took from the bank of the stream some soft clay, and formed out of it twelve sparrows; and there were other boys playing with him. Then Jesus, clapping the palms of his hands, called the sparrows, and said to them: "Go fly away; and while ye live remember me." So the sparrows fled away making a noise. (1:1–9)

Apparently, the koranic verses in which Jesus spoke as a baby in the cradle and made a bird figure from clay and gave life to it by leave of Allah were inspired by the apocryphal "First Gospel of the Infancy of Jesus Christ," written long before the emergence of Islam. What Ahmet Ebu Idris had stated was indeed true; evidently, Muslims—who had a close relationship with Christianized Arabs—had used the apocryphal "Arabic Gospel of the Infancy of the Savior." Accordingly, when we bear in mind the Islamic belief that all koranic verses originated from Allah and were transmitted by Gabriel, then these verses should in no way exist in the Koran. Therefore, we may suggest that, tempted by Lucifer, one of the early caliphs of Islam might have ordered the scribes to insert these and maybe even other verses into the Koran when they made copies at a later time. Actually, it is a known fact that Caliph Utman gathered the earliest copies of the Koran and ordered that new copies be written. [18]

---

18 The earliest Korans were compiled by gathering verses written on various materials and from a few Muslims who had memorized them. They were then sent to centers such as Jerusalem and Damascus and gathered later by Utman, who ordered new copies to be written. This shows that the present

Clearly, these explanations do not intend to criticize the Koran or to find fault in it. Muslims proudly insist that Allah inspired every single koranic verse and that Gabriel transmitted them directly to the Prophet. However, the existence of these verses—undeniably inspired by an apocryphal Gospel that was in existence at the birth of Islam—suggests that other verses have been inserted into the Koran by people who had recompiled or made copies of it after the Prophet's lifetime. Therefore, these verses, disguised as original verses, infiltrated the Koran under luciferic influences. Bearing in mind that one of Lucifer's chief characteristics is deception, we can surmise that the caliphs and transcribers of the Koran must have been enticed by Lucifer and took the liberty of inserting these verses into the Koran. (In a later section, we will touch upon a certain claim, or rumor, concerning the Prophet that suggests how "the devil" intervened while the Prophet was receiving certain inspired verses.) Gabriel Sawma reveals an example of tampering with the koranic verses that took place at a later time:

> According to Arab historians, the Calipha "umar bin al-Khattab, after the death of the Prophet, personally went to the city of Jerusalem to receive its submission. The [al-Aqsa] mosque was built during the reign of Calipha al-Walid...i.e., more than seventy years after the death of the Prophet, which indicates that the verse did not exist before the construction of al-Aqsa Mosque.... Critics say that someone must have added this verse to the Qur'an.[19]

If luciferic influences were only effective on the Koran and Islamic teachings, it would have been easier to avert them, but in our encounters with radical and extremist Muslims we cannot avoid facing certain unpleasant manifestations of luciferic influences. In the conduct of extremist and jihadist Muslims we are not only facing the reverberations of luciferic influences but also the ahrimanic influences that enter our dimension via the portal opened by Lucifer—that is, when their haughty convictions and prejudices, blended with hatred and

---

Koran has a "terrestrial" history (in contrast to Muslims' claim that it is the result of being transferred directly from Allah.) This also means that the "human factor" is inherent in the present Koran, and the human factor connotes luciferic influences.

19 Sawma, *The Qur'an,* p. 92.

rage, are transformed into hostility, terrorism, and jihads, then we are also witnessing the ahrimanic influences that manifest in the personality and deeds of these Muslims. Valentin Tomberg spoke of Ahriman's interference on the evolution and affairs of humankind: "If it were not for Lucifer's shadow, Ahriman would have been unable to interfere in evolution; he would have always been eclipsed and dazzled by the light of the hierarchies."[20]

We may suggest that initially the Islamic impulse had been permeated by luciferic influences, but as time went by ahrimanic influences also took effect on this monotheistic Moon religion. Consequently, a certain part of Islam began to provide an entrance for ahrimanic interferences. This is probably why the world has faced hostile Muslims, Islamic terrorism, and fanatic jihadists in recent years.

Folk spirits have been continuously effective on certain groups of Muslims, also. As we recall, every tribe and nation has a folk spirit that induces certain influences on that tribe or nation. As there are progressive folk spirits that guide humans in accordance with the goals of human evolution, there are also retrogressive folk spirits who influence the people or nation they lead in accordance with their "fallen nature." When we bear in mind that Islam—in its present state[21]—is not progressing in harmony with the Christ impulse, and when we also observe how Islamic understanding manifests (for example, in the implementation of inhumane *sharia* laws like lapidation, flogging, and mutilation of certain parts of the body), we can state that certain peoples of the Islamic world are influenced by retrogressive folk spirits. Since folk spirits are beings behind a large or small group of people, they can be influential on the group souls of people. For example, when a crowd of Muslims gathers to stone a woman to death, their individual states of consciousness and conscience are, as it were, eclipsed, and they are acting as a group soul with diminished consciousness and conscience. The driving force of any group soul is the folk spirit who influences that group from the background. But it

---

20 Tomberg, *Christ and Sophia*, "The Spiritual Triumph of Jacob," p. 43.

21 Today, Muslims who belong to different sects have become relentless enemies of each other, as witnessed in the Middle East, and have been killing members of other Islamic sects and even non-Islamic people.

must be emphasized that the more people of a certain tribe or nation are individualized and acquire a developed individual "I," the more such persons act according to their own free will and transcend the guidance they receive while they belonged to the group soul. This is precisely the freedom—freedom from having to belong to the group soul—provided by the Christ impulse. Islamic teachings—especially those that are misinterpreted and misunderstood—can hinder the development of the individual "I" of its members and leave them prone to the influences of retarded folk souls. To be able to make the transition from belonging to a group soul to being an individual who has independently developed thinking, feeling, and will, it is necessary that Muslims open themselves to the influences that emanate from the Christ impulse. Reflecting on Islamic terrorism, perverted and inhumane deeds of jihadists, and the brutal aspects of Islamic *sharia*, we may suggest that, at present, luciferic and ahrimanic influences and the influences of folk spirits are somehow blended and have a combined effect on certain members of Islam.

Is Islam related to Christ in any way?

In what way do Muslims understand and evaluate the Christ[22] and is Islam related to him in any way? The answer to this question is quite simple and straightforward. Since Muslims have always denied the concept of the Holy Trinity, there is no place for the concept of the Son–God (the Cosmic Christ) or for his true representative—the Christ-being (the Sun God) in Islam. Therefore, a concept of Christ as an exalted divine–spiritual being does not exist in the Islamic teachings or belief system; Allah is the only deity who is recognized as God and is acknowledged to be the creator who encompasses the universe, the Earth, and all the beings that live on Earth. As far as Muslims are concerned, there is only one God and that is Allah. The *azan* trumpets this Islamic belief five times a day. This is why it was previously said that "the impartiality of the meaning of *azan* is disputable, for it has a more serious connotation than we imagine." The following

---

22 Christ, in the sense that—as the second divine person of the Holy Trinity—he is the Son of God, bringer of the Christ impulse, and the redeemer of humanity.

excerpt from one of Steiner's lectures gives us a better idea about how Islam is related to Christ:

> [John the Apocalyptist's] prophetic glance now fell on the teachings that were coming into being around the year 666 and that harked back to the mysteries that knew nothing of the Son—the Muslim teachings. Muslim teachings do not know the structure of the world I have just been speaking of; they do not know the two realms—that of the Father and that of the Spirit; they know only the Father. They know only the rigid doctrine, "There is one God, Allah, and none besides him, and Muhammad is his Prophet." From this perspective, the teachings of Muhammad are the strongest polarity to Christianity, for the will to do away with all freedom forever is in them, the will to bring about determinism, for nothing else is possible if you can imagine the world solely in the sense of the Father–God.[23]

As indicated by Steiner, Muslims speak of a single God, but it is necessary to emphasize that when Muslims refer to God, they never mean the Father–God, who is the first person of the Holy Trinity. The concept of a Father–God, who has seen the necessity of a radical change in the universe and has made incredible cosmic preparations so that the Son–God (who is the representative of new cosmic principles) would succeed him in the far future, is beyond their comprehension. Nevertheless, Muslims do have a certain concept of an almighty God, but their understanding only encompasses Allah—as noted, the Arab equivalent of the Hebrew God Yahweh, transformed into the God of Islam and Muslims. As elucidated by anthroposophic wisdom, Yahweh was one of the seven Elohim, who are from the second hierarchy and are the true revealers of the Eternal Son. Muslims are not cognizant of the fact that Yahweh—whom they got to know as Allah—is one of the seven Elohim; they regard him as the one and only God of the universe, and proclaim that there is no other divinity besides him. This belief is not open to discussion. Consequentially, there is no mention of the other six Elohim or the other Form Spirits from the ranks of the Exousiai in the Koran. Thus, because of their

---

23 Steiner, *The Book of Revelation*, lecture 7, p. 102.

strong denial and rejection of the Holy Trinity, Arabs' comprehension of an almighty God has not been able to reach as far as the Father–God of the Holy Trinity.

Why do Muslims believe that Allah is the one and only God in the universe? Long before the emergence of Islam, Yahweh's mission was to prepare the Hebrews for the Advent of Christ. During this long preparatory period—a transitory period—Yahweh had to assume the role of an omnipotent Father–God. This was necessary because absolute obedience had to be expected of the Hebrews. To be able to achieve this, a vivid image of an omnipotent God (a Father–God) had to be perpetually reflected onto them. Otherwise, it would not have been easy to establish and implement the strict spiritual discipline that was necessary throughout "forty-two generations" to prepare the physical body of Jesus. For instance, only the figure of an omnipotent Father–God—whom they feared—could have commanded Hebrews to circumcise generations of males. Circumcision and several other strict disciplines found in the Talmudian law were the reasons that Hebrews perceived Yahweh as an omnipotent Father–God who created humankind, the Earth, and the universe. Later, Muhammad came with his inspired messages and began to influence the Arabs. Among the messages he proclaimed, the most effective one was: Abraham is also the ancestral father of the Arab tribes, and his God, omnipotent Yahweh (presented as Allah), is now calling Arabs to believe in him and to surrender to him. Since Muhammad's inspired verses emphasized that these messages came directly from Allah, as a result of his call—and after many battles—Arabs finally acknowledged Allah. As a result, *he also became the omnipotent God of Muslims.* But since what Muslims knew about Yahweh fundamentally came from Judaism, they never had the chance to realize that Yahweh was not "the omnipotent Father–God of the universe." Thus, Muslims have always associated the image of the omnipotent God, who is the creator of everything, only with Allah. The concept of an omnipotent God—Allah—is at the foundation of their uncompromising monotheistic religion. As mentioned earlier, throughout the Koran Yahweh is never referred as *Yahweh* or *Jehovah*. Even in the verses, which refer to the former relationship of Yahweh and the Hebrews, his name is always *Allah*.

Accordingly, although the archangel Michael—formerly the countenance of Yahweh—had been associated with Yahweh for several centuries, his name is only mentioned once in the Koran.[24] Apart from this, there is no indication concerning Archangel Michael's connection with humanity.[25] Islamic teachings have also bypassed the important fact that, when the Mystery of Golgotha began to unfold, Michael became the countenance of Christ. The profound fact—and its implications—that Michael began working as the spiritual regent of our time in the year 1879 has eluded Islamic teachings.

Consequences of the reappearance of Abraham's monotheistic faith

Abraham's monotheistic faith reappeared as a result of the Islamic impulse, but now in a different form. This time, descendants of Ishmael became adherents of the new religion. However, there were some consequences of the reappearance of Abraham's faith as a new monotheistic religion six hundred years after the Advent of Christ and the Christ impulse. As we recall, the universe prior to the Earth stage of evolution was a universe of wisdom, and the ruling power in this universe was the omnipotent Father–God. The divine beings of the spiritual hierarchy had inspired evolution up to the Earth stage in accordance with this former principle that was prevalent in the universe. But the divine–spiritual beings had actually intended to create a new universe that was to be governed by new principles, and, to this end, it was necessary that this former principle—which was previously an integral part of the quintessence of the earlier universe—was transformed into something totally new. The new principles of the future universe were *freedom* and *love*. Accordingly, from the Earth

---

24 Verse 2:98 "Whoever is an enemy of Allah, His Angels, or His apostles, or of Gabriel or Michael, shall make Allah himself his enemy: Allah is the enemy of the unbelievers."

25 Steiner indicates, "When the middle of the nineteenth century had not yet quite been reached, in fact more or less at the beginning of the 1840s, a certain spiritual being...[the Archangel Michael] prepared himself to evolve gradually from an archangel to a Time Spirit to undergo an evolution that would enable him to work into human life, not merely from the superearthly point of view, but directly from the earthly standpoint" (*The Archangel Michael*, p. 80).

stage onward, the Christ, as the true representative of the Eternal Son, was to give a new direction to human evolution by incorporating the new principles of freedom and love.[26]

Yahweh, who had worked closely with the other six Elohim up to the Hyperborean stage of the Earth evolution, did not proceed with the other six Elohim to the Sun sphere. In accordance with the requirements of his mission he had to stay connected to the Earth in the Moon sphere. It was Yahweh's mission to train the Hebrews as a group soul and prepare them throughout the centuries for the future event of Christ's advent. Besides his "external" relationship with the Hebrews, his multidimensional arrangements were also effective in the background and were preparing them for the arrival of the Christ and the Christ impulse, which was to bring about the individualization of the "I"—as opposed to remaining in a group soul imprisoned under the "law." The new law—contrary to Islamic *sharia* law, which hinders the development of the essence of a free human "I"—was *"no law."* Valentin Tomberg writes:

> The theme of the Old Testament is the preparation and realization of the advent of Christ in the human body; that of the New Testament is the advent of Christ in the human "I." The "new law" is, in fact, no law, but the formation of the essence of a free human "I." This cannot happen unless the human "I" absorbs the being that is the "new law." This absorption must involve something that does not arise externally, but that comes from the depths of the world in which the human "I" is rooted. A plant receives its sap from the soil in which it is rooted, and likewise the being of the Christ impulse should enter the human "I" from the "soil" in which the "I" is rooted.[27]

The Christ-being brought the Christ impulse to the world to implant the relevant seeds of this "cosmic transformation" into the Earth stage of evolution; Earth had been interconnected with this cosmic transformation from the very beginning of human creation. Thus,

---

26 Among other significant factors inherent in it, freedom, love, and forgiveness were the main principles that formed the core of the Christ impulse.

27 Tomberg, *Christ and Sophia*, "Pentecost as the Realization of the New Testament," p. 308.

the Christ impulse is a spiritual force that is in accordance with the necessities of the phenomenal change that is taking place in the universe. For this reason, the principle of worshipping a single God—and the figure of an almighty God—upon which monotheism is founded is no longer in harmony with the Christ impulse and with these crucial cosmic changes. From the point of view of the ongoing cosmic processes, adhering to the concept of monotheism would only bring about deterioration and regression. Therefore, as long as Muslims cling to a belief solely based on the one-and-only omnipotent God doctrine, they will be held back from comprehending the truth of the Son–God (the Christ-being), as well as the truth of Yahweh. Rigid adherence to the monotheistic Father–God principle means that their gaze is—as it were—directed toward the former structure of the universe in which the Father–God's role was prominent and the Son–God was not yet in the foreground. In other words, having their gaze fixed on the past stage of evolution precludes them from comprehending the fact that as of the First Coming of Christ, Earth has become the Son–God's sphere of action. However, Muslims' irrevocable convictions deprive them of receiving the divine light of the Son–God.

As a result of rejecting the Christ and the impulse he brought to the world, the reemerged form of Yahweh's Moon religion bypassed the Christ impulse, and—in a way—reverted to the past stage of evolution that was supposed to be left behind. Divine–spiritual beings had not intended to revive and bring back this past phase of evolution by inaugurating the Islamic impulse. Their original purpose was to transform the former principles governing the universe into new principles. Therefore, Islam was the inevitable outcome of an extraordinary measure that they had to implement to resolve the unavoidable crisis of Sorath's intervention.

Why are adherents of the reemerged Moon religion of Islam so strongly inclined to turn their gaze to the past stage of the evolution? Why do they reject the Christ impulse? The reason for this will become more apparent when we recall that Lucifer's involvement was required to be able to solve the crisis of Sorath's intervention. Since Lucifer was a fallen spiritual being who had remained in a past stage of his evolution, his involvement meant that through him certain influences from the past stage of evolution would inevitably infiltrate the Islamic impulse. Thus, a significant consequence of this extraordinary measure (the Islamic impulse) was that under the retarding and hindering luciferic influences adherents of the revived Moon religion of Yahweh were not able to recognize and understand the Christ and the Christ impulse. Rudolf Steiner spoke of this matter in one of his lectures: "The people of Europe were well aware that no concept of the Christ could come from the Arabs. If they had anything to say, their ideas would not accord with the true Christ idea."[28] Upon reading verse 5:110, it becomes clear that Steiner's statement conveys the truth:

> 5:110 Allah will say: "Jesus son of Mary, remember the favor I have bestowed on you and on your mother: how I strengthened you with the Holy Spirit [correct rendering: Gabriel or Ruh-ul Kudus], so that you preached to men in your cradle and in the prime of manhood; how I instructed you in the Scriptures and in wisdom, in the Torah and in the Gospel; how by My leave you fashioned from clay the likeness of a bird and breathed into it so that, by My leave, it became a living bird; how, by my leave, you healed the blind man and the leper, and by My leave restored the dead to life; how I protected you from the Israelites when you brought them veritable signs: when the unbelievers among them said: 'This is nothing but plain magic'; how when I enjoined the disciples to believe in Me and my apostle they replied: 'We believe; bear witness that we submit to you [to Allah] utterly.'"

The first part of this verse is intended to form a persuading association between Allah and Jesus, but this message (Jesus making birds out of clay) actually refers to the false information that came from the aforementioned apocryphal Gospel. The statement "how I protected you from the Israelites" refers to the Islamic belief that Jesus was not crucified by the Jews, for Allah protected him from this fate.[29] In the latter part of the verse, Jesus is depicted as a prophet who was struggling to persuade the Jews to believe in Allah, as if the Hebrews were insistently denying Yahweh (as the Arab unbelievers had firmly denied

---

28   Steiner, *Excursus on the Gospel according to St. Mark*, lecture 7.
29   This message is found in verse 4:157 and shall be discussed in a later section.

Allah). The way this verse is composed gives the impression that upon seeing that Jesus was having difficulties in persuading the Jews, Allah commanded the disciples to believe in him and in Jesus. The disciples took heed of Allah's command and announced that they do believe and submitted to Allah—they became Muslim. In comparison with the image of Jesus Christ radiating from the Gospel, how different and distorted is the image of the Jesus depicted in this and many other koranic verses. It is not hard to see that this was one of those verses formulated with the hope that it might help Muhammad while he was struggling to persuade Arabs to believe in Allah. Thus, in this verse it is apparent that "when Arabs did say anything, the ideas put forward were incompatible with the true Christ idea." This was one of the most significant consequences of the reappearance of Abraham's monotheistic faith in the form of the Islamic religion.

Why is the Antichrist (Dajjal) *mentioned in Islam?*

What does Islam have to say about the Antichrist?[30] That is to say, does the Antichrist really have a place in Islamic teachings? An analysis of Islamic teachings reveals the Antichrist does not belong to Islamic teachings and, therefore, it is not a subject that has any importance in Islam. No true information concerning the Antichrist can be found in the fundamental Islamic teachings. Accordingly, the Antichrist (*dajjal*) is not a topic that has a place in Muslims' general religious understanding, and few have any idea about what the name *dajjal* really signifies. Rarely, an *imam*, or scholar, may speak about the *dajjal* in his talk, trying to relate it to the Antichrist. Upon hearing certain comments made by the imam (who is actually an Islamic preacher),[31] one may assume that the Koran must refer to the Antichrist and that Muslims are familiar with a similar kind of information to that

---

30 In Arabic, the word that approximately corresponds to Antichrist is the *dajjal*, or the false messiah, *Masih ad-Dajjal*.

31 Every imam is not properly informed about the subject of the Antichrist in the sense it is known in Christianity. Even if some are familiar with the word *Antichrist* (*dajjal*), they often confuse it with the "devil." Only those who have had some connection with the Christian world might have something to say about the Antichrist, but this will nevertheless reflect only their own Islamic interpretation of the Antichrist.

originally found in St. John's Apocalypse. But throughout the Koran, there is no mention of *dajjal*. If the Antichrist does not show up in the Koran, from where did Muslims get this information? Actually, the Islamic understanding of *dajjal* is somewhat comparable to the figures of Armilus (the anti-Messiah figure) and the Antichrist in Jewish and Christian eschatology, respectively. However, Muslim scholars and imams claim that their information comes from the *hadith*—revered sayings of the Prophet Muhammad. So, let us delve into the etymological meaning of *dajjal* to find out how this Arabic word has become the term that corresponds to the Antichrist. This may also help us understand whether the *hadith* that refer to *dajjal* are authentic or not.

Prior to its use as a name, which somewhat corresponds to the Antichrist or Armilus, *dajjal* was not used as a name. Before Muslims began to use it in this way, this word connoted "deceiving." In Arabic, *dajjal* was used in the sense of covering something—that is, to plate something (for example, an ordinary metal) with silver or gold. Also, traders used to smear tar over a camel's skin so that it covered a skin disease before it was taken to the bazaar to be sold; this was regarded as an act of "deceiving." So, since the word *dajjal* was associated with deceiving, and since Arabs had learned from Christians that the Antichrist was a "deceiver," Muslim scholars and interpreters of the Koran began to use it as a name. As a result, *dajjal* became the suitable word that corresponds to the Antichrist. It is believed, according to one of his *hadith* that Muhammad had said, the "*dajjal* will be the last of the series of 'thirty *dajjal*,' or 'deceivers,'" which means: "The *dajjal* that comes in the future will be the last of the series of false prophets."

Muslims have also heard that, when he comes, the Antichrist will be a false prophet. There are some vivid Islamic descriptions of the *dajjal*. For instance, according to some *hadith,* when Ali (Muhammad's nephew who also became his son-in-law) referred to *dajjal*, he was reported to have said that the color of his skin will be reddish-white. His forehead will be prominent and neck would be wide, and he will be powerfully built. His right eye will be blind (bulging out), and his left eye would be raised to his forehead and will be sparkling like a star. Only the believers will be able to read the word *Kufr* (disbelief), inscribed in bold letters, on his forehead. There will be big mountains of smoke at both front and backsides of his caravan. He will be riding on a huge white colored "donkey" that will cover a mile in a single stride. All rivers, falling in his way, will become dry and he will call upon people in a loud voice, "O my friends come to me! I am your lord who has made your limbs and given you sustenance."

As can be seen, this exaggerated depiction of *dajjal* reveals that he is a gruesome being and, as a false prophet, he is potentially dangerous, for he will attempt to lure and persuade people to believe in him. Apparently, the idea of the *"beast"* found in this superficial depiction of *dajjal* has been inspired from the depictions of the beast found in St. John's Revelations, especially in chapters 14 to 17. In contrast, St. John's words are not just superficial descriptions; many significant and profound meanings are inherent in them. So, we can see that the *hadith* can contain inaccurate information and thus are not reliable. Throughout the centuries after Islam was founded, the *hadith* have been used as a reference and guide along with the Koran. However, thousands of *hadith* exist, and any conscious Muslim learned-man and well-educated scholar surely knows that the majority of these *hadith* are fallacious and unreliable. Although some original *hadith* surely exist, it is very likely that there are also several false *hadith* that are claimed to have been uttered by the Prophet. It is likely also that some of Muhammad's sayings must have been distorted during the span of approximately 1,400 years. In a way, the content of some of the *hadith* can be likened to the twisted information found in the apocryphal Gospels. For instance, when we recall that Jesus had supposedly performed many miracles as a child in the apocryphal *First Gospel of the Childhood of Jesus,* and how these false stories influenced early Christians and made false impressions on them concerning the child Jesus, we can imagine how false *hadith* have been influential on Muslims throughout the centuries.

Although the church fathers meticulously examined all existing Gospels and only selected the four canonical Gospels while they were compiling the New Testament, caliphs (leaders of Islam after Muhammad) and Muslim scholars—and even Islamic scholars—have never done such a necessary culling of the *hadith*. In fact, as we look into the content of some of them, it becomes apparent that many appeared after the Prophet, and this is one of the reasons why many are distorted and untrue. All the *hadith* that refer to the Antichrist belong in the category of fallacious *hadith*. This can be said without any doubt whatsoever, because to be able to assert anything about the Antichrist in the first place, *there ought to be an indication about the true Christ in the Koran.* Since the name *Christ* or any concept pertaining to Christ does not exist in the koranic verses, we can rightfully conclude that the Prophet never uttered anything concerning the Christ and could not have possibly mentioned anything about the Antichrist in his sayings (*hadith*) either. As far as we can understand from the koranic verses, Muhammad's authority was well defined by Allah, and his task was not to contribute complementary sayings to compensate for that which is lacking in the koranic verses.

From the Islamic point of view, nothing is lacking in the Koran, so it is unthinkable and unacceptable that someone other than Allah would convey guidelines that should be taken into consideration along with Allah's guidelines. Thus, it is not likely that Muhammad proclaimed such *hadith* concerning the Antichrist. We can conclude that since no information concerning the Antichrist (*dajjal*) exists in the Koran, all information concerning the Antichrist must have entered Islamic teachings at a much later time, and that Muslims must have initially acquired this information from the Christians who were neighbors of Arab tribes. Also, we can surmise that certain *hadith* referring to the Antichrist must have been incorporated into the Prophet's sayings by multiple Muslim scholars, for when we examine the content of these *hadith*, they reflect the different personal sympathies, antipathies, and religious convictions of varied persons. The existence and the content of such fallacious *hadith* about the Antichrist also show that Muslims have never developed any true concept of the Christ or Jesus, and accordingly they have created an Islamized idea of the Antichrist. So it can be stated that *dajjal* is a kind of imaginary, Islamized Antichrist.

How do Muslims interpret the Second Coming of Christ?

In Islam, an apparent confusion and wrong interpretation exists concerning the Second Coming of Christ. As a matter of fact, when we probe the Koran we find no mention whatsoever of Christ's Second

Coming. On the other hand, according to some *hadith*, Jesus—*not Christ, but only Jesus*—will come again to the world, this time to establish his sovereignty. Muslims who rely on these *hadith* assume that Jesus will come to the world again in a physical body. Bearing this in mind, let us examine how some Muslims conceive and interpret the event of the Second Coming (in relation to the *dajjal*).

Jesus will descend on Mount Afeeq, on the white eastern minaret of Damascus. He will descend during morning prayer, and the leader of the Muslims will address him thus: O Prophet of God, lead the prayer. Jesus will decline with these words: The virtue of this nation that follows Islam is that they lead each other—implying that he will pray behind the imam (the man who leads the prayer), just as the word of God was completed after revelation of the Koran and Muhammad as the last prophet of God.

After the prayer, Jesus will prepare himself to do battle and shall take up a spear. An army shall return from a campaign launched before his arrival. *Dajjal* will lose the battle and retreat to Israel.[32] Jesus shall set out in pursuit of the *dajjal*. All those who embraced the evil of the *dajjal* shall perish even as the breath of Jesus touches them. The breath of Jesus shall precede him as far as the eye can see. The *dajjal* will be captured at Lud. The Antichrist shall begin to melt, as salt dissolves in water. The spear of Jesus shall plunge into the *dajjal*'s chest, ending his dreaded reign. The followers of the *dajjal* will be rooted out, for even the trees and rocks will speak out against them. Jesus will break the cross[33] and kill the pig,[34] which will be an indication that his teaching did not include the legitimacy of these two. Then all battles shall cease and the world will know an age of peace. Truly the sheep will lie in the shadow of the wolf without fear. The

---

32 Some Muslims believe that *dajjal* will initially show up in Israel and then will proceed with his plans to rule the world from Israel.

33 Jesus will make sure that the cross will not be used as the symbol of Christianity anymore; in other words, he will put an end to Christianity.

34 Let us recall verse 5:60, which says: "Shall I tell you who will receive the worst reward from Allah? Those on whom Allah laid His curse and with whom He has been angry, transforming them into apes and swine, and those who worship false gods [like Jesus as the Son of God]. Worse is the plight of these, and they have strayed from the right path."

rule of Jesus will be just, and all shall flock to him to enter the folds of the one true religion, Islam. Jesus will live for forty years among the Muslims, and he will die in Medina. After his funeral *namaz*,[35] Muslims will bury him next to the Prophet Muhammad. During the time he lives, he will adhere to Islamic beliefs and abide Islamic rules. Consequently, Christianity will be wiped off the earth.

We can surmise that such an imaginary prophesy probably came into being by compiling false *hadith*. Apparently, the way Muslims interpret the return of Jesus is peculiar to Islamic teachings. To start with, they presume the one who is coming to the world is Jesus, definitely not the Christ, because—as we recall—Christ does not exist in Islamic teachings. Secondly, in relation to the absence of the concept of Christ as a spiritual being—since the concept of spirit is also lacking in Islam—it is difficult for Muslims to conceive that, in his Second Coming, Christ will manifest in a spiritual form and will be present in the etheric aura of the Earth—that is, his ethereal presence will pervade the Earth. Therefore, besides the fact that the concept of the Etheric Christ is hard to come to terms with, even the idea that Jesus will return in a physical body to the physical world is acceptable only by a minority, with much reservation and doubt. Furthermore, in this fictional prophesy Jesus is given a role similar to Muhammad's—that is, he will have a sword in his hand and will be involved in battles against the enemy. Moreover, according to this prophesy, besides killing the *dajjal*, Jesus will not hesitate to use his sword to vanquish all his former followers, the Christians, from the Earth.[36]

One may think the accounts conveyed in this Islamic prophesy concerning the fate of Christians and Christianity in relation to the Second Coming of Jesus are only astounding fantasies and no Muslim would take them seriously. But when we recall how radical, fundamentalist, and even conservative Muslims have been seriously claiming "Islam is the last and the most perfect and sacred religion

---

35 The Islamic ritual of prayer performed five times a day to worship Allah, by symbolically prostrating before him.

36 As we recall, according to Koranic verses, Jesus tried to guide the Jews to Allah's straight path and persuade them to surrender to Allah, but he was unsuccessful. Thus, according to the Koran, Christianity was the outcome of a misinterpretation of Allah's messages as proclaimed by Jesus.

in the world, for it was decreed by Allah," it becomes apparent that in accordance with this claim, some Muslims are likely to believe that when Jesus returns to the world, he will put an end to Christianity and annihilate adherents of this religion. Such fantasies might sound implausible, but the image of a Jesus who comes to Earth as an ally of Islam is likely to be taken very seriously by some Muslims, since such claims justify their dogmatic Islamic beliefs. Nonetheless, could it be that this unusual and astonishing Islamic reverie of a Jesus figure who is connected to Islam and Muslims and is henceforth allied with them implies a deep unconscious wish to have a closer relationship with Jesus Christ?

5.

How Is Jesus of Nazareth Conceived in Islam?

Apart from their ideas concerning the Second Coming of the Islamized Jesus, how do Muslims conceive and evaluate Jesus of Nazareth? Are they able to envisage Jesus of Nazareth in the same way as the Gospels depict him? In the Koran, there are many verses that refer to Jesus, but the reason he is mentioned so often is not really clear to most Muslims. Although the koranic verses have simplified the matter of Jesus by presenting him solely as a prophet of Allah, there is an ambiguity about his identity and role as a prophet.

When we analyze the Koran carefully, we notice a significant difference between the Prophet Muhammad and the Prophet Jesus. The Koran explicitly presents Muhammad as the first and the last prophet of Islam, whereas while it acknowledges Jesus as a prophet, *he is never presented as the prophet of Christianity.* This is because, according to Islam, Jesus was a prophet who was trying to deliver Allah's messages to the Jewish people (similar to Muhammad, who was also assigned to deliver Allah's messages), but Jews had misunderstood his messages, and, as a result, some of them became Christians. Since Christianity came into being as a result of this big misunderstanding—and since Allah had not originally intended to found a religion like Christianity—Islamic teachings and Muslims have difficulty approving the existence of the Christian religion and its members. This is basically why Jesus is not presented as the prophet of Christianity in the Koran. In other words, if Jesus was acknowledged as the prophet of Christianity in the Muslims' sacred book, they would have no excuse to deny the existence of Christianity and its holy book, the Gospels. Thus, if Christianity is not supposed to exist as a legitimate religion, then there cannot be a legitimate prophet of this religion either. According to Islam, Jesus was only a prophet sent by Allah—in service of Allah like the other prophets.

One might ask: Were Christians not acknowledged in the Koran as the People of the Book? Doesn't this mean that the Koran accepts their religion? It is true that koranic verses refer to Christians as People of the Book, but this should not be taken as a firm and final confirmation of their religion; it is simply a way of referring to them. If we analyze the Koran carefully, it can be seen that although Jesus was acknowledged as a prophet in the Koran, more emphasis is placed on Abraham, Moses, the Jews, and their monotheistic religion. As a prophet from the lineage of Ishmael, Muhammad sympathized more with Judaism and its holy book, the Old Testament. As far as Abraham was concerned, more than having sympathies, Muhammad venerated him. The fact that Jewish people had a "law" given by Allah contributed to his sympathies. Therefore, the expression *People of the Book* refers more to the Jews, but since those who later become Christians were originally Jews, Christians were also included in this expression.[1]

It is significant that in the Koran no reference is made to the names of the original authors of the Gospels—Matthew, Mark, Luke, and John. Koranic verses indicate that it was Allah who gave the Gospel to Jesus, just as he issued the koranic verses to Muhammad. Therefore, People of the Book could be understood as a group of people who had been given a holy Book by Allah through Jesus. However, this group of people misinterpreted Allah's messages—revealed by Jesus—and ended up becoming Christians, even though Jesus had no role in the founding of this religion. Such inconsistent and contradictory information conveyed by the koranic verses create serious confusion, and consequently Jesus and Christianity become more unintelligible to Muslims. Koranic verses neither identify Jesus with

---

[1] According to Muslims, the reason Allah sent Muhammad to establish the unspoiled religion of Islam was because Allah was not content with the results of Jesus' endeavor to establish the religion he desired. The prevalent idea among Muslim scholars and commentators on Islam is that it was Muhammad who was successful in eventually founding Allah's religion, whereas Jesus had failed.

How Is Jesus of Nazareth Conceived in Islam?

Christianity nor refer to him as the prophet of the Christian religion; furthermore, they try to sever Jesus' connection with Christianity.[2]

As a result of the Koran's deceptive and erroneous portrayal of Jesus, Muslims—who have little idea about the content of the Gospel—know of a totally different Jesus—that is, not the image of Jesus of Nazareth and Jesus Christ emanating from the Gospel, but *an Islamized version of him.* Muhammad's verses do no refer to Christ at all; there is no indication of the name Jesus Christ or Christ Jesus throughout the Koran. Certain verses refer to the Messiah, but since there is no mention of the Christ, there is no connection or association between the Messiah and the Christ.[3] As a result of not having a true concept of Jesus and refuting the truth pertaining to Jesus Christ, Muslims did not have a chance to realize that Jesus was not just a prophet whose mission was to convey a teaching to the Jews, but that *he brought the "spirit of the cosmos" to the world.* Before he came to the world, the human connection with the divine realm was totally severed; he renewed this connection. While everything he uttered was an invaluable teaching and was inscribed in the Gospel, *he himself—his very being—was the living teaching, the living cosmic Word.* This is why his words have been eternally inscribed in the Akasha Chronicle. Muslims also did not comprehend that the Advent of Christ was not a single event that happened once and was then finished. The strength and magnitude of its effects have continued growing ever since he came into the world.

We may encounter some surprising verses in the Koran. Apart from a number, each of the 114 suwar has a name. Strangely, the name of the nineteenth surah is attributed to Mary, the mother of Jesus. However, the name of this surah is not Mary, but *Maryam,* for throughout the Koran Mary's name is always referred to as *Maryam.* In the nineteenth surah, detailed information about Maryam and her family is given. It should not be assumed that this surah is only about Mary; as in other suwar, it broaches a variety of subjects. We might

---

2 Let us recall how—in the aftermath of his battle with *dajjal*—Jesus breaks the cross and wipes out all Christians who insist on adhering to their former Christian beliefs.

3 As previously mentioned, in the Koran the term *Messiah* is used only as an alternative name for Jesus.

wonder why Mary, who actually belongs to the Christian tradition, is written about in Islam's sacred book. Furthermore, the third surah, which is named "The Imrans," is connected with the nineteenth surah in a way, for Mary is also often mentioned in it. These two suwar illustrate Mary's virginal conception of Jesus after her meeting with Gabriel. Apparently, there is no dispute about the exoteric belief of Mary's virginal conception. That is to say, according to the Koran, a physical father had no role in the birth of Jesus.

> 19:19 He [Gabriel] said: "I am only a messenger of thy Lord that I may bestow on thee [Mary] a pure son."
>
> 19:20 She [Mary] said: "How can I have a son when no man has ever touched me, neither have I been unchaste?"
>
> 19:21 He [Gabriel] said: "So (it will be) Thy Lord said: It is easy for Me."
>
> 19:22 And she conceived him [Jesus], and she withdrew with him in a far place.

These verses underscore Mary's virginal conception, but the claim that Jesus had no physical father contradicts the truth regarding the lineages of the Solomon Jesus child and the Nathan Jesus child conveyed in the Gospels Matthew and Luke and the truth imparted by anthroposophic wisdom. Moreover, in some of the verses serious confusion concerning Mary's identity exists. At the foundation of this confusion is the anachronism that in these verses Mary's father is confused with Amran (*Imran*, in Arabic), who was the father of Moses, Aaron, and Miriam (Maryam). Mary, the mother of Jesus, is confused with Miriam, sister of Moses and Aaron, and thus she is named Maryam in the Koran. As a result of this confusion early Muslims must have presumed that Amran (Miriam's father) was Mary's father. Accordingly, the name of the third surah, Al-Imran, was inspired by Miriam's father's name—Amran.

> 66:12 And Maryam (Mary), the daughter of Imran who guarded her chastity; and We breathed into (the sleeve of her shirt or her garment) through Our Ruh [i.e., Jibrael (Gabriel)].[4]

---

4   N. J. Dawood's English translation of the Koran has been used in this book. However, cognizant of the anachronism concerning Mary's name,

According to the Koran, after Maryam (Mary) gave birth to Jesus and brought the baby to her people, they realized that the baby had no father. As a result, members of her tribe made reproaches:

> 19:28 "O Aaron's sister, your father was not a bad man, nor was your mother unchaste."

The noteworthy point is that Jesus' mother Mary has become "Aaron's sister" in this verse. It was perhaps this unacceptable anachronism and the many other inconsistencies found in Muhammad's inspired verses—in comparison with the Bible—that made the Jews refuse to become Muslims.

Besides those that mention Mary and the birth of Jesus, there are other intriguing koranic verses. Some in the third and nineteenth suwar refer to the incident in which an angel heralded the birth of John the Baptist (*Yahya*[5]) to his father. The same incident is found in the Gospel but is narrated somewhat differently in the Koran. In this context, the content of verse 3:39 is significant, for the term *word* is mentioned in it. This brief reference is not associated with any other information that might indicate that the *word* mentioned is the cosmic "Word" or Logos written about in the beginning of St. John's Gospel. Evidently, the *word* used in this verse is used in a literal sense and has no connection with the Christ as the second person of the Holy Trinity.

> 3:39 And as he [Zechariah] stood praying in the Shrine, the angels called out to him saying: "Allah bids you rejoice in the birth of John [the Baptist], who shall confirm the word of Allah. He [John] shall be princely and chaste, a prophet and a righteous man."

This verse basically conveys that angels heralded the birth of John the Baptist (*Yahya*) to his father and told him that his son would be a

---

in verse 66:12, Dawood has used the English name *Mary* so that the name *Maryam* does not give way to confusion. In Mohsin Khan's translation, the original name *Maryam*, as written in the Koran, has been used correctly, and Khan has put *Mary* in brackets. Therefore, in the quotation of 66:12 here, Khan's rendering is used. We can also see that he has correctly used the term *ruh* and not *spirit* and has indicated in brackets that the term *ruh* used in this verse actually corresponds to *Jibrael* (Gabriel).

5 John the Baptist's name is *Yahya* in Arabic.

prophet in the future and "shall confirm the word of Allah." No other complementary verses relate to it that would explain what this "word" really means. When we bear in mind that every koranic verse is conveying Allah's "words," one might assume that as a prophet of Allah[6] John the Baptist was assigned by Allah to deliver certain messages—or words—from him. The ambiguous and elusive way this verse is composed does not give us any clue that the "word" is the cosmic Word—the divine creative cosmic force[7]—for it does not clearly state: "He will confirm the arrival of the Word." Thus, we may conclude that "the word of Allah" only means the messages of Allah, which he sends via prophets like Moses or Muhammad—or in this case via John the Baptist. Therefore, the true concept or the profound meaning of the cosmic Word (logos) does not exist in Islamic teachings. Accordingly, the Koran fails to state that Christ is the living cosmic Word, and that the Word had incarnated in the three sheaths of Jesus at the baptism in the Jordan River.

As we analyze the Koran, something one does not fail to notice is the apparent endeavor to present Jesus merely as the son of Mary. His profound connection with the divine–spiritual world and his tremendously significant role in the evolution of humankind is not emphasized or even briefly mentioned. On the contrary, an ambiguity is created concerning his connection with the divine–spiritual world. One also notices the effort to present him as a mortal human prophet. For example:

> 3:58 *This revelation, and this wise admonition, We recite to you:* 59 *Jesus is like Adam in sight of Allah. He created him out of dust and then he said to him: "Be" and he was.* 60 *This is the truth from your Lord: therefore do not doubt it.*

---

6   Within the context of the ongoing explanations, this statement is made in accordance with the Islamic teachings based on the Koran; it does not reflect the narrations found in the four canonical Gospels.

7   Besides the other three cosmic etheric forces of warmth ether, light ether, and sound ether that had been active in the Old Saturn, Old Sun, and Old Moon stages of humankind's creation, the "Word" was the most significant cosmic force, for *the Word* was actually "life ether," the source of vibrant, weaving life.

> 5:75 The Messiah [Jesus], the son of Mary ["Maryam" in the original koranic text], was no more than an apostle; other apostles passed away before him. His mother was a saintly woman. They both ate earthly food.

The statement in 3:59—"Jesus is like Adam in sight of Allah"—refers to another koranic verse that indicates that Allah had created Adam out of dust or mud—that is, Adam was initially created on Earth by Allah, and during the process of creation Allah provided him a mineral or earthly body. In the Koran, there is no reference to the three former planetary stages of evolution. When we study the Koran we get the impression that Allah initially created humans on Earth. Verse 3:59 emphasizes that Jesus was created in the same way as Adam: "...then he said to him: 'Be' and he was." By emphasizing the physical aspect of Jesus—contrary to what we know from anthroposophic wisdom—it is implied that *a divine aspect is not inherent in him*. Verse 5:75 strongly states that the role of Jesus, who had a human mother, was nothing more than to serve Allah as an "apostle.'" The statement "Jesus and his mother Mary ate earthly food" underscores that neither Jesus nor his mother had a spiritual aspect; they were both ephemeral earthly beings.

Among the unusual verses found in the Koran is a verse that claims Jesus had heralded the coming of the Prophet Muhammad:

> 61:6 And of Jesus, who said to the Israelites: "I am sent forth to you by Allah to confirm the Torah already revealed and to give news of an apostle that will come after me whose name is 'Ahmad' [a derivative of the name Muhammad]."

Since it is an undisputable fact that Jesus had not predicted the coming of a messenger from Allah named Ahmad in the canonical Gospels, we may wonder from which source this verse was inspired. Although it is not possible to know who placed this verse in the koranic text and at what stage of the history of Islam it was placed, we can state definitively that it was not inspired by Yahweh/Allah. Nevertheless, we can deduce why it was placed in the Koran. If it is proclaimed in a verse inspired by Allah that Jesus predicted the coming of Muhammad, this would have made a valuable contribution to Muhammad's credentials as a prophet. It is also possible that 61:6 was added to the Koran at a later stage of its compilation. The Greek term *Paraclete*[8] had been somehow rendered into Arabic as "the awaited one." The *Paraclete*, which is actually the Holy Spirit, was going to be sent to the world by Jesus Christ after he had left the world. Therefore, in a sense, the *Paraclete* was in fact the awaited one. It is likely that this rendered Arabic meaning of *Paraclete* along with Jesus' promise that the *Paraclete* would be sent by him in the future induced one of the Islamic caliphs or transcribers to insert this persuading but false information into the Koran, proclaiming that the Prophet Muhammad was "the awaited one."

This verse reminds us of similar claims concerning Muhammad as the latest prophet of Allah. In an earlier chapter it was discussed that apocryphal Gospels inspired some koranic verses. Conversely, there are reasons to believe that certain koranic verses inspired an apocryphal Gospel. When we analyze and compare the apocryphal Gospel with these koranic verses, we see the outstanding similarity of the subjects within each and how harmoniously they are related. This apocryphal Gospel is known as "The Gospel of Barnabas." Although the name Barnabas may suggest that Barnabas, who had traveled with St. Paul and had written the Epistles of Barnabas, wrote it, the author is not the Barnabas mentioned in Acts in the New Testament. Some sources indicate that the author of this Gospel was either a Jew or even a Muslim, but surely not a Christian. Reliable estimations reveal that the Gospel of Barnabas was written in the fourteenth century. This is the main reason it cannot be claimed that verse 61:1 and other koranic verses were inspired by it, for the Koran was compiled at a much earlier time. Although Muslims have not used it as a holy book, the Gospel of Barnabas could be regarded as a "Muslim Gospel," because it is very much in accordance with Islamic teachings. For example, it presents Jesus merely as a human prophet who is the forerunner of Muhammad, not as the Son of God. It also always refers to Jesus Christ only as *Jesus* and never associates him with his divine aspect, the Christ—that is, the name Christ is never used in this Gospel.

---

8   *Paraclete* (*Paracletos*) has been rendered into English variously as helper, comforter, and advocate.

In the Gospel of Barnabas, Jesus often humbly states that he is only a herald of the prophet who is to come in the future (i.e., Muhammad). He also rejects the notion that he is the Messiah, indicating that the prophet who is to come is the real Messiah. Still, there is no such claim in the Koran suggesting that Muhammad is the Messiah. When we analyze this pseudo-epigraphical Gospel, it becomes apparent that the author made a kind of patchwork by taking certain parts from the Old Testament, the canonical Gospels, and the Koran and wrote an imaginary Gospel that supports Islamic doctrines. This Gospel was written in a way that it would especially please Muslims, and presently some Muslims believe it to be an authentic Gospel.

It is also noteworthy that in the Gospel of Barnabas the one who was crucified was definitely not Jesus Christ, because Allah and his angels had saved Jesus by—somehow—hoisting him up from the window of his house. Furthermore, Allah used his power to make Judas Iscariot look exactly like Jesus so that, according to this Gospel, Judas was the one caught by the persecutors and crucified, not Jesus. As we recall, koranic verses deny that Jesus was crucified. As a result of constantly denying this profound truth pertaining to Jesus Christ,[9] Muhammad and believers of Islam were not able to realize that Jesus was not just a prophet who was serving Allah like the other prophets, but *"in Jesus the Word was made flesh" and through Jesus Christ the first example of the future Son of Man had come into being.*

Reasons behind the denial of the Holy Trinity and God's Son

At the time when the Prophet Muhammad was declaring his teachings and trying to establish a monotheistic belief, his neighbors—the Nestorian Christians, the Coptic Christians, and some Christianized Arabs, all who had been influenced by apocryphal Gospels—clung to an erroneous idea about the members of the Holy Trinity. As previously mentioned, according to their conception of the Trinity, it consisted of a Father–God, Mary (Maryam) the mother, and Jesus the Son. However, although a truer wisdom concerning the divine persons of the Trinity was available in the canonical Gospels, Muhammad did not have direct access to this wisdom. Since he was illiterate,

---

9 Denial of the Crucifixion event will be dealt with later.

he had to rely only on the spoken accounts of the Gospel. It is likely that since he was able to communicate with Christianized Arabs, he was influenced by the accounts that came from the apocryphal Gospels, such as the Arabic Gospel of the Infancy of the Savior. Since the Christians he encountered believed this erroneous version of the Trinity, Muhammad must have thought that their depiction of the Trinity was how it also existed in the other canonical Gospels. He must have overlooked the fact that, at that time, Christianity was a comparatively new religion, and since such concepts were also relatively new for the Christians, this made them prone to erroneous beliefs. In any case, whether this form of the Trinity was true or erroneous, any belief that proclaimed that God[10] exists as three distinct persons must have been perplexing for Muhammad. He must have realized that if he had to deal with the concepts of the Trinity and the Son of God while he was trying to persuade pagan Arabs to believe in a single deity, this would complicate matters to a great extent and endanger the success of his task. Muhammad's priority was to establish the belief in a monotheistic God—the one and only Allah—among the Arabs, who were idolaters until that time and had never believed in only a single God. He must have sensed that the concept of three Gods in one Godhead would have been very confusing for the pagan Arabs.

From a certain point of view, it seems that the Prophet was justified in opposing the erroneous image of the Trinity prevalent among some Christians, but his real concern was not to correct what was wrong about this belief and present the truth. Muhammad chose instead to refute the existing erroneous conception of the Trinity, and, consequentially, he ended up rejecting the true concept of the Holy Trinity also. This was quite a radical resolution, but by adopting this attitude Muhammad managed to avoid entangling himself in further complications that could have confronted him in the future. Accordingly, two verses emphasize that Allah does not approve the belief of the Trinity and that the ones who insist on saying he is part of it have to suffer the consequences.

---

10 As far as Muhammad was concerned, "the concept of God" only corresponded to Allah, for there is no deity other than Allah.

5:72 Unbelievers are those that say: "Allah is one of three." There is but one God. If they do not desist from so saying, those of them that disbelieve shall be sternly punished.

4:171 O people of the Book [Jews and Christians]! Do not exceed the limits in your religion. Speak nothing but the truth about Allah. The Messiah Jesus, son of Mary [Maryam], was no more than a Messenger of Allah and his word, which he conveyed [cast] on Mary [Maryam] and a Spirit [Ruh] from him; so believe in Allah and his messengers, and do not say: "Three" [Trinity]! Forbear and it shall be better for you. For Allah is the only Ilah [God]. Allah forbids that he should have a son. To him belong all that is in the heavens and all that is in the earth. And Allah is the all-Sufficient Protector.

Allah's disapproval of the belief of the Trinity and the claim that Allah is one of three can be clearly seen in the verse above. It also reflects his reproach and repudiation concerning the claim that he has a son. There are other verses that convey similar messages, but it is significant and noteworthy that although Allah rejects being part of the erroneous depiction of the Holy Trinity, *throughout the Koran he never declares anything concerning the true Holy Trinity.*

In the history of Islam, there is another incident that caused much controversy and probably strongly influenced Muhammad in his firm denial of the concept of the Trinity, leading him to adopt such a radical resolution of denial. Some Islamic sources claim that the leaders of Arab tribes who had declined to believe in Muhammad's messages at the beginning had proposed that they would believe and surrender to Allah if Muhammad would not refuse the three female deities they had been worshipping and would allow them to continue doing so. These deities were Al-Lat, Al-Uzzah, and Al-Manat, and they were regarded as El-Ilah's[11] daughters. According to certain claims related to the emergence of Islam, while Muhammad was having a meeting with the leaders of these tribes and reciting certain inspired verses, he said some words of affirmation concerning these three female deities along with the verses he recited; these words seemed to be part of the

---

11 According to some Islamic scholars, prior to the outset of Islam, El-Ilah was a deity found among the 360 deities surrounding the Kaaba. In the Arabic language, the word *Ilah* literally means "deity."

verse he had been reciting at that moment. Upon hearing the Prophet's words of acknowledgement in a verse inspired by Allah, members of the tribes regarded this as an approval of their deities and, complying with their agreement, they prostrated[12] along with the Prophet. Later, Gabriel warned Muhammad that these verses were not inspired by Allah but by *Shaytan* (Satan). A verse that came later (22:52) indicates that Muhammad was not the only Prophet who was influenced by the devil's tampering:

> 22:52 *We have never sent any messenger or prophet before you [Muhammad] into whose wishes Satan did not insinuate something, but Allah removes what Satan insinuates and then God affirms his message. Allah is all knowing and wise.*

The verses in question are known in Islamic history as "the verses of the devil" or "satanic verses." It is said that they were later permanently removed from surah 53; however, verse 17:73 must have somehow escaped their attention. As a consequence, the Prophet must have found himself in a difficult position. He was a prophet chosen by Allah, yet he had failed to discern that these verses were inspired by the devil, and this disappointed Allah. A verse indicates Allah's disappointment concerning this matter:

> 17:73 *They [pagan Arab tribes] sought to entice you from Our revelations, hoping that you might invent some other scripture in Our name, and thus become their trusted friend. Indeed had we not strengthened your faith you might have made some compromise with them and thus incurred a double punishment in this life and the next. Then you should have found none to protect you from our wrath.*

Although some Islamic scholars detail this incident later in their commentaries, devout Muslims have strictly refused that it ever took place. The latter say that the devil could not possibly have interfered

---

12 Prior to Islam, pagan Arabians used to prostrate before their idols, but after Muhammad established Islam they began to prostrate before Allah in the direction of Mecca (Kaaba). As a matter of fact, at the very beginning of Islam they were prostrating in the direction of Jerusalem, but after the Jews refused Muhammad's calls, they were instructed by an inspired verse to prostrate in the direction of Mecca instead of Jerusalem.

while Allah transmitted a verse. The following is an example of verses in the Koran that strictly reject the erroneous belief that Allah has daughters:

> 17:40 What! Has your Lord blessed you [unbelievers] with sons and he himself adopted daughters from among the angels? A monstrous blasphemy is that which you utter.

After he was deceived by the verses inspired by the devil and faced Allah's anger, Muhammad must have realized that it would not be wise to test Allah's patience any further by bringing up the issues of the Holy Trinity and God's Son, or show any sign that he is swayed by such claims and beliefs. Another verse gives a warning from Allah:

> 6:100 Yet they regard the jinn [elementary spirits] as Allah's equals, though he himself created them, and in their ignorance ascribe to him sons and daughters. Glory to him. Exalted be he above their imputations!

These are among the reasons why the koranic verses never approve or support the concepts of the Holy Trinity or God's Son. As a consequence, Muhammad's refusal of the Holy Trinity and Jesus as God's Son formed a permanent obstruction against comprehending the truth of the Holy Trinity and the Son–God. Verses 5:72 and 73 depict how these blasphemous ideas evoked Allah's anger.

> 5:72 Unbelievers are those that say: "Allah is the Messiah [Jesus], the son of Mary." For the Messiah himself said: "Children of Israel, serve Allah, my Lord and your Lord." He that worships other gods besides Allah shall be forbidden Paradise and shall be cast into the fire of Hell. None shall help the evildoers.

> 5:73 Unbelievers are those who say: "Allah is one of the three." There is but one God. If they do not desist from so saying, those of them that disbelieve shall sternly be punished.

At the same time that the Koran firmly stands against these concepts, it accuses the Jews of corrupting the Scriptures and the Christians of worshipping Jesus as the Son of God—even though Allah had strictly commanded them to worship none but him. Throughout the Koran, one can clearly see the endeavor to correct the so-called blasphemous convictions of the Jews and Christians. For instance, verse 9:30 portrays such an accusation.

> 9:30 *The Jews say Ezra is the son of Allah,[13] while the Christians say the Messiah [Jesus] is the son of Allah. Such are their assertions, by which they imitate the infidels of old. Allah confounds them! How perverse they are.*

In the following verse, Allah has given further explanations concerning this matter:

> 9:31 *They worship their rabbis and their monks, and the Messiah [Jesus] the son of Mary [Maryam/Miriam], as Gods besides Allah; though they were ordered to serve God only. There is no God but him. Exalted is he above those whom they deify beside him!*

Existence of such verses shows that Muhammad's role as a messenger of Allah also involved passing judgment on the religious beliefs and teachings of Jews and Christians and pointing out where they have gone wrong according to his Islamic convictions. Note that, in the previous verses, the names *Jesus* and *Messiah* are used synonymously. In verse 43:81, Allah says his last word concerning God's Son:

> 43:81 *"If Most Gracious (Allah) had a son, I would be the first to worship him."*

These verses, claimed to be inspired by Allah and transmitted by Gabriel, form the core of the dogmatic teachings of Islam. At present, all conservative, fundamentalist, radical, and extremist sects of Islam believe in the truth of these teachings. This may help us understand why fundamentalist, radical, and extremist Muslims cannot tolerate Christianity and insist that Christians should accept Islam as their religion. As far as they are concerned, Allah's messages clearly explain all relevant matters in the truths spelled out in the Koran.

What did Abraham's monotheistic faith mean to Muhammad and to Muslims?

The Prophet was aware that he had a certain task to accomplish, and he knew that he could not afford to be unsuccessful. His prime

---

13 This charge concerning Ezra does not appear to have any basis in Jewish religious teachings.

concern was to persuade the pagan Arabs to believe in a single deity. To guarantee success, it was necessary that fear of God and obedience be introduced once again in this new version of Yahweh's Moon religion. Muhammad must have been aware that sooner or later he had to confront the teachings and beliefs of other religions adhered to by his Jewish and Christian neighbors. These problems had to be resolved one way or another, and the result he achieved would justify the means. During these critical times, the Prophet did not think that concepts such as God's Son and the Holy Trinity were indispensable. Muhammad was trying to follow the example of his ancestral father Abraham, and he struggled to direct the pagan Arabs' attention to Abraham's monotheistic faith. The nature of this new faith did not allow space for other beliefs or concepts. The following verse represents this brief and steadfast message:

> 3:95 Say, "Allah has declared the truth. Follow the faith of Abraham. He was an upright man, no idolater."

Allah's decree is quite clear: Muslims had no choice but to follow the monotheistic faith of Abraham and avoid entanglement with blasphemous concepts such as the Holy Trinity and God's Son. However, while Muhammad was struggling to establish this new faith, he was not cognizant of the fact that the actual reason behind the impulse of Islam was solely to deaden Sorath's intervention. Nonetheless, he managed to found the religion that successfully served this purpose, for the kind of force inherent in this particular form of religious belief and the momentum it created were exactly what were needed in the process of blunting Sorath's intervention. In one of his lectures Rudolf Steiner indicates:

> Above all, in the areas where there was a desire to spread the Gnostic wisdom of Gondishapur, Muhammad took the ground from under its feet. He skimmed the cream off it, and so the Gondishapur influence was left to trail behind and could accomplish nothing in the face of what Muhammad had done.[14]

---

14 Steiner, *Three Streams in Human Evolution*, lecture 5.

Again, Muhammad did not know the actual reason why he was fulfilling such a task. As far as he could understand, Yahweh had revealed himself as Allah to descendants of Ishmael and now the time had come for Ishmael's descendants to reestablish the faith of their ancestral father Abraham since the Jews and Christians had corrupted Abraham's faith and failed to cooperate with Allah's messengers—for example, back when Jesus tried to persuade them—in founding a monotheistic religion of total obedience and surrender. Verse 2:127 characterizes the Muslims' belief that Abraham and Ishmael had a special relationship, and that Abraham and Ishmael had together built the sacred building of Kaaba. However, it does not seem likely that this sentimental story could be true. Claiming that Abraham and Ishmael, as an adult, had a close relationship could be interpreted as an endeavor to compensate for the fact that Ishmael and his mother, Hagar, were asked to leave Abraham's household when he was a child. The story of Abraham's sacrifice of Isaac has also been transformed into an Arab (and Islamic) version. Muslims believe that it was Ishmael whom Abraham was going to sacrifice for Allah (Yahweh)—not Isaac. As a result of their beliefs, Muslims fail to realize that the story of Abraham's sacrifice of Isaac is not just an ordinary story but has a profound truth behind it. In his "Anthroposophic Meditations on the Old Testament," Valentine Tomberg writes:

> The son of Abraham indicated (to him personally and objectively to humanity) not only an event in his personal life, but also a revelation by means of an actual event. The birth of Isaac was itself a revelation, awaking in Abraham's soul an understanding of the mystery of the relationship between the Eternal Father and the Eternal Son.... Thus, through the "I," or Ego, of Isaac, Abraham discerned the Father's thought of the Son. Abraham was able to recognize in the birth of Isaac the mystery of the Eternal Son's earthly birth and sacrifice. Isaac's star revealed to him the mystery of the Son's sacrifice, and this revelation became the essence of Israel's whole history.[15]

---

15 Tomberg, *Christ and Sophia*, chapter 3, "Abraham, Isaac, and Jacob," pp. 35–36

Although Allah had neither made a covenant with the Prophet Muhammad while he was alive nor with any of the caliphs after his death, Muhammad probably surmised that after having founded the religion in accordance with the monotheistic faith of his ancestor Abraham, *he and his descendants were going to be the chosen ones* who would ensure the continuation of Abraham's faith. At this point, let us recall verse 3:95, which says: "Allah has declared the truth. Follow the faith of Abraham. He was an upright man, no idolater," and 3:67: "Abraham was neither Jew nor Christian. He was an upright man, who had surrendered himself to Allah."

These verses show that, according to Muhammad, the most crucial point of the newly founded religion was *to follow the faith of Abraham*, for this was the guideline declared by Allah. Since Abraham had nothing to do with the erroneous beliefs of Jews or Christians ("Abraham was neither Jew nor Christian"), the quality of his faith was not spoiled; Abraham had managed to surrender to Allah entirely. Therefore, Muslims were to use his faith as an example. Muhammad believed that Abraham's pure and unspoiled faith went through a deformation when his descendants disobeyed Allah and strayed from the right path—that is, by adhering to Christianity and believing in blasphemous concepts. These are the convictions and beliefs that formed and strengthened the core of the Islamic doctrine at the outset of Islam, and these convictions remain unchanged in today's Islamic teachings. This is one of the main reasons why it seems a chance of reconciliation between Islam and other religions—especially Christianity—shall not be easy.

The Prophet Muhammad's two sons

After he assumed the role of the Prophet from the lineage of Ishmael and laid the foundations of Islam, Muhammad was persuaded that he was "the chosen one" who would continue the lineage of Ishmael and carry Abraham's faith into the future. And for this to be actualized, he had to have a son. Therefore, it was necessary that Allah bestow a son to the Prophet as he had to Abraham. However, Muhammad's first son did not live long but died when he was a small child, and for a long time the Prophet did not have another son. Eventually, toward the end of his life, a Coptic slave girl—whom the Byzantine Christian governor of Egypt sent him as a present—bore him a son. This made the Prophet very happy, and he named his son Ibrahim, after Abraham—the prophet he deeply venerated. Sadly, after a short time, in January 632, his son Ibrahim died. (A few months later, in July 632, the Prophet also died.)

His son's death had been a serious blow for Muhammad, as it was very important for him to have a son. In addition to the fact that this was necessary for the continuation of future generations, in Arab culture not having a son was a humiliating situation for a man. One may wonder why Allah's chosen Prophet was not granted a son, and the Prophet must have been baffled by this question as well. As previously mentioned, the Prophet Abraham had recognized the mystery of the birth of the Eternal Son on Earth and his sacrifice. This profound truth had been revealed to him. However, although Muhammad had received certain revelations through Gabriel, this mystery was not revealed to him. Therefore he never had an insight into the mystery of the Eternal Son and the profound meaning of Christ's sacrifice, and how—from the very beginning—this mystery was particularly related to the Israelites: Abraham, Isaac, Jacob, and their descendants. Muhammad did not realize that the Hebrews' ultimate mission was to form the threshold through which Christ could enter the Earth sphere. Moreover, the Prophet also did not conceive that the Christ-being had already accomplished his cosmic mission on Earth and had turned human evolution in a totally new direction, and that the impact of his Advent was going to continue with the Christ impulse. Valentin Tomberg highlighted this fact: "For the Christ impulse is the voice of the Shepherd sounding in the world and throughout history."

Muhammad's uncompromising declaration, "If Most Gracious (Allah) had a son, I would be the first to worship him," brought about an eclipse between him and the mystery of the Christ. As a result, he was unable to hear the voice of the shepherd. It would do him justice to underline that his mission was not to hear the voice of the shepherd. At this point let us recall that Christ was a divine being from the Sun sphere—he was a Sun God. It is noteworthy that on January 27, 632, the day that the Prophet Muhammad's second son Ibrahim died, there was an eclipse of the Sun. Did the tragedy of his son's death have anything to do with his uncompromising denial of God's Son?

When we recall that one of the most important aims of the Sun God was to replace the principle of retribution with the principle of forgiveness and love, it becomes evident that Muhammad's denial of God's Son could not have possibly played any role in his son's death. Therefore, there must be a more feasible reason why Muhammad was not granted a son. If Muhammad's son had lived and begun the lineage of the Prophet, his descendants would have generated into the future. However, it would not have been in accordance with the aims of the divine–spiritual world to have another ancestral father, whose descendants would inevitably proclaim to be Allah's new chosen people. The transitory period in which a special ancestral blood tie enabled the chosen people to be related to God had only belonged to the Hebrews, and it had come to an end. It was replaced by the Christ impulse, which granted every human being the opportunity to be related to God through the Christ—through the spirit. However, since Muhammad's understanding was firmly fixed on how the Hebrews were formerly related to Yahweh, he could not perceive that an immensely significant transition had begun to take place starting with Christ's Advent, nor have Muslims comprehended this profound truth since.

After Muhammad's death, his relatives hoped to form a lineage through the sons of Muhammad's daughter, Fatima, who was married to Muhammad's cousin Ali. However, archenemies of Muhammad assassinated Ali. Then, one of Ali's sons, Hasan, was poisoned. Later, his other son Hussein and Hussein's son were slain in a place called *Karbala*. The incident in Karbala brought the possibility of the symbolic continuity of Muhammad's linage through his daughter to an end. This incident was also the reason for the major division among Muslims and within Islam itself. As a consequence, *Shi'ite* and *Alawi* Muslim sects emerged on the one side, and the *Sunnite* Muslim sect emerged on the other.

Further consequences of adhering to the old principle, "I and Father Abraham are one"

Before Christ came to the world and brought the Christ impulse, Hebrews were conscious of the fact that their connection to Yahweh was maintained through their unspoiled blood ties, which went back all the way to their ancestral father, Abraham. This special principle of blood ties was very important to them. However, now that Christ has returned to the world in the etheric, henceforth those who are imbued by Christ will have a spiritual connection to the Father. This became possible because Christ brought a new principle, deeper than the physical ties, as a result of which humankind is no longer obliged to be connected through a special ancestral blood tie. This fact, often explained by Rudolf Steiner and Valentin Tomberg, was initially indicated in John 14:6: "Jesus answered, 'I am the way and the truth and the life. No one comes to the Father except through me.'" After Christ's proclamation, instead of being obliged to form a connection to an ancestral father (as in the statement "I and father Abraham are one"), humankind was now able to say, "I and the Father–God are one." As Christ gave the petitions of the Lord's Prayer to humankind and said "Our Father in heaven," he made it possible for human beings to address Father–God directly. These were the significant new principles that Christ brought to the world.

However, Muhammad's verses did not allow for the mystery of the Son, or the mystery of Christ, to prevail in the Islamic teachings. In verse 2:116 he proclaims, "They say: 'Allah has begotten a son.' Allah forbids! [or, Nay!]" The verse cited earlier: "If Allah had a son, I would be the first one to worship him," shows his uncompromising denial of God's Son. Since Muhammad always refused to acknowledge God's Son, he could never attain the following profound insight: that with the coming of the Son, humankind did not have to worship God in the former ways, and God was not incessantly demanding the kind of worship based on fear and obedience. Instead of fear and obedience, through the grace of the Son, a person's meeting point with God was to be spiritualized love. The koranic verse below shows Muhammad's lack of understanding about the divine aspect of Jesus.

Evidently, what the "Islamic Jesus" utters in this verse is not in harmony with the truth radiating from the canonical Gospels:

> 5:72 Unbelievers are those who say: "Allah [God—i.e., Godly aspect of Jesus] is the Messiah [Jesus], the son of Mary." For the Messiah himself said: "Children of Israel, serve Allah, my Lord and your Lord." He that worships other Gods besides Allah shall be forbidden Paradise and shall be cast into the fire of Hell. None shall help the evildoers.

Much confusion and misunderstanding are inherent in this verse. We can see that besides an erroneous depiction of Jesus—that is, Jesus Christ—it has integrated both a fear of Allah and the threat of Allah's Hell. It's apparent that Muhammad and the original source from which this verse issued have no doubt that Jesus was just an ephemeral earthly being, a messenger whose only task was to deliver Allah's messages. Apparently, the Prophet could not sense that there was a phenomenal combination of a god and a physical human being in "the Prophet Jesus," and that his mission surpassed being solely a messenger of Allah, involving *the redemption of humanity from the material world and the clutches of adverse beings such as Lucifer and Ahriman*. Muhammad also failed to realize[16] that humankind would not remain perpetually earthbound. Before the "Fall," humans belonged to the divine–spiritual world, but although they became earthly beings after the Fall, divine–spiritual beings expected and hoped that humans would take their rightful place among them in the divine–spiritual world in the distant future.

An exalted God—who was from the ranks of the progressive divine beings and who had been active in every stage of the creation and evolution—could not possibly wish that ephemeral beings fear him and prostrate before him, for it is the aim of the beings of the divine realm to be united with humanity at a higher spiritual dimension of consciousness and love, achieved through the love impulse brought by Christ.

---

16 Let us recall that Muhammad's messages always had two aspects: Muhammad was the one who received and recited the messages on the Earth plane, but they were originally conveyed by Allah via Gabriel. Therefore, when we speak of Muhammad's lack of understanding of certain spiritual matters, we must also take into consideration that the suprasensory world was the main source from which these messages were issued.

However, the Prophet did not have the insight that spiritualized love was the essential divine quality that could help humankind's redemption from its earthly grave.[17] Muhammad's (and his followers') total elimination of the Son God (and the Sun God) from Islamic teachings also precluded Muslims from understanding the profound mystery of death and resurrection. Consequentially, the cosmic truth inherent in this most vital and significant event, Christ's Resurrection, has not been comprehended by Muslims.[18] The only concept of resurrection (likely inspired by the Christian concept of resurrection) that exists in Islamic teachings has to do with the time when the world comes to an end—the Last Day discussed earlier. This will be the "Day of Resurrection" for Muslims—that is, they will be resurrected to be judged by Allah.

Denial of the Crucifixion and its consequences

The subject of resurrection brings us to Muslims' denial of the event of the Crucifixion—the denial of Jesus Christ's death on the cross. As a matter of fact, besides denying the event of the Crucifixion, Muslims also try to refute it. Why do Muslims controvert this event and even try to prove that it did not take place? One reason at the base of their denial and refutation is the refusal of the phenomena of reincarnation and incarnation. A previous chapter examines how the refusal of the phenomena of reincarnation is a consequence of being under the influence of Arabism. Muslims' obliviousness to the fact of reincarnation has acted as an obstacle and prevented them from gaining an objective insight into the anthroposophic aspect of reincarnation and incarnation. In this context, Muslims never ask questions such as "Why is there reincarnation and what purpose does it serve?" and "What actually is involved when a soul reincarnates?" As a result of their complete refusal to give any consideration to the truth of these concepts, it has

---

17 As we recall, under the circumstances prevalent during the emergence of Islam, the Prophet's task was to establish "fear, obedience, and surrender" so that Arabs became Muslim. His endeavor had to remain within the limits of a well-defined framework and in no way exceed it.

18 Jesus Christ's Resurrection does not mean resurrection of only the physical body; insofar as human beings are concerned, it means the resurrection of the human "I" in a highly spiritualized form in a distant future. This is why Jesus Christ declared, "I am the resurrection and life" (John 11:25).

not been possible for them to understand that a sublime divine–spiritual being incarnated into the physical body of Jesus. Any knowledge concerning reincarnation is contradictory to their rigid teachings and beliefs; according to their convictions, there is no probability of reincarnation, and this subject is thus not open to discussion.

Why is their belief so rigid and unchangeable? Actually, it is because of their fatalistic convictions about human death. According to Islamic teachings, once a person dies, that is the end of that person, excepting the Last Day—Resurrection Day—when Allah will bring everyone back to life and judge them. Only the latter part of this belief—that people will be judged at the end of their time on Earth—comes somewhat close to the truth. However, since this partial truth is blended with erroneous information, it loses its power to convey the truth concerning *humankind's alternating states of being*. Islamic dogmas proclaim that Allah will bring everyone back to life to judge them on the Last Day, and after being judged and sent to Paradise or Hell, humankind's cosmic saga will come to an abrupt end. The vital concept of progression of the soul through higher stages of consciousness in its spiritual evolution does not exist in the Koran, and Islamic teachings do not indicate that humankind will continue to move on to further stages of its evolution after the Earth (fourth) stage.

One of the most vital aspects of human evolution is that it will not finish abruptly at the end of the fourth (Earth) stage of evolution, but rather the perishable human members[19] that presently constitute the human being will be transformed into a nonperishable spiritual form: the "resurrected human being."[20] As a consequence of refusing the concept of reincarnation and remaining uninformed about the vital details of humankind's evolutionary process, Muslims are unaware that, if people were given a single random lifetime on Earth and eventually end up in Paradise or Hell, they would not have enough time or opportunity to achieve this essential transformation. Moreover, Islamic teachings do not provide the knowledge that Christ's Crucifixion, death,

---

19 The perishable members of the human being are: the physical, etheric, and astral bodies and the ego (one's sense of self formed in the material world).

20 In the far future, the spirit self, the life spirit, and the spirit body will constitute the "resurrected" human being.

and Resurrection were actually cosmic events, the results of which will enable humanity to reach further spiritual stages of evolution.

Could there be other reasons that contribute to Islam's denial of the event of the Crucifixion? Muslims insist that Jesus, son of Mary, did not die on the cross, because they are persuaded that omnipotent Allah could not have been helpless in preventing his prophet's Crucifixion. In verse 4:157, Allah firmly denies the event of the Crucifixion:

> 4:157 "They declared: 'We have put to death the Messiah Jesus the son of Mary, the apostle of Allah.' They did not kill him, nor did they crucify him, but they thought they did [or, 'he was made to resemble another for them']."

This verse clearly states that, according to Allah, Jesus was not crucified—that is, he was not put on the cross, nor did he die on a cross. Clearly, as long as such a statement exists in the Koran, it will be impossible for Muslims to comprehend and come to terms with an explanation contrary to this statement. Muslims believe that koranic verses transmit Allah's correct and indisputable messages. An interpretation of a *hadith* that is very much in accord with the meaning conveyed by the verse above can be found in Tafsir Ibn Kathir:

> The king became angry and wrote to his deputy in Jerusalem to arrest the rebel leader [Jesus, or 'Isa, as he is named in the Koran] stop him from causing unrest, crucify him and make him wear a crown of thorns.... That day was a Friday, in the evening. They surrounded 'Isa in the house, and when he felt that they would soon enter the house or that he would sooner or later have to leave it, he said to his companions, "Who volunteers to be made to look like me, for which he will be my companion in Paradise?" A young man volunteered, but 'Isa thought that he was too young. He asked the question a second and third time; each time the young man volunteered, prompting 'Isa to say, "Well then, you will be that man." Allah made the young man look exactly like 'Isa, while a hole opened in the roof of the house, and 'Isa was made to sleep and ascended to heaven while asleep... but they killed him not, nor crucified him.[21]

---

21 Ibn Kathir. *Tafsir Ibn Kathir*, "The Evil Accusation the Jews Uttered against Maryam and Their Claim that They Killed 'Isa."

This interpretation is very similar to the aforementioned narration found in the apocryphal Gospel of Barnabas. The assertions in verse 4:157, in the Gospel of Barnabas, and in the imaginary account of Ibn Kathir's interpretation are contrary to the truth of the event of the Crucifixion found in the canonical Gospels. *Apparently, whoever originally inspired this verse ignored and refused the true account of this event.* Therefore, we must ask this question: Can we possibly imagine that Allah (Yahweh) imparted such revelations contradicting the truth pertaining to the Crucifixion, *because he was oblivious to the events that unfolded on Earth as manifestations of the Mystery of Golgotha?* Clearly, Allah (if he is God Yahweh, as koranic verses claim) could not have possibly issued such a message. Then, what is the source of inspiration for verse 4:157 that has led Muslims to believe Jesus was not crucified? Again, we may suggest that such distorted information has infiltrated the Koran as a result of luciferic machinations. Traces of pride can be detected in the conviction that omnipotent Allah—the God of the Muslims—was not helpless and powerless against the persecutors of his Prophet Jesus; therefore, he did not allow Jesus to die on the cross.

Valentin Tomberg illustrates Lucifer's deep realization upon seeing Jesus Christ suffering on the cross: "When looking at the Crucifixion on Golgotha, it pierced him with the insight that it was in fact he who should have experienced those sufferings. And now the other was bearing them *in his place.*"[22] Could it be that such a profound cosmic fact was too much for Lucifer to bear since *with one side of his nature he loved the Christ,* and for this reason he wished that the event of the Crucifixion did not really take place? Since the authentic God, Yahweh, could not have denied the event of the Crucifixion[23] and convey such verses that contradict the truth, how else can we explain the existence of Allah's strong denial in the koranic verses, the *hadith*, and other scriptures such as the apocryphal Gospel of Barnabas?

According to Tomberg's explication, "Lucifer is a Janus-like character; with one side of his nature, he loves the Christ, while with the

---

22 Tomberg, *Christ and Sophia,* "The Mystery of Golgotha," p. 296.

23 It was Yahweh who prepared the Jews in a multidimensional way so that the Christ could come among them and the event of the Crucifixion would eventually take place.

other he has affinity with Ahriman."[24] Could there be another reason for the denial and refutation of the event of the Crucifixion that carries traces of Lucifer's other side—his affinity with Ahriman? When we bear in mind that Muslims deny not only the Crucifixion, but also the event of the Resurrection, another reason for their behavior begins to materialize. Muslims are well aware of the Christian proclamation that Jesus Christ was resurrected after he died on the cross—indeed, *as a consequence of dying on the cross*. Therefore, according to Islamic logic,[25] if Jesus were not crucified and did not die on the cross, then the Christian claim of his Resurrection would have to be classified as an unfounded (imaginary and false) belief. Additionally, if Allah has explained the truth and brought clarity to this matter through the messages he transmitted to Muhammad,[26] it would be "going against Allah" to continue to believe in such things as the Crucifixion and Resurrection. Muslims thus think Christians should also take note of Allah's explanations and turn away from their "blasphemous beliefs." These explanations are in accordance with what Allah previously stated about Jesus:

> 5:75 The Messiah [Jesus], the son of Mary, was no more than an apostle; other apostles passed away before him. His mother was a saintly woman. They both ate earthly food [i.e., he was created from dust and therefore was merely an ephemeral apostle].

What this message really wishes to convey is that Jesus did not have a divine aspect; therefore, his death was an ordinary death like the other apostles who passed away before him. Accordingly, these messages imply that since the central beliefs that form the quintessence of Christianity—that is, the Crucifixion and the

---

24 Tomberg, *Christ and Sophia*, "The Mystery of Golgotha," p. 295.

25 In fact, in this case scheming and devious "luciferic logic" has found expression in Islamic logic. When such delicate issues as the Crucifixion and Resurrection of Christ are concerned, we can sense that luciferic intelligence and logic are capable of devious maneuvers in accordance with Tomberg's explanation, which claims: "Lucifer has an affinity with Ahriman." If there is one being in the cosmos who did not wish for the Resurrection to take place, it is Ahriman.

26 4:157: "They did not kill him, nor did they crucify him, but they thought they did."

Resurrection—are proved to be false and erroneous by Allah's messages, there are no grounds for the existence of Christianity or for insistence on adhering to it.

Rejection and refutation of these events can be regarded as an outcome of luciferic and ahrimanic inspirations, but it must also be borne in mind that, in the long run, such prejudiced convictions function as an obstruction that prevents Muslims from comprehending the fact that Christ came to Earth to confront and defeat death, and his Crucifixion, death, and Resurrection were the central and most important events of the Mystery of Golgotha. Instead of denying the truths inherent in the Gospel, if Muslims studied and analyzed it objectively, they would realize that the Christ came to the world with the undisputable knowledge that he was going to be crucified. It is also possible for them to see that everything Jesus said and every deed he performed—like the miracles—carried him step by step to his Crucifixion. In fact, in the Gospels on various occasions he indicates that he was going to be crucified. The event of the Crucifixion was not just an accidental or random happening; it was originally conceived by the beings of the divine–spiritual hierarchy long before the fourth evolutionary stage. In other words, this event that was going to take place on the Earth plane in the future had been formerly contemplated in the divine realm. Muslims are oblivious to the fact that *if Christ's Crucifixion and Resurrection were not cosmic events that were actualized on Earth, the future of human evolution would have been gravely imperiled.*

In contradistinction to these Islamic convictions, in his first Epistle to the Corinthians, St. Paul's words reflect his deep insight of the event of the Resurrection: "And if Christ had not been raised, then our preaching is in vain and your faith is also in vain.... And if Christ had not been raised, your faith is worthless; you are still in your sins" (1 Cor 15:14, 17).

The Resurrection of Jesus Christ was the central event[27] of human evolution, and this suprasensory result was achieved for the redemption of humanity. Apparently, Islamic thought could not comprehend

---

27 It would not be wrong to proclaim that Christ's Resurrection was the central event or, in a sense, the "zenith event" among all the other very crucial and important spiritual developments that constitute the Mystery of Golgotha.

that Christ's death on the cross and his Resurrection was a victory over death—a victory over Ahriman's power over humankind—and that this event provided an example for humankind's potential resurrection in the future. Christ named the example he provided for us the "Son of Man." The profound words *Per Spiritum Sanctum Reviviscimus* indicate humankind's future revival in the spirit. Islamic thought also fails to understand that, to be able to revive in the spirit, human beings first have to die in Christ (*In Christo Morimur*). In other words, oblivious to the meaning of Christ's profound sacrifice, Muslims have missed out on what his Crucifixion, death, and Resurrection really mean for humanity and for the cosmic evolution.

Since the koranic verses are far from revealing the truth about Christ, Muslims are not able to apprehend certain significant and profound spiritual truths. This is one of the reasons why they do not have any yearning to understand the Christ—who came to the world for them also—or the Sun God. Some verses in the Koran inevitably fetter them to the old belief of a monotheistic God who should be feared and worshipped by the beings he has created. Jesus has somehow been integrated into these rigid teachings.

> 5:116 Then Allah will say: "Jesus son of Mary, did you ever say to humankind: 'Worship me and my mother as gods besides Allah?'" "Glory to you," he will answer, "how could I say that to which I have no right? If I ever said so, You would have surely known it. You know what is in my mind, but I cannot tell what is in Yours. You alone know what is hidden. I spoke to them of nothing except what you bade me. I said: 'Serve Allah, my Lord and your Lord.'"

In this verse even Jesus, as a Prophet of Allah, cringes when Allah sternly questions him. If we compare the image of Jesus depicted in the Koran with the image of Jesus Christ emanating from the Gospels, it will become evident that the koranic depictions are far from reflecting his true image and relationship with the Father–God.

> For the Father loves the Son and shows him all he does. Yes, and he will show him even greater works than these, so that you will be amazed. (John 5:20)

> I have given them the glory that you gave me, that they may be one as we are one—I in them and you in me—so that they may be brought to complete unity. Then the world will know that you sent me and have loved them even as you have loved me. Father, I want those you have given me to be with me where I am, and to see my glory, the glory you have given me because you loved me before the creation of the world. (John 17:22–24)

The Gospels clearly convey on many occasions that Christ is the Son of God and that he is very close to the Father–God. Many other profound facts uttered by Jesus Christ give us an insight pertaining to their multidimensional relationship, as well. When we bear in mind that the Son has such a profound and suprasensory relationship with the Father, it can be concluded beyond any doubt that he could not possibly cringe before the Father in fear as depicted in the koranic verse 5:116. In truth, their relationship is not based on fear, intolerance, scolding and punishment, and threats of destruction. But how could Muslims ever consider freely delving into the Mystery of the Jesus Christ and form a true idea of him without fearing Allah's wrath, when it is indicated in verse 5:17 that even Allah's Prophet Jesus is liable to suffer serious consequences if he ever angers Allah?

> 5:17 Unbelievers are those who declare: Allah is the Messiah, the son of Mary. Say: "Who could prevent Allah from destroying the Messiah, the son of Mary, together with his mother and all the people of the Earth?" His is the kingdom of heavens and the earth and all that lies between them. All shall return to him.

When we ponder on the message imparted by this verse—while recalling that the relationship of the Father–God and the Son (together with the Holy Spirit) manifests as cosmic laws and principles that uphold the universe—it becomes evident that a verse such as 5:17 could not have been conveyed by Yahweh, who is a pure revealer of the cosmic Christ (the Son). Muslims, on the other hand, who never question how an exalted deity could possibly be so intolerant and radiate so much wrath, readily believe that this verse was originally inspired by Allah (Yahweh). Since they have not studied the Gospel objectively, Muslims have had no opportunity to compare the two Jesus figures found in the Koran and in the Gospel so that they may realize the Jesus Christ figure emanating from the canonical Gospel is the true Jesus and does not cringe before the Father–God. A profound spiritual love exists between him and the Father–God, the quality of which—at this stage of our evolution—is far beyond our comprehension. As we analyze the Koran, we come across several other verses that inhibit Muslims from making the transition from their concept of a monotheistic God—complete with former influences from the Moon sphere and in which a person's relationship to God is based on fear and obedience—to the Sun religion of Christ, stocked with revitalizing spiritual influences from the beings of the divine–spiritual hierarchy and *based on reciprocal love.*

Conclusion

When dealing with the subject of Islam, it is not easy to say the last word or reach a conclusion, for there are many intricate details and connections that need further explanation. Nevertheless, when we bear in mind the foregoing explanations concerning Islam, we see that the main purpose of the Islamic impulse can be summarized as an unavoidable and necessary measure that was instigated by the divine realm to blunt the Sorathic intervention. Although it was absolutely necessary to instill the Islamic impulse as a preventive measure, beings of the divine–spiritual realm had not intended it to be a substitute for the Christ impulse either for the Arabs or for those who later became Muslim, for it was necessary that Muslims also receive the redeeming and transforming influences of the Christ impulse. In spite of this fact, the divine realm knew from the beginning that the Islamic impulse was not going to unfold in harmony with the Christ impulse, since the special spiritual quality and power required for transmitting the influences of the Christ impulse to Muslims was not inherent in it. As a consequence of having been permeated by such an impulse, Muslims' soul–spiritual constitutions remain "closed" and, consequentially, some of them have not been able to receive their share of what Christ and other members of the divine realm bestow on humanity. Nevertheless, whether Muslims are receptive to that which emanates from the divine beings or not, the Christ impulse is a kind of spiritual force that also embraces them. Actually, we can sense that the Christ and the Christ impulse has already begun to influence them when we find that—excepting fundamentalist, radical, and extremist Muslims—we are surrounded by countless friendly and good-willed Muslims whom we embrace as kinsfolk.

We shall continue with further considerations on Islam's "spiritual history." According to anthroposophic revelations, Lucifer had to be involved from the very beginning in order to deaden Sorath's intervention.

It was inevitable that there would be certain consequences of Lucifer's help, as well as further consequences when Muslim Arabs encountered the Sorathically inspired knowledge as they laid siege and got hold of the Academy of Gondishapur. Rudolf Steiner and Valentin Tomberg express in detail that all these factors put together later played an important role in the shaping of the future European culture according to *weight, measure, and number.* In other words, Islam—infused by Sorathic wisdom and permeated by Arabism—caused the emergence of materialism in Christian European civilizations. Steiner spoke of how Muhammad's deed influenced these European civilizations:

> Anyone who studies the civilization of our own time will misjudge many things if he or she ignores the influences which, having received their initial impetus from the deed of Muhammad, penetrated into European civilization as the result of the Arab campaigns, although the actual form of religious feeling with which these influences were associated did not make its way into Europe.[1]

Steiner also drew our attention to the fact that, although a certain part of the Arab influence found its way into Europe, manifesting as materialism and a scientific worldview, "the actual form of religious feeling with which these influences were associated did not make its way into Europe." Here, Steiner is referring to the teachings of Islam and indicates that the content of the Islamic teachings was not able to permeate and influence European cultures— that is, the essence of Islamic teachings was not able to expand in Europe because Europeans were already permeated with the Christ impulse and were Christianized. In other words, European civilizations were not supposed to be influenced by the religious teaching and feeling inherent in Islam. Therefore, it must be emphasized that the representatives of the Islamic impulse were not destined to be the representatives of humanity's spiritual progression. However, it cannot be denied that descendants of Ishmael played a very important role in the outer history of humankind and brought about significant and necessary changes at a specific stage of human

---

1   Steiner, *Karmic Relationships,* vol. 1, pp. 159–160.

evolution. Steiner's elucidations shed light on the impulses brought by Arabism into Europe:

> Old concepts that had been current among the Egyptians and Chaldeans were denuded of their visionary, pictorial content and recast into abstract forms. They reappear in the wonderful scientific knowledge of the Arabs who made their way into Europe via Africa and Spain. Whereas Christianity brought an impulse connected essentially with a person's soul life, the greatest impulse given to the human intellect was brought by the Arabs. Without thorough knowledge of the course taken by the evolution of humanity it is impossible to form any idea of what the worldview that arose in a new form under the symbol of the Moon has given to humankind. There would have been no Kepler and no Galileo without the impulses brought by Arabism into Europe. For the old mode of thinking appears again, but now denuded of its ancient clairvoyance, when the third post-Atlantean cultural epoch celebrated its resurrection in our own Fifth post-Atlantean cultural epoch, in our modern astronomy, in our modern science.[2]

From the point of view of human spiritual development, Arabism was a hindrance, but from the standpoint of the development of the human terrestrial "I" and the necessary formation of a materialistic world outlook, it brought the previously mentioned impulses into Europe. However, while the great achievements of sciences and the newly emerged scientific worldview have been highly regarded by Europeans, from a spiritual viewpoint the impulses of Arabism prematurely induced the intellect, which is a manifestation of the Sorathic knowledge that issued from the Academy of Gondishapur. Moreover, since this intellect was able to apprehend only the outer world of nature, Europeans became increasingly identified with the material world and adopted a scientific worldview. That Christian European cultures became entangled in materialism in a variety of ways cannot be regarded as a spiritually progressive aspect

---

2   Steiner, *Background to the Gospel of St. Mark*, lecture 9. In relation with these explanations, see Steiner, *Universe, Earth, and Man*, lecture of Aug. 11, 1908.

of human evolution. This entanglement meant that the process of *involution*[3] was going to continue. However, if this development is considered from an anthroposophic point of view, it becomes evident that involution was required within the flow of the evolution so that humanity would gain more freedom from the divine–spiritual world, enabling further development of the "I"-consciousness in the fifth post-Atlantean culture—the epoch of the consciousness soul (or spiritual soul).

In considering Islam and recalling that every human being is entitled to the freedom of belief—granted by the divine–spiritual world—we cannot criticize Muslims for identifying deeply with a religion founded on venerating a single deity. We cannot blame them for their unwillingness to acknowledge the Christ and closing themselves to the outflow of the Christ impulse. Also, we cannot expect them to look in the same direction as Christians do, for everybody is free to believe in or deny whatever they wish. Let us also remember Tomberg's indication that the new law is *no* law—that is, there is no compulsory law that a group of people can impose on any other group of people, for conscience will eventually be humankind's inner law. Perhaps, from a karmic point of view, some people are not destined to find the Christ in their present incarnation. Concerning this inability to find the Christ and the spirit, Rudolf Steiner explains: "Not to find the Father is a sickness of the soul; not to find the Christ is a misfortune (a karmic misfortune) of the soul, and not to find the Spirit is a deception of the soul."

Steiner demonstrates that the situation for adherents of Islam signifies "a misfortune of the soul" and "a deception of the soul." Steiner's words may help us form a more optimistic outlook concerning Muslims. As each human being has many incarnations ahead of him or her before the end of the Earth stage of evolution, Muslims, too, have more time and more reincarnations on Earth to be able to

---

3   Steiner often expresses that, although we speak of human evolution as if it is a continuously "progressive" development, from the spiritual viewpoint the term *involution* would be more correct to describe this ongoing cosmic process, for during this evolution humankind has totally lost its connection with the divine–spiritual realm and has gradually hardened as it continues its entanglement in materialism. However, human involution will transform into evolution again in the future.

find the Christ and the spirit. In addition, now that Christ is present in the etheric body of the world and is seeking for his "lost sheep," he will surely grant every human being more chances so that each will be able to find him. We can deduce that if a Muslim incarnates into a Christian culture in one of his or her future incarnations, that person may have a chance to get to know the Christ and other divine beings like the Holy Spirit and the divine Sophia.

In this context, Steiner commented on the idea that some Christians who are born into a Christian culture do not seem to have a deep insight of the Christ:

> People may sense the Divine but may have no possibility to sense the Christ.... Only through their participation in the cultural life have they become accustomed to speak of Christ, of freedom, and so forth... They call themselves "Christians" even though they cannot find the transition from the God they sense, to the Christ.[4]

Steiner's words point to the fact that some Christians living in Western Christian cultures are not able to find the Christ. We can surmise that these people were probably adherents of other religions such as Islam in a past life, for a human soul is likely to reincarnate in a different culture in each incarnation—that is, in a completely different setting from what one knew in the previous incarnation. Now that they are born in a Christian culture, this gives them the chance to sense the Christ. It is likely that some were Muslims or belonged to other religions in their previous incarnation. In his lecture series *Karmic Relationships,* Steiner offers various examples that show that this has often been the case: the Arabian commander Tarık ibn Ziyad[5] reincarnated as Charles Darwin; Muawie (an Arabian caliph) reincarnated as Woodrow Wilson; and Haroun-el

---

4 Steiner, *The Archangel Michael,* p. 158.

5 Tarık ibn Ziyad was the commander of Muslim Arabs who came to Spain at the beginning of the eighth century from North Africa and crossed the Strait of Gibraltar (Gebel al Tarik—which was named after him). Arabian armies fought many wars in Spain. Eventually, Tarik's armies were victorious. This was the beginning of the 500 years of Arabian rule in Spain and how the impulses of Arabism entered European cultural life and influenced the Europeans.

Rashid (a renowned caliph) reincarnated as Lord Bacon of Verulam. These were reincarnations of renowned Muslims. We may deduce that many more Muslims, who are not particularly renowned, reincarnate in Christian countries. In this way, the divine–spiritual realm provides these souls the opportunity to have a close relationship with Christianity and balance their deeply ingrained Islamic beliefs. It stands to reason that a soul who had been Muslim in a former reincarnation, permeated with Islamic teachings and influences, faces difficulties in the new incarnation in finding the transition from the God one senses to the Christ. It is also noteworthy that many people who were born as Christians in Western countries willingly renounce their creed and become adherents of Islam.

Although several incidents of Islamic terrorism and hostile behavior by extremist Muslims may lead peoples of Christian cultures to form negative impressions about Islam and Muslims, it is important and necessary that we try not to generalize. As a matter of fact, countless Muslims—for example, those who live in a laicized Islamic country like Turkey—do not wish to get involved in extremist behavior, for they strongly disapprove of the hatred and hostility of radical and fundamental Islamists. They are also opposed to the aggression and terrorism of extremist and fanatical jihadists and other Islamist factions. Moreover, these people are not at all in favor of the implementation of *sharia* law. They might not have had the chance to comprehend deeper spiritual aspects of Christianity or to recognize the Christ in their present incarnation, but they consciously choose to have a peaceful and humane relationship with Christians and adherents of other religions. Therefore, a generalized judgment about all adherents of Islam would not do justice to the large number of Muslims whom we would wish to continue having as our kinsfolk.

Encouraging Islamophobia and forming a negative attitude against Muslims will not be helpful in establishing reconciliation between Christianity and Islam. Muslims, too, show that they share our human values and are in agreement about what is good and what is evil. There is no doubt that Muslims who value common sense, peace, and kinship will clearly show their disapproval when extremist or fanatical Islamist terrorists brutally kill dozens and even hundreds of Muslims who belong to other sects of Islam;[6] or when extremists use bombs or weapons to attack public places[7] and kill Christians; or when they see fundamentalist Muslims trying to impose Islam on members of other religions. Their disapproval will demonstrate that, although we do not share the same religious beliefs, we share the same human values.

Fundamentally, we are all human beings living in the same world, and at least this much solidarity is necessary to be able to live in peace and harmony. However, although a large number of Muslims disapprove of the wrongdoings of extremist, radical, and jihadist Muslims, they often choose to turn a blind eye, for they are afraid to show their disapproval within their Islamic community (*ummah*). But if Muslims do not hesitate to underline their objective differentiation between that which is right and wrong—and that which is good and bad—this might help fundamentalist and extremist Muslims to realize that their belief that Islam is superior and holier than other religions, and that this gives them the right to demand that other people accept Islam is not only wrong and unfounded, but from a religious (spiritual) point of view, it is a "trespass." Finally, it might be helpful if we recall that Muslims are generally afraid to delve into the teachings of a religion other than Islam, for Islam is not a permissive religion. As long as Muslims abide by a verse such as "The only true faith in Allah's sight is Islam.... He that denies Allah's revelations should know that he is swift in reckoning," how can they be expected to analyze the profound truths regarding Christianity[8] in freedom and acquire an objective understanding about it?

---

6 These are precisely the kind of incidents that have been occurring in the Middle East since the summer of 2014.

7 For example, in recent years churches were attacked and bombed in Egypt at Christmastime, and many Christians attending the services were killed or wounded.

8 In the sense used here, Christianity does not have any specific connotation with the Catholic, Orthodox, or Protestant sects. What is meant here is the anthroposophic concept of "cosmic Christianity," which transcends sects and denominations and embraces humanity as a whole.

Can Christianity and Islam find a key to reconciliation?

When we ponder on the preceding explanations concerning Islam and Muslims, it becomes apparent that the deeply ingrained convictions of radical and fundamental Islamists—and to a certain extent the opinions of conservative Muslims—cannot be altered by any suggestions, discussions, or arguments, for Muslims are living in a "separate reality" that is not in harmony with Christ's statement, "I am the way, the truth, and the life." In other words, as long as Muslims are closed to the cosmic reality that Christ (God's Son) is not only the way to the Father, but is the ultimate cosmic truth—the Word—as well as *the cosmic etheric power that grants life*, then Muslims will continue living in a different realm where the inherent consciousness is not in harmony with the essential truths and consciousness of the divine-spiritual hierarchy. Steiner states a truth that relates closely with this situation: "Fundamentally there is nothing in the universe but consciousness. Everything outside the consciousness of beings—of whatever order—belongs to the realm of *maya*, the great illusion."

One of the main characteristic of maya (created by Lucifer and Ahriman) is that it induces "sleep" in a spiritual sense and gives the impression that this illusion is reality. One can wake up from this sleep only if one is able—using one's own free will—to form an inner urge to wake up. However, no one has the right to wake up another person forcibly from this sleep. Just so, no one can interfere directly with the Islamic beliefs of any Muslim. Therefore, we cannot expect to witness any major changes in their thoughts or beliefs over a short span of time. We can also deduce that, since the koranic verses are believed to be direct revelations of Allah, the majority of Muslims will never consider revising the Koran to make beneficial alterations, such as discarding verses that incite hatred and inspire certain Muslims to wage jihad on imaginary enemies of Islam; or those in which it is stated that Jews and Christians are pigs and apes, and are enemies of Allah; or verses that give the false impression that Muslims have the right to convert members of other religions to Islam.

Many influences impose inflexible limitations on Muslims and hinder them from the moment they are born in an Islamic community.

Knowing this might help us understand why they[9] are not able to sympathize with members of other religions and embrace them with tolerance and sympathy. The fact that their difficulties derive from being permeated by Islamic dogmas since childhood does not necessarily provide a justification for certain Muslims' unacceptable negative feelings and actions. When we recall the devastating attacks carried out by Muslim terrorists against not only the members of other religions but other Islamic sects as well, we would be justified in asking: When extremist terrorists and fanatical jihadists are consumed with hatred, aggression, and violence and then go out and kill people, is this not the manifestation of evil? An undeniable dark side is inherent in Islam. How are we to relate to Islam's dark side, which has an affinity with *ahrimanic evil?* First, it would be helpful to understand what evil is and how it comes into being. Rudolf Steiner spoke of evil and its relation to human evolution:

> In the ancient Persian or Aryan view, evil arises when a previously benevolent element retains the same form later on—that is, rather than changing and progressing, it remains adapted to an earlier time. The ancient Persians viewed evil and darkness as the consequence of good remaining the same rather than changing appropriately with time. The conflict between good and evil arises from the encounter between an outdated but enduring form of being and one that has advanced.[10]

Steiner explains precisely where our difficulties lay concerning our encounters with the dark and evil aspect of Islam, which have been manifesting in diverse ways lately. Steiner's explanation points out these five stages: something good coming into being, serving its purpose, stagnation, becoming retrogressive, and then being prone to evil. As we recall, Islam came into being because it had a definite purpose—and it has successfully fulfilled this purpose. In a way, the impulse of Islam was alive as long as the Prophet was alive. Because Muhammad had the profound experience of closely encountering the spiritual world,

---

9   The word *they* does not connote all Muslims, but only fundamentalist, extremist, radical, and fanatical jihadist Muslims.

10 Steiner, *According to Matthew*, p. 32.

certain spiritual merits and maturity were inherent in him. Thus, the early Muslims experienced Islam in a different way while their leader Muhammad was alive. Directly following his death, koranic verses, which inevitably had a static structure, had to be put into use. Yet the hard times and compulsory battles that Muhammad and his followers had fought were over; his task was accomplished. Verses like the one below did not need continuous recitation, for the battles and hostility had ended and peace reigned among the Arab tribes.

> 5:51 Believers, take neither Jews nor Christians for your friends. They are friends with one another. Whoever of you seeks their friendship shall become one of their number. Allah does not guide the wrongdoers.

Nevertheless, when the Koran was compiled, such verses were placed in it permanently, and throughout the centuries Muslims have been reading these relics over and over again. This has inevitably had a negative effect on them regarding their perception of Jews and Christians and people of other religions.[11] Unfortunately, instead of focusing on verses that foster peace, friendliness, and compassion, radical, extremist, and fanatical Muslims concentrate on the negative meanings inherent in some verses, heeding them as Allah's words, believing they give them the license to strike and kill. They do not take into consideration that these verses belong only to the past, to the time when Islam was emerging.

There is no doubt that the inculcation of the Islamic impulse, which came shortly before AD 666, was in accordance with the requirements needed to blunt the Sorathic intervention. But since that time, Islamic teachings—the core of Islam—have not been changed, reformed, or ameliorated. Islamic dogmas and the Islamic way of life have remained more or less the same since the time of Muhammad. In other words, the content of Islamic teachings—while befittingly in accordance with the requirements of Muhammad's time—*has remained exactly the same.* Harking back to Steiner's five stages of how evil comes into being, we see that Islam went through the

---

11 Some years ago a notorious Islamic militant leader blew up a colossal statue of Buddha in Afghanistan, a historical icon that belonged to the world's cultural heritage.

stages of stagnation and decline throughout the centuries. Then, due to luciferic influences, it became prone to ahrimanic influences. Presently, the world is encountering the "ahrimanic and asuric evil" that manifests in the "thoughts, feelings, and acts" of some Muslims.[12]

Bearing in mind the principle of the freedom of belief, if a group of people do not wish to be involved in the spiritual development engendered by the progressive divine–spiritual beings of the cosmos, it cannot be expected of them to change their outlook and ameliorate their dogmatic opinions. Nobody can force them to do so. However, the failure to do so will bring about more stagnation in their soul–spiritual constitution, and the inevitable consequence of stagnation will be *retrogression*. It is noteworthy that according to the Arab or Islamic calendar, the *Hijri*, the Western Gregorian calendar year 2015 is 1436.[13] There is a difference of 579 years between the Gregorian and *Hijri* calendars. Islamic countries and Muslims everywhere on Earth use this calendar[14] to determine Islamic holy days and the beginning day of Ramadan. The first day of this calendar starts in the year AD 622, when the Prophet immigrated to Medina (Yathrib). Muslims also take into consideration the Western calendar—for it brings a certain convenience to their dealings with the Western world—but they regard the *Hijri* as their official calendar. As we recall, around 1436 is the time when the epoch of the intellectual soul ended and the epoch of the consciousness soul began. (To be more precise, the epoch of the intellectual soul ended in 1413.) This means—from an anthroposophic point of view—that if Arab Muslims are claiming that the

---

12 These explanations do not intend to associate evil only with Muslims or with Islam. The truth is, evil can come from any human being or from members of any other religion on Earth. As humankind is constantly under the influence of Lucifer and Ahriman, we are all liable to make mistakes (trespasses) and be inclined to do evil. When we look at the state of the world, we see that evil is manifesting everywhere. It is important to comprehend how evil manifests in persons or in communities and try to nullify it with consciousness and love.

13 Since the Arabian calendar is basically a lunar calendar, its conversion into the Gregorian calendar (or vice versa) involves more than just adding 622 years.

14 Whereas the Christian (Gregorian) calendar is a solar calendar based on Christ's birth, the *Hijri*, or Islamic calendar, is based on the lunar year and has about 354 days broken down into 12 months, each with 29 or 30 days.

Islamic world is presently in the year 1436 (rather than 2015), they are 579 years late in entering the epoch of the consciousness soul. In other words, it has only been 22 years since they entered the epoch of the consciousness soul. This may explain why some Muslims have difficulties in keeping up with the spiritual developments brought about by the Christ impulse, which actually unfolds in accordance with the time designated by the Western calendar.

It does not seem likely that there will be changes in the convictions and conduct of radical, extremist, and jihadist Muslims, and these representatives of the kind of soul and spiritual constitution that has antipathy, intolerance, hatred, and hostility at its core will probably grow in number in the future. Thus, it would not be realistic to expect these Muslims to begin to love adherents of other religions, but if they do not acquire at least a minimum amount of tolerance and respect toward members of other religions, it is likely that there will be more serious confrontations between them and Christian cultures in the future.[15] When we recall the grave and disturbing incidents that have happened thus far, we see that a struggle between cultures is already occurring. But it is most important that the Western Christian world avoids reverting to hostility or using weapons in such confrontations. Muslim terrorists may have a strong tendency to use weapons, but it is not the task of progressive humanity to destroy the *demonic manifestations of evil* by using similar weapons. Instead, in our endeavor to transform evil into good, adopting peaceful and humane ways to deal with this problem would be more harmonious with the spirit of *true cosmic Christianity*,[16] as well as with the principles of the Christ

---

15 Steiner and Tomberg indicates that members of the Philadelphia Community would have to face an unavoidable spiritual struggle involving everyone—the war of all against all—at the end of the sixth cultural epoch.

16 As a consequence of Christ's First Coming, the seeds of Christianity were sown, but the initial form in which Christianity came into being was destined to be fettered to the physical world, inevitably exposed to luciferic and ahrimanic influences, and transformed into an institutionalized form founded on ritual and rhetoric. However, owing to the fact that new seeds are being sown by the "Risen One," who will be accompanied by the divine Sophia, the seeds that will be sown after his return in the etheric will acquire a different quality, as a result of which earthly Christianity will make the transition to "cosmic Christianity." Therefore, to leave all weapons aside—at all costs—is in harmony with the future cosmic Christianity.

impulse. In Matthew 26:52 Jesus Christ uttered a warning and a guideline for humanity concerning the use of weapons: "Put your sword back in its place, for all who draw the sword will die by the sword."

Bearing in mind Steiner's foregoing explanation concerning evil and recall that Islam was the outcome of the preventive measure so that human evolution was not imperiled, we cannot afford to superficially judge Muslims, declaring them enemies of Christianity. As we recall, Steiner said that "the teachings of Muhammad are the strongest polarity to Christianity." This statement does not mean that Muslims are enemies of Christianity. It actually means that Islamic teachings happen to be in the position of showing strong opposition to Christianity since they came into being under extraordinary and crucial circumstances—that is, Muslims had unavoidably found themselves in the middle of this situation. Therefore, due to the manifestations of the consequences of what they experienced, they deserve more conscious understanding and help from us, and we should try to solve this problem together. Muslims who have absolutely nothing to do with extremist or fundamentalist Muslims and, on the contrary, have an affinity with the Christian world, must be considered valuable and indispensable in bridging the gulf between the Christian and Islamic cultures.

It would be more just and helpful to bear in mind the spiritual-historical fact that some human beings did not have a choice regarding their involvement in the struggle of deadening Sorath's intervention, and there would have been serious consequences if this demonic intervention had not been blunted. So we cannot ignore the fact that the Prophet Muhammad and the Arabs successfully accomplished this important task. If Muslims only knew that the Prophet's actual accomplishment was not in establishing a new religion but in warding off a demonic intervention, they would have a deeper feeling of veneration for him. Therefore, it would do him justice if we acknowledge that, from a certain aspect, what he did was indeed a great service for humanity. This is why Christians should not blame Muhammad or hold him responsible for the degenerate acts done by radical and extremist Muslims at present. Accordingly, although everyone undisputedly has the right and freedom to state their criticism on any subject, we must admit that the way the Danish cartoonist depicted the Prophet

Muhammad as a bomb about to explode was unfair and undeserved. The artist might have had justified sentimental reasons for drawing such a caricature, but he could have considered the fact that Muhammad was a prophet who is deeply venerated by Muslims and that such a drawing would offend them. On the other hand, however, can we justify certain Muslims' harsh reaction toward this artist? Even bearing in mind that Muslims judge according to Islamic laws based on retribution, condemning him to death for a drawing was unfounded and unjustified, for the "dose of the retribution" they demanded was very much exaggerated.[17] If they had calmly expressed that the way the Prophet Muhammad was depicted was impolite, prejudiced, and insulting rather than threatening war with Christians, they would have gained much support from Christian peoples. Why were the extremist, and to a certain extent conservative, Muslims so offended and angry—to such a degree that they wanted to kill the artist?

Muslims received certain spiritual teachings by way of Muhammad's inspirations from the suprasensory world when the Islamic impulse was engendered, and this helped them to establish a religious aspect in their lives that they did not have prior to Islam. What they received was not enough to prompt them to seek deeper spiritual truths and establish substantial contact with the beings of the divine–spiritual world. Islamic teachings, based on the fear of Allah, were just enough to turn their attention from carved idols to the monotheistic concept of a single deity who encompasses the whole universe. Lucifer was involved from the very beginning of the Islamic impulse, and it was as if a "veil" of darkness was cast over them. (Later, this veil was also cast over people who became adherents of Islam in different parts of the world.) Thus, Muslims never became aware of the truth of numerous spiritual issues, since they were always obscured by the darkness induced by this veil. This is one of the reasons why they have not questioned what kind of spiritual forces govern at the background of Islam. Moreover, they have been under the impression that Islam

---

17 Besides, this artist was a Christian who lived in Denmark; therefore, he was not under the rule of *sharia* and should not be judged by Islamic laws. If those who were offended demanded fair justice, they could have taken him to court and asked for a trial.

is the most holy and perfect religion and, consequentially, have been proclaiming that everybody on Earth must become its adherents. Let us be more specific about what this "dark veil" is and what makes it so powerful. This veil and the darkness inherent in it came into being through "luciferic pride," and it has remained in existence by continually succumbing to this same pride.[18] Since this dark veil formed a blockage between what Muslims believe to be true and what the truth really is, it has prevented them from fathoming profound secrets pertaining to "cosmic Christianity," Jesus Christ, the Sun-God Christ, the Holy Trinity, God's Son, the divine Sophia, and the other divine–spiritual beings who have been closely involved in humankind's creation and evolution. Let us once again remember Steiner's words concerning how this "darkness" originated: "But the influence that was to go out from Gondishapur was deadened, held back by retarded spiritual forces—which were nevertheless connected—although they form a kind of opposition with the outflow of the Christ impulse."

When we recall that Lucifer has a permanent seat in the human astral body, it becomes evident that it was Lucifer who initially cast this dark veil over them. The astral bodies of Arab Muslims were influenced by Lucifer, especially as a group soul, because of their "close encounters" with him during this period. This influence was not limited to the beginnings of Islam, but continued into the future. Islam could not have come into being in any form other than what it is now, for help came from retarded luciferic forces that form a kind of opposition with the outflow of the Christ impulse. In this context—as we bear in mind the aforementioned Islamic dogmas and observe how these teachings manifest in the thought, feeling, and will of Muslims—it becomes apparent that their understanding of what is truly spiritual and what has no spiritual value was formed in such a way that constant denial of Christ and opposition to the Christ impulse had to inevitably exist at the background of their understanding. Because of their intrinsic nature, Islamic teachings could not have possibly represented the progressive spiritual aspect of human evolution. However, let us recall that *it was not*

---

18   Let us recall that *pride* is among the seven capital vices, or the Seven Deadly Sins.

their conscious choice to be in this situation. Accordingly, as we look back to the Old Moon stage of our evolution, we are able to say: "At that stage, certain spiritual beings had to remain behind in their evolution because of cosmic necessities, and this deed was a sacrifice." Now, during the Earth stage of our evolution, again a sacrifice has been taking place, but this time we are witnessing the sacrifice of human beings in a more conscious state. During the Old Moon stage, human beings did not have the consciousness to realize the meaning of such cosmic events as the sacrifice of Lucifer and luciferic angels; but at this stage of our evolution, humans do have the necessary consciousness to comprehend what is enacted in front of them. When we consider these facts and our microcosmic and macrocosmic[19] responsibilities, what are we to think and feel about Muslims? We could begin to seek the answer to this question in the Gospels.

Jesus Christ proclaimed, "Do not judge, and you will not be judged. Do not condemn, and you will not be condemned. Forgive, and you will be forgiven" (Luke 6:37). He also said, "To you who are listening I say: Love your enemies, do good to those who hate you, bless those who curse you, pray for those who mistreat you. If someone strikes you on one cheek, turn to him the other also" (Luke 6:27–29). When he was on the cross, Christ forgave those who had unjustly condemned him to death, saying, "Father, forgive them, for they do not know what they are doing" (Luke 23:34). Who but an extremist Muslim or fanatical jihadist could claim that "Islamic terrorists know what they are doing"? The thinking, feeling, and willing faculties of Islamic terrorists—those who believe that their jihad is justified and that it will provide them tickets to Allah's Paradise—are under a very deep sleep induced by Lucifer and Ahriman. Christ gave humanity one of the most important messages of the Christ impulse: "*Love your neighbor as yourself*" (Matt. 22: 31).

---

19 At this stage of evolution, humankind is in the position of being the microcosm; but in the future Jupiter, Venus, and Vulcan stages of evolution humankind will gradually assume its real place in the macrocosm. The preparations of this future development have already begun on Earth. The Advent of the Christ initiated this change of human direction from the microcosm to the macrocosm. Thus, humanity will likely also be challenged with macrocosmic responsibilities while it is still going through the Earth stage of evolution.

Conclusion

It is true that Islamic terrorist attacks and the tragic deaths of many people have influenced us inevitably to form negative impressions regarding Muslims and Islam. We may be inclined to feel that it is not so easy to implement the guidelines given by Christ under these circumstances. However, we do not have the time or luxury to indulge in this kind of pessimism. The time given to us in every reincarnation is limited, and it is necessary that we take what confronts us as a challenge—a challenge that is in accordance with our microcosmic and macrocosmic responsibilities. What Steiner expressed in his Fifth Gospel could help to show us that it is not impossible to achieve what Christ demonstrated, for the Apostles had already attained such wisdom:

> They [the Apostles] felt as if something had come to them from the universe that we can only call all-prevailing love.... Now, however, they seemed transformed, like individuals who had really and truly entered a completely new state of mind, a new soul mood. It seemed they had left behind all narrowness and self-seeking and gained infinite greatness of heart, complete inner tolerance, and real heartfelt understanding of all that is human on Earth.[20]

The endeavor to acquire "largeness of heart, all-embracing tolerance, and a deep understanding for everything that is human on Earth" could be a challenge that would lead us to the entrance of the "narrow gate," for Christ stated: "Enter through the narrow gate. For wide is the gate and broad is the road that leads to destruction, and many enter through it. But small is the gate and narrow the road that leads to life, and only a few find it" (Matt. 7:13–14).

Also, recalling Christ's new commandment in St. John's Gospel may also help to reevaluate and even forgive our neighbors' trespasses. "A new command I give you: Love one another. As I have loved you, so you must love one another" (John 13:34). St. John's farewell message was also in harmony with Christ's new command: "Love one another." Jesus Christ said,

> Jerusalem, Jerusalem, you who kill the prophets and stone those sent to you, how often I have longed to gather your children

---
20 Steiner, *The Fifth Gospel*, pp. 14–15.

together, as a hen gathers her chicks under her wings, and you were not willing. Look, your house is left to you desolate. For I tell you, you will not see me again until you say, "Blessed is he who comes in the name of the Lord." (Matt. 23:37–39)[21]

Jesus Christ's declaration regarding Hebrews who did not recognize that he was the "Revealer" of the Son of God is also valid for Muslims who do not acknowledge him and are not willing to say, "Blessed is he who comes in the name of the Lord." Muslims, under the influence of hindering forces and eclipsed by certain Islamic teachings that came into being apropos of the task of blunting Sorath's intervention, did not have the opportunity to comprehend the Mystery of Golgotha and the Mystery of Christ. They were not able to find the transition from the deity they sense, to the Christ. It is most probable that some Muslims will continue denying Christ and the spirit in their future incarnations, and that in the long run this will inevitably bring some karmic consequences for them. But some Muslims will undoubtedly have the karmic luck in finding Christ, for this opportunity is as available to them as it is to every other human being on Earth. There is no doubt that if Muslims seek him, they will find Christ, *since he has also been seeking for his "lost sheep."*

In accordance with the fact that Christ united himself with humankind's—and Earth's—destiny, every human being, regardless of which religion one belongs to, now has the chance to find him and say: "Blessed is he who comes in the name of the Lord." Christ declared these words in his First Coming and put particular emphasis on *the requirement to be able to behold him* by saying, "I tell you, you will not see me again until you say." In the statement, "Blessed is he who comes in the name of the Lord," he indicates that the requirement be able to *"see"* him is *to recognize and acknowledge him.*

---

21 When we carefully read these words of Jesus Christ, we can see that it is actually God Yahweh who is speaking through Jesus (remember, Yahweh is closely connected with the hexarchy and supports the pleroma of the Christ-being), and such an occasion where Yahweh speaks is very rare in the Gospels. When we ponder these words, it becomes clear that it was not Jesus Christ but God Yahweh "who had very often longed to gather Hebrew folk together as a hen gathers her chicks under her wings," but sadly perceived that they were not willing.

Although Christ knew that he was going to return to the Father after his Crucifixion and Resurrection, the fact that he still drew attention to *"seeing" him* can be taken as an indication that he shall return to the world. Since the phrase "until the time" points to a future time, his statement can be regarded as a clear indication of his Second Coming in a future time. Within this context, these words could also be heard as *Christ's call*, sounding forth for the whole of humanity during the time between his First Coming and his Return in the Etheric. According to Steiner and Tomberg, the Christ has returned to the world since the beginning of the 1930s, and this means that the ones who consciously lend an ear may be able to hear this call that now echoes from the spiritual dimension of the world's etheric body. If Muslims are able to open their hearts to the truths inherent in Christ's saying, "Blessed is he who comes in the name of the Lord," they will realize that there is another profound truth inherent in this statement. In this sentence the divine person who is referred to as "him" is the Christ (the fullness (*pleroma*) of the six Elohim that came from the Sun sphere). However, the second part of the sentence, *"who comes in the name of the Lord"* indicates that he (the Christ) has come to the world in the name of "the Lord." Who is "the Lord" mentioned in this sentence? At this point, let us look into what Valentin Tomberg delineates about the seven Elohim

> The Exusiai (Elohim) are pure representatives of the Son [the Second divine Person of the Holy Trinity], within the hierarchy of the Son.... If we wish to understand the cosmic Christ [from the Holy Trinity] correctly, we must look to the seven Elohim, as the revealers of Christ in the cosmos.[22]

Tomberg's words reveal the fact that the Christ (the fullness—*pleroma*—of the seven Elohim, including Yahweh Elohim who joined his forces with the other six Elohim) has come in name of the cosmic Christ—the cosmic Word (logos). And the cosmic Christ is at the same time the Son—*God's Son*—and the second person of the Holy Trinity—the Godhead. Therefore, Jesus Christ's statement indicates

---

22 Tomberg, *Christ and Sophia*, "The Jehovah Being in Cosmic and Human History," p. 14.

that since he belongs to the Godhead, "the Lord" is "the Son" and henceforth his presence will be felt in the physical world.

This is why we hope that adherents of Islam will become more conscious of Christ, the Sun being, with the realization that he is the divine being who represents God's Son in the Earth sphere and that he is with us now in the transitory world and will be with us all the way until humankind succeeds in becoming eternal beings ("sons of man") in the future stages of human evolution. We could also wish that Christ's profound words, "Blessed is he who comes in the name of the Lord," shall eventually rise from the depths of every Muslim's soul. Such a heartfelt wish concerning our human kinfolk would be in harmony with the outflow of the Christ impulse and with the responsibilities brought by "the times of the Sun Regent Michael." To hope that Muslims join us in acknowledging the great cosmic event of Christ's Return in the Etheric would also be in harmony with the preparations of the coming age of the *divine Sophia*.

On the one hand there is no doubt that these hopes concerning our Islamic kinsfolk are heartfelt and in harmony with the Christ impulse. On the other hand, however, although such positive wishes are needed, it is doubtful if mere optimism could succeed in hurdling the formidable barriers that have formed between Christianity and Islam over the centuries. From time to time leaders of the Christian and Muslim religions get together and—surely with good intent—speak about establishing "a dialogue between religions." However, nothing substantial or long-lasting is achieved as a result of these meetings, for they never progress beyond rhetorical speeches. It is not surprising that they cannot find any common meeting point, because it is not possible to form a true and everlasting understanding between two religions that hardly recognize each other or revere each other's beliefs. Besides, how some members of Islam try to debase and negate Christianity and how Christians feel about Islamic dogmas are facts nobody can deny. As long as no deep understanding or sympathy between Christianity and Islam springs up at the foundation of their relationship, can there be any hope of reconciliation? Under these circumstances, could Anthroposophy possibly offer a "common reality" or a common meeting point—that is, some profound truth that transcends religious beliefs and embraces both religions—in fact, all religions on Earth—and the whole of humanity? Anthroposophic wisdom can indeed reveal a profound and crucial cosmic truth that can dissipate the *maya*, the great illusion, if a deep comprehension of it is attained. This could alter untrue and distorted beliefs and opinions that have been leading members of religions and even nations to antipathy, hatred, hostility, aggression, killing, and war. How are we to approach and understand this truth? To start with, it is necessary that we delve into some significant questions: What is *maya*? How does *maya* engulf humankind? What is lacking in maya?

The "illusion" that surrounds us, constantly energized by luciferic and ahrimanic forces, generates a certain kind of *false reality* that humankind assumes to be real without any doubt or questioning. For example, the way we describe the material world using weight, measure, and number[23]—that is, all our information, concepts, and theories concerning the world—as well as the spatial space we perceive with our physical eyes belongs to the realm of maya. We could attempt to describe how maya surrounds and engulfs humankind by way of analogy. The ocean—the underwater world surrounding the fish—is apprehended by the fish as the one and only reality, since the fish do not have the degree of consciousness that would enable them to be aware of a separate reality like the humans' above-water world. Likewise, humans presume that the visible world of the mineral, plant, and animal kingdoms that surround them, the high-tech machines they have molded, and the complex life they lead in the cities that they themselves have built are all undisputable realities, because they do not yet have the necessary degree of consciousness to perceive the reality and truth of the invisible divine–spiritual world. Indeed, since humans have acquired and developed their "I" in the visible and material world that surrounds them, this world has become the one

---

23 Tomberg's elucidations concerning the true quintessence of "weight, measure, and number" can be found in *Christ and Sophia*, part 3, chapter 1. Also, one of Steiner's explications about "measure, number, and weight" can be found in his *Anthroposophical Leading Thoughts*, specifically the lecture of January 4, 1925, "Heavenly History–Mythological History–Earthly History."

and only reality as far as they are concerned. Yet, when seen in the broader scope of the reality and truth inherent in the divine–spiritual realm, all of this is nothing but an illusion, or maya. However, at this stage of evolution humans have not been able to discern what maya is, for they are yet "asleep" in a spiritual sense.

The culture in which we are born also contributes to this illusion. For instance, when we are born in a certain community (be it Christian or Muslim, Jewish or Buddhist), we are raised with the religious teachings and dogmas that are inherent in that community, and the essence of this instruction permeates our souls from childhood onward. Just so, when we are born in a certain nation, we unconsciously believe in the nationalistic opinions and prejudices ingrained in that community. In both cases, the "maya of religion and nationality" conceals the truth that we are all essentially spiritual beings that manifest in a physical world that has been created for a very special purpose. Our religious and nationalistic beliefs mean absolutely nothing to the divine–spiritual beings that have created humankind. In this context, we often speak of "the world of Christianity" and "the world of Islam," as if homogeneous and consistent worlds of Christianity and Islam exist, whereas these concepts are only an illusion. Christianity and Islam are each divided into multiple sects that do not share a common, consistent belief. We can witness today how members of different Islamic sects are at war with each other.[24] Apparently, the fact that "the enemy" on both sides happens to be Muslim seems to mean nothing. The Islamic dogma that claims "there is only one Allah and Muhammad is his Prophet" should be the common maxim that binds all Muslims, yet it does not help them wake up from the "dream" induced by maya. As we recall, in former times similar wars lasted decades between members of Christian sects.

When Christians and Muslims realize that we are all surrounded and engulfed by a powerful illusion and that the cosmic spiritual truths that belong to the eternal reality of the beings of the divine–spiritual realm are not under this illusion, then it will become

---

[24] The war that has been going on in Iraq and Syria since 2014 is, in fact, a war between different Islamic sects.

apparent that this is precisely the reason why we have been evaluating "other" human beings in an untrue and distorted way, preventing us from seeing the truth that *we are all spiritual beings*. As a result of this realization, we might wish to disabuse ourselves of the beliefs and concepts that energize the negative maya, keeping it alive and upright. When we study Steiner's detailed elucidations about the three previous stages of humankind's evolution,[25] we can see that in the former evolutionary stages of Old Saturn, Old Sun, and Old Moon, certain higher beings of the divine–spiritual hierarchy at the periphery poured something from their own being into the space of each evolutionary stage,[26] and certain spiritual beings from the lower ranks of the hierarchy were present inside that space to receive the inflowing forces of these higher beings. After working with these forces, the results of their work streamed out from them—from the center—back to the divine–spiritual beings who were situated at the periphery of that particular evolutionary phase. In the Earth stage, this pattern has changed, and beings of the divine–spiritual hierarchy are no longer present in the central area of the fourth evolutionary stage. Instead, humanity is at the periphery of the activity of the fourth main evolutionary stage, but they do not presently have any connection with the divine creators who are at the periphery of Earth as was the case in the previous stages of evolution.

At the beginnings of the fourth stage, humans were yet in a dream state. Later, when they attained a certain degree of consciousness in their "self," their "I," their connection with the divine realm was severed. Then, certain spiritual beings who do not belong to the divine–spiritual hierarchy and had no role in the creation gradually began to be involved in humankind's fourth evolutionary stage, and some of these beings became influential on the human astral body. Some of them took their place in the core of the world, constantly radiating degrees of "evil" from different stratums of the

---

[25] It was possible to give only a very brief explanation about this complicated subject; further details are beyond the scope of this book. Steiner's elucidations can be found in *An Outline of Esoteric Science*, ch. 4; and in *The Spiritual Hierarchies and the Physical World*, part 2.

[26] At each evolutionary phase, different divine beings poured (or granted) different forces from their innermost being.

Earth.[27] These are, successively, luciferic and ahrimanic beings. In other words, humanity stayed "within the bosom" of the beings of the divine hierarchy until the middle of the third main epoch of the Earth evolution. The third main epoch was Lemuria. In the middle of Lemuria, the event of humankind's "Fall from heaven" took place. During the first and second stages of the Earth evolution,[28] divine–spiritual beings gradually departed from the Earth evolution. From this point onward (from the middle of Lemuria) it was necessary that the last spiritual beings,[29] who had remained with humankind until the middle of Lemuria, gradually exit the Earth phase of the evolution also.[30]

Steiner indicates, "In the outwardly apparent [world is] no longer the Divine itself but only the forms of the Divine are there."[31] In the modern conception of Nature humankind has no relation to the divine, but only to the accomplished work of the divine. Therefore, since the divine qualities that form the essence of the divine–spiritual realm are lacking in this Earth phase of humankind's evolution, and because non-divine spiritual beings are present in the Earth sphere and have been exerting strong influences on humankind, Jews, Christians, Muslims, Buddhists, and peoples of every other religion *are facing each other in a state of "sleep" induced by the maya and generated by these adverse beings*. In this state of sleep, it is very difficult for us to become conscious of the true reasons why we exist on Earth as ephemeral beings trapped in the dimension of time, although we are surrounded by eternity. However, exposure to the influences of an illusion induced by Lucifer and Ahriman was not the only consequence of being severed from the divine–spiritual realm. After humans became earthly beings and developed their "I" within their

---

27 Steiner's lecture of Sept. 4, 1906, in *Founding a Science of the Spirit* discusses the subject of evil (ahrimanic) influences radiating from the core of the Earth.

28 The Polarian and Hyperborean ages, respectively.

29 These were the Exousiai, the spirits of form.

30 Among them only Yahweh, the leader of the Seven Elohim, stayed behind in the Moon sphere; this was as close as he could get to the Earth plane, which would be the sphere of activity of adverse spiritual beings in the future.

31 Steiner, *Anthroposophical Leading Thoughts*, p. 85.

earthly conditions, they became spiritually very vulnerable and were susceptible to suffering, illness, and death. They were also now under the cosmic "law of karma." Valentin Tomberg's explanation indicates humankind's critical situation: "The karma of Earth, however, is death, which is the only reality of everything that is purely of the Earth. And in the field of death, everything sown is reaped first by death. Those who truly understand this, therefore, cannot help feeling that the Earth is one vast grave."[32]

But human beings (who were formerly pure spiritual beings) did not become terrestrial beings only to perpetually suffer and die on Earth. It is essential to comprehend that humanity was not created so as to become adherents of this or that religion—while presuming their religion is the best religion and favored by God—and that *God (or Allah) did not create humankind to serve him*. As a matter of fact, in accordance with the purposes and aims of the divine realm, humankind, the other three kingdoms of the Earth, and all the beings of the divine–spiritual hierarchy are involved in a magnificent cosmic process that is actually *a great cosmic transformation of the universe*. This great transformation unfolds as a cosmic evolution in which humankind has been given a very important task. One's personal evolution is essentially related with this cosmic transformation and humans can only be "real beings" if their personal evolutions progress in accordance with the purposes and aims of the divine–spiritual realm. This is one of the main reasons behind the reality of our existence. Thus, our creators are not in the least interested in what our religious beliefs are but *in our conscious contribution* to this ongoing awesome divine cosmic process.

If human beings are fettered to prostrating before an Islamic God (or a God venerated in other religions) in fear of that God, this will hinder their capacity of understanding the profound cosmic developments that are in progress, and it will also eclipse the truth that our creators do not want us to fear or serve them or prostrate before, but actually wish to meet and unite with humanity in "love." Therefore, if Muslims wish to be part of this divine cosmic process in harmony with the purposes and aims of the divine–spiritual

---

32 Tomberg, *Christ and Sophia*, "Higher Stages of the Passion," p. 298.

realm, it is necessary that they leave the law of retribution and all other *sharia* laws behind, which will bring about *the development of consciousness, conscience, forgiveness, and love*. However, this result cannot be easily achieved while humankind is under very strong luciferic and ahrimanic influences. Looking at the state the world is in, we can sense that we definitely need help from the divine realm—that is, from our creators—to be able to succeed in our cosmic task. As a matter of fact, this crucial help has already come to the world. The divine–spiritual realm has sent us *the Christ*.

The foregoing explanations draw our attention to "the cosmic reality," which needs to be comprehended by humanity and can be commonly shared by peoples of every religion and nationality since it encompasses every human being on Earth without differentiation. In addition to many other profound spiritual facts, this is the truth that Anthroposophic wisdom reveals, and hopefully it will be able to provide the missing "common meeting point," the truth that is a common reality for members of all religions and humankind—in other words, "the key for reconciliation." We really do not have any time to waste with hatred, aggression, and hostility, for these belong to *the realm of luciferic and ahrimanic maya*. When humans adopt this kind of negative behavior toward others, they continue to be fettered to the world of maya and are likely to generate more bad karma, which in the long run will cause retrogression in their personal evolution.

At first glance these explanations may not mean much to some Muslims, nor may it interest them, because they might associate its terminology with terms and concepts found in Christianity. However, since the koranic verses form the foundation of their religion, Muslims could instead ponder on the profound meaning inherent in one of Allah's messages, which connotes similar meanings. This significant verse reveals that Allah had something very special in mind when he created humankind and that he has high hopes concerning these beings. According to this verse, upon looking at the being that Allah initially created, the angels had some doubts about it and voiced their hesitations. Allah told them that they did not know what he knew. In this way he implied that there was something special concerning the being he created and let the angels know that he had confidence in it.

> 2:30 When your Lord [Allah] said to the angels: "I am placing on the Earth one that shall rule as My deputy [humans]," they replied: "Will You put there one that will do evil and shed blood, when we have for so long sung Your praises and sanctified your name?" He said: "I know what you do not know."

In this verse, Allah does not distinguish between the religions or nationalities adopted by human beings on the Earth plane. Nor does he indicate or underscore that Islam is his favorite religion and that Muslims are going to be his "deputies" on Earth. He speaks about humankind in an undifferentiated way. Therefore, such a verse, which embraces every human being, is one of the most important verses in the Koran, for such a message is in harmony with the Christ impulse. Since Allah did not keep his thoughts and hopes to himself and especially sent this verse to Muslims as a guideline, we can deduce that he expects Muslims to ponder on it and take heed of its deeper meanings. It is hoped that all Muslims will have the opportunity to consider the meaning of this verse someday. When we contemplate on it now, we can state that whether we are Jewish, Christian, or Muslim, Allah's phrase, "one that shall rule as my deputy," actually denotes *humankind*. What does Allah really mean by "my deputy"? Although Allah knew from the beginning that humans would do evil and shed blood on Earth, he still trusted in them, for he knew that this would be only a transitory period and was confident that humans would transform into completely different beings in the future.

Thus, Allah also knew that for humans to be able to become his deputy, it was necessary that the human soul and spiritual configuration experience radical changes in order to acquire certain divine qualities. Otherwise, in their present state of perpetrating evil and shedding blood, they cannot represent Allah. So Allah knew from the beginning that humankind would eventually reach this highly spiritual stage in the future. This is why he says to the angels: "I know what you do not know." According to anthroposophic elucidations, the future times in which humankind will acquire divine qualities and transform into true divine beings are the Jupiter, Venus, and Vulcan stages of evolution. During these stages humans will acquire their higher divine aspects of spirit self, life spirit, and spirit body.

However, it is necessary that humans consciously work on themselves to be able to transform their souls and achieve these higher divine qualities. Since at present humans are unconsciously perpetrating evil and shedding blood, how and from which point shall they begin this transformation?

Let us bear in mind that the epoch of the consciousness soul or the spiritual soul of human evolution had actually begun, as noted, in the fifteenth century and that the spiritual powers inherent in this epoch[33] would provide humans the necessary impetus to "wake up" into their thinking, feeling, and will. During the former epochs, the human physical body, soul body,[34] sentient soul, and intellectual soul or mind soul had each developed. Therefore, during the fifth post-Atlantean epoch, when development of humankind's consciousness soul takes place, human beings would have the faculty of intelligence and logic at their service. At this point in their evolution, they will not receive any guidance or admonition from the divine–spiritual realm in the sense of Talmudic or koranic verses, for the divine realm would grant them absolute freedom of choice in a spiritual sense. At this crucial point, which can be likened to being at a fork in the road, humans shall either choose to be conscious helpers to the achievement of the purposes and goals of the divine–spiritual hierarchy and progress further in their individual evolution, or refuse to take part in this cosmic progress and consequentially regress.

The point of beginning our work for further spiritualization of our soul is to ameliorate the way we see and evaluate those other human beings who do not belong to our religious sect or to our nationality. It is essential that radical and extremist Muslims and fanatical jihadists take heed of the deeper meaning of verse 2:30 and understand that Allah does not differentiate between any religion or nationality and sees only *human beings*—the spiritual beings he created—when he looks at humanity, and that Allah is confident that someday in the

---

33 Rudolf Steiner and Valentin Tomberg revealed that Christ's "return in the etheric" would commence in the 1930s.

34 The soul body or sentient body is another distinct member of human constitution and is actually the finer part of the ether body, which forms a unity with the sentient soul. The soul body manifests in the human senses—the sense organs.

future human beings will also be able to see *spiritual beings* when they look at one another, realizing that every other person is also a creation of Allah. Once extremist Muslims understand that Allah does not hate non-Muslims or regard them as his enemy, and that he is opposed to bloodshed and therefore does not wish jihadists to kill in his name, it would not be unreasonable to hope that they will cease seeing other humans as their enemies, as infidels, or as enemies of Allah. It is absolutely necessary that they understand that, when Allah uttered, "I am placing on the Earth one that shall rule as My deputy," the "deputy" he had in mind was not a relentless Islamist jihadist, for the times of jihad were only relevant to the times of the Prophet and should not be continued today. It is essential to comprehend that Allah's ideal of a "deputy" actually connotes *a highly spiritualized human being who approaches Allah's creation (humankind) with consciousness, conscience, compassion, and love.* Nevertheless, in accordance with the "freedom" brought about by the Christ impulse, members of Islam are free to choose between becoming jihadists and serving adverse beings of darkness or allowing Christ, the Holy Spirit, and the divine Sophia to permeate their souls so that they may embrace every other human being with spiritualized love.

In the following Gospel proclamation, we can see that Jesus Christ does not force us to act in this way or that, yet he has given a very clear and objective warning concerning the consequences of choosing to become a servant of adverse spiritual beings of darkness:

> I am the true vine, and my Father is the gardener. He cuts off every branch in me that bears no fruit, while every branch that does bear fruit he prunes so that it will be even more fruitful. You are already clean because of the word I have spoken to you. Remain in me, as I also remain in you. No branch can bear fruit by itself; it must remain in the vine. Neither can you bear fruit unless you remain in me.
>
> I am the vine; you are the branches. If you remain in me and I in you, you will bear much fruit; apart from me you can do nothing. If you do not remain in me, you are like a branch that is thrown away and withers; such branches are picked up, thrown into the fire, and burned. (John 15:1–6)

Zarathustra was one of the greatest initiates in the history of humanity and was also endowed with the faculty of clairvoyance. What did this great initiate proclaim thousands of years ago? He declared that within the cosmos exist specific forces of "good" (light) and "evil" (darkness) and that these are two principles that proceed from the primal universal principle of *Zeruane Akarene*—the undisturbed and uncreated cosmic time. He also indicated that the name of the divine spiritual being who was the representative of the "good principle" of the universe is *Ormuzd–Ahura Mazda*—the Great Aura of the Sun—and that the forces of darkness are named *Angru Manyu*, also known as Ahriman. Zarathustra proclaimed that the good forces were involved in a continuous struggle with the evil forces in the cosmos and that human beings were also involved in the battle, which continued on Earth, for this conflict could be only resolved in the physical plane, in the stream of on-flowing time.

Thus, during our lifetime human beings have no other choice but to choose between good and evil and side with one of them. However, the aim of this battle is not to destroy the evil forces, but is rather an endeavor to transform them, for the new must come into being while the old must not be swept away. Those who took heed of his teachings and became his adherents were known as Zoroastrians. In contrast with the Buddhists and followers of some other Far Eastern teachings, Zoroastrians did not seek enlightenment, deathlessness, or liberation from the perpetual wheel of death and reincarnation on the Earth plane; rather they believed and sensed that they were on Earth to take part in the ongoing cosmic moral battle between good and evil. Muslims have not been able to convert Zoroastrians to Islam during their conquests, so they have categorized Zoroastrians as fire worshippers, which connotes that Zoroastrians practice idolatry. However, for Zoroastrians fire is actually a visible symbol of the "inner light" that burns within each person and is also a physical symbol of the divine-being (Ahura Mazda) found in the Sun sphere. Thousands of years ago, Zarathustra indicated that Ahura Mazda was going to leave the Sun sphere and come to the physical plane in the distant future. This exalted being indeed came to the world at a later time, but with a different name. During the three-year period of his ministry on Earth he was known as *Jesus Christ*.[35] Accordingly, since this "cosmic moral battle" between good and evil is still going on, humans have no other choice but to side with either the good principle or the evil principle found in the cosmos. On the other hand, as they stand at the fork in the road at this stage of their cosmic evolution, humans are absolutely free to choose or not choose good or evil. Having analyzed the prevalent circumstances that confront humanity and the deeper meaning of their mission in the cosmos, let us leave the last word to Rudolf Steiner's Michaelic revelations and to Christ, to illuminate where humanity stands:

> Christ bears within himself, in a manner true to the whole Cosmos, the impulses for the future of humanity. To unite with Christ signifies for the human soul to receive into itself, in a manner true to the Cosmos, its own seeds for the future...to unite ourselves with Christ in the right way is also to preserve our-selves in the right way from Ahriman.[36]

John 14:6: Jesus replies, *"I am the way and the truth and the life; no one comes to the Father except by me."*
John 11:25: *"I am the Resurrection and Life."*

---

35 Unfortunately, because of Lucifer's interference his name does not rightfully appear in the Koran as *Christ*, but only as Jesus, son of Mary. Jesus was the physical body in which Christ incarnated during the three years he stayed on Earth until he was crucified.

36 Steiner, *Anthroposophical Leading Thoughts*, p. 114.

Bibliography

The Holy Bible. Oxford, UK: Oxford University Press, 1978.

The Koran. New York: Penguin. 1974.

The New English Bible. Oxford, UK: Oxford University, 1975.

Chittick, William C. *Sufism: A Short Introduction.* Oxford, UK: One World, 2001.

Cook, Michael. *Muhammad.* Oxford, UK: Oxford University, 1983.

Durant, Will. *The Age of Faith: A History of Medieval Civilization—Christian, Islamic, and Judaic—from Constantine to Dante, AD 325–1300.* Scranton, PA.: Haddon Craftsman, 1950.

Frieling, Rudolf. *Christianity and Islam: A Battle for the True Image of Man.* Floris Books, 1980.

Ibn Kathir, Hafiz. *Tafsir Ibn Kathir: A Compilation of the Abridged Tafsir Ibn Kathir* (vols. 1–10, English language with Arabic verses). Houston, TX: Dar-us-Salam Publications, 2000.

Luxemburg, Christoph. *The Syro-Aramaic Reading of the Koran: A Contribution to the Decoding of the Language of the Koran.* Berlin: Verlag Hans Schiler, 2007.

Sawma, Gabriel. *The Qur'an: Misinterpreted, Mistranslated, and Misread: The Aramaic Language of the Qur'an.* Plainsboro, NJ: Gabriel Sawma, 2006.

Schuon, Frithjof. *Understanding Islam.* London: George Allen, 1976.

Steiner, Rudolf. *According to Matthew: The Gospel of Christ's Humanity.* Great Barrington, MA: SteinerBooks, 2003.

———. *Anthroposophical Leading Thoughts: Anthroposophy as a Path of Knowledge: The Michael Mystery.* London: Rudolf Steiner Press, 1973.

———. *Anthroposophy (a Fragment): A New Foundation for the Study of Human Nature.* Hudson, NY: Anthroposophic Press, 1996.

———. *The Apocalypse of St. John.* London: Rudolf Steiner Press, 1977.

———. *The Archangel Michael: His Mission and Ours.* Hudson, NY: Anthroposophic Press, 1994.

———. *Background to the Gospel of St. Mark.* London: Rudolf Steiner Press, 1968.

———. *The Christ Impulse: And the Development of Ego-Consciousness.* London: Rudolf Steiner Press, 2014.

———. *Death as Metamorphosis of Life.* Great Barrington, MA: SteinerBooks, 2008.

———. *Deeper Secrets of Human History in the Light of the Gospel of St. Matthew.* Hudson, NY: Anthroposophic Press, 1985.

———. *Evolution of Consciousness: As Revealed through Initiation Knowledge.* London: Rudolf Steiner Press, 2006.

———. *Excursus on the Gospel according to St. Mark.* Rudolf Steiner Publishing, 1938.

———. *Founding a Science of the Spirit.* London: Rudolf Steiner Press, 1999.

———. *From Jesus to Christ.* London: Rudolf Steiner Press, 1973.

———. *The Evolution of Consciousness.* London: Rudolf Steiner Press, 1979.

———. *Genesis: Secrets of the Bible Story of Creation.* London: Rudolf Steiner Press, 1982.

———. *The Influences of Lucifer and Ahriman: Human Responsibility for the Earth.* Hudson, NY: Anthroposophic Press. 1976.

———. *Inner Impulses of Evolution: The Mexican Mysteries and the Knights Templar.* Hudson, NY: Anthroposophic Press, 1984.

———. *Karmic Relationships: Esoteric Studies,* vol. 1. London: Rudolf Steiner Press, 1972.

———. *An Outline of Esoteric Science.* Hudson, NY: Anthroposophic Press, 1996.

———. *The Occult Significance of Blood: An Esoteric Study.* London: Theosophical Publishing, 1912.

———. *The Reappearance of Christ in the Etheric.* Hudson, NY: Anthroposophic Press, 1983.

———. *The Spiritual Foundation of Morality: Francis of Assisi and the Christ Impulse.* Hudson, NY: Anthroposophic Press, 1995.

———. *Theosophy: An Introduction to the Spiritual Processes in Human Life and in the Cosmos.* Hudson, NY: Anthroposophic Press, 1994.

———. *Three Streams in Human Evolution: The Connection of the Luciferic–Ahrimanic Impulses with the Christ–Jahve Impulse.* London: Rudolf Steiner Press, 1985.

Tomberg, Valentin. *Christ and Sophia: Anthroposophic Meditations on the Old Testament, New Testament, and Apocalypse.* Great Barrington, MA: SteinerBooks, 2011.

www.ingramcontent.com/pod-product-compliance
Lightning Source LLC
Chambersburg PA
CBHW022056160426
43198CB00008B/248